Muslims in Scotland highlights the distinctive features of both Scottish identity and Scotland's Muslim communities, demonstrating the relatively benign relationship between the two, in contrast to the situation in some other parts of the UK and Europe.

Professor Hugh Goddard, University of Edinburgh

This up-to-date analysis rests on a historical and demographic foundation. Its account of the Muslims of Scotland and their experiences, often so different from the rest of the UK, is a welcome addition to the literature on Muslims in Europe.

Professor Jørgen S. Nielsen, University of Birmingham

This is an important, fresh and pioneering study of the Muslim community in Scotland. It should be required reading for policy makers and academics as well as all those interested in the changing social shape of Scotland today.

Professor Sir Tom Devine, University of Edinburgh

In a world riven by ethnic and religious conflict, Stefano Bonino's *Muslims in Scotland* gives us a convincing, fascinating and inspiring example of how an indigenous society can live in harmony with immigrant communities. It should be compulsory reading for those concerned about the future of our world.

Professor Akbar Ahmed, American University (Washington, DC) and formerly Pakistan's High Commissioner to the United Kingdom

MUSLIMS IN SCOTLAND

The Making of Community in a Post-9/11 World

Stefano Bonino

EDINBURGH
University Press

Edinburgh University Press is one of the leading university presses in the UK. We publish academic books and journals in our selected subject areas across the humanities and social sciences, combining cutting-edge scholarship with high editorial and production values to produce academic works of lasting importance. For more information visit our website: www.edinburghuniversitypress.com

Edinburgh University Press Ltd
The Tun – Holyrood Road
12 (2f) Jackson's Entry
Edinburgh EH8 8PJ

Typeset in 11/15 Adobe Garamond by
Servis Filmsetting Ltd, Stockport, Cheshire,
and printed and bound in Great Britain by
CPI Group (UK) Ltd, Croydon CR0 4YY

A CIP record for this book is available from the British Library

ISBN 978 1 4744 0801 1 (hardback)
ISBN 978 1 4744 0802 8 (paperback)
ISBN 978 1 4744 0803 5 (webready PDF)
ISBN 978 1 4744 0804 2 (epub)

Published with the support of the University of Edinburgh Scholarly Publishing Initiatives Fund.

CONTENTS

TABLES AND FIGURES

ABBREVIATIONS

AISF	All-India Seamen's Federation
AIUS	All-India Union of Seamen
BBC	British Broadcasting Corporation
BNP	British National Party
EDL	English Defence League
ELREC	Edinburgh and Lothian Regional Equality Council
EU	European Union
IFC	Islamic Finance Council
MCB	Muslim Council of Britain
MCS	Muslim Council of Scotland
MP	Member of Parliament
MSP	Member of the Scottish Parliament
NATO	North Atlantic Treaty Organization
PEGIDA	Patriotic Europeans Against the Islamisation of the West
PTI	Pakistan Tehreek-e-Insaf
SDL	Scottish Defence League
SIMD	Scottish Index of Multiple Deprivation
SNP	Scottish National Party
SSP	Sipah-e-Sahaba Pakistan
StWC	Stop the War Coalition
UK	United Kingdom

GLOSSARY

Ahmadiyya	An Islamic movement founded by Mirza Ghulam Ahmad
Banlieues	Suburbs
Barelvi	A traditionalist and populist version of Sunni Islam
Bhangra	A Punjabi disco club
Biraderi/Biradari	The extended kin and tribal network in a Pakistani community
Burqa	A loose garment worn by Muslim women: it covers the head and the face (sometimes the full body)
Citoyenneté	Citizenship
Dar	A South Asian Islamic study curriculum
Da'wa	Islamic proselytism
Deobandi	A revivalist version of Sunni Islam
Fatwa	Islamic legal pronouncement
Fiqh	Islamic jurisprudence
Gulab jamun	A popular South Asian dessert
Halal	Permissible under Islamic law
Hanafi	One of the five Sunni schools of jurisprudence
Hanbali	One of the five Sunni schools of jurisprudence
Hijab	Headscarf worn by Muslim women

Iftar	The evening meal that breaks the daily fast at sunset during Ramadan
Imam	Prayer leader in a mosque
Isma'ilism	A branch of Shi'a Islam
Izzat	Honour in Pakistani and North Indian culture
Ja'afari	One of the two Shi'a schools of jurisprudence
Lingua franca	Common language
Masjid	Mosque
Musallā	A non-designated, temporary space for ritualistic prayer which does not meet the criteria for a mosque
Purdah	A custom in some Muslim and Hindu societies of using clothes to conceal women from men or strangers
Qur'an	The holy book of Islam
Ramadan	Month of fasting
Salaam	Muslim greeting
Salafism	A conservative branch of Sunni Islam
Shalvar kameez	Traditional South Asian dress
Shari'a	Islamic law derived from the Qur'an and the teachings and traditions of the Prophet Muhammad (Sunna)
Shi'a Islam	The second-largest denomination of Islam
Sufism	A mystical school of Islam
Sunna	The teachings and traditions of the Prophet Muhammad
Sunni Islam	The largest denomination of Islam
Tablighi Jamaat	An orthodox revivalist Sunni Islam movement
Topi	A South Asian cap
Ulama	A group of Muslim legal scholars
Umma	The global Muslim community
Wahhabism	A conservative branch of Sunni Islam
Zakat	Alms giving (Third Pillar of Islam)

ACKNOWLEDGEMENTS

I am indebted to those kind and patient Muslim men and women who took part in my research fieldwork in Edinburgh between 2011 and 2013 and to the two gatekeepers who facilitated interviews with a good and balanced pool of voices across the gender, ethnic and age spectra. Alistair Henry and Susan McVie's academic expertise guided me through the successful completion of the doctoral research conducted at the University of Edinburgh (2010–14) that provides much of the material for this book. Advice received from Nasar Meer, a world-renowned expert on Muslims in Europe, has been instrumental in developing this book. Timothy Peace and Fayaz Alibhai deserve a special mention for the invaluable scholarly support that they have provided throughout my years of research. I am grateful to Nicola Ramsey and the staff at Edinburgh University Press for their assistance.

Lastly, I would like to thank the following publishers for permission to reproduce material for which they hold copyright: Edinburgh University Press for sections of Chapters 2, 3 and 6 that first appeared in 2015 as 'Scottish Muslims through a Decade of Change: Wounded by the Stigma, Healed by Islam, Rescued by Scotland', *Scottish Affairs*, 24 (1): 78–105; and the Taylor and Francis Group for a large section of Chapter 5 that first appeared in 2015 as 'Visible Muslimness in Scotland: Between Discrimination and Integration', *Patterns of Prejudice*, 49 (4): 367–91.

Stefano Bonino – Planet Earth, September 2016

FOREWORD

D espite the seeming ubiquity of the constitutional question in Scotland, scholarship focusing on territorial politics has told us remarkably little about the changing character of Scottish identity. Scholarship in the tradition of sociologies of nationalism, meanwhile, has largely (though not entirely) focused on the responses of white majorities, sometimes in different regions of Scotland. What this means is that we still do not really know whether – in the late Stuart Hall's terms – Scotland has 're-written the margin into the centre, bringing the outside into the middle' (Hall 2005: 31). By making central what is at the periphery, therefore, in this widely researched monograph Stefano Bonino unsettles the prevailing *doxa*.

The story of Muslims in Scotland, or of Scottish Muslims, is a rich account illustrative of tendencies that are both common to, as well as divergent from, patterns elsewhere in Europe. *Muslims in Scotland: The Making of Community in a Post-9/11 World* is one of the first sustained scholarly studies through which we can substantiate and explore that claim with a sufficiently 'thick description' of the Scottish case. It is published at a welcome time. As Bonino notes, religious pluralism is not new to Scotland. Irish Catholics secured various gains down the years as part of the Catholic emancipation in Scotland, most clearly symbolised by the restoration in 1878 of the hierarchy of the Catholic Church in Scotland. The typical response to bringing Muslims into such settlements, however, is that 'it would be extremely depressing,' as a

Member of the Scottish Parliament (MSP) once told me, 'to think that in 50 or 60 years' time we'd repeated the mistakes in terms of other ethnic groups and other religions' (Meer 2015a: 1493). In this respect it may be the case that, as the late Bashir Ahmad, Scotland's first ethnic minority MSP, put it in 1995, 'it isn't important where you come from, what matters is where we are going together as a nation'. But it is necessary that this journey occurs within democratic and inclusive terms, in a manner that allows us to remake not just people's Scottish national identities but also the identity of Scotland. This book will support us to consider why and how this can occur.

Just as Scottish identities change over time, so do Muslim identities. As Bonino shows quite clearly, what have emerged alongside 'religious' Muslim identities in Scotland are political 'associational' identities, where increasing self-identification of Muslims in Scotland *as Muslims* reflects a story of socialisation in Scotland. This is a sociological dynamic that is not unique to Scotland and was first shown by Knott and Khokher (1993) in how young Muslim women in Yorkshire drew a distinction between 'religion' and 'ethnicity' in rejecting their parents' subscription to traditions that the young women thought were less consistent with their own aspirations. Jacobson (1997) later referred to this development as a 'religion-ethnic culture distinction' and contrasted it with a 'religion-ethnic origin distinction'. While the former involves a perception of identity in terms of one's attachment to a place, the latter points to one's identity as a Muslim in a manner that denotes belonging to a global community, which transcends ethnic and national boundaries and takes us forward to a new community identity. Here, Bonino takes this further in charting such tendencies across a variety of formal and informal settings in Scotland, social conventions and notions of piety. In so doing, he makes a very valuable contribution to our understanding of each.

Professor Nasar Meer
University of Strathclyde

We have held the peculiar notion that a person or society that is a little different from us, whoever we are, is somehow strange or bizarre, to be distrusted or loathed. Think of the negative connotations of words like alien or outlandish. And yet the monuments and cultures of each of our civilizations merely represent different ways of being human. An extraterrestrial visitor, looking at the differences among human beings and their societies, would find those differences trivial compared to the similarities. The Cosmos may be densely populated with intelligent beings. But the Darwinian lesson is clear. There will be no humans elsewhere. Only here. Only on this small planet. We are a rare as well as an endangered species. Every one of us is, in the cosmic perspective, precious. If a human disagrees with you, let him live. In a hundred billion galaxies, you will not find another.

Carl Sagan – *Cosmos* ('Who Speaks for Earth?')

INTRODUCTION

T he terrorist attacks on the United States on 11 September 2001 spotlighted the real and perceived tensions in Western–Islamic relations,
once again catapulting Samuel Huntington's (1993) controversial idea of a
clash of civilisations between the West and the Muslim world to the forefront
of public debate. A wide array of academics, politicians, journalists and pun-
dits have taken an interest, at times of a genuine kind and at times dictated
by personal or political agendas, in discussing the role played by Muslim
communities within Western society. In Europe, Great Britain maintains a
key position in this debate, largely for historical and geopolitical reasons. The
British Raj (1858–1947) ruled over the Muslim (and non-Muslim) populations of the Indian subcontinent for almost a century. Since the British
Empire disintegrated seventy years ago, the Muslim population in Great
Britain has grown exponentially, from as little as around 21,000 people in
1951 (Peach and Gale 2003), accounting for about 0.05 per cent of the
British population at the time, to over 2.7 million in 2011, making up 4.8
per cent of today's British population (Ali 2015). Ethnic grocery stores, restaurants and takeaway shops have made Muslim presence a vivid reality in
British society.

But the key feature that has turned former colonial subjects into full
members of the country is the symbolic and physical presence of Islam in
most British cities and towns. With over 1,800 mosques and spaces for

prayer across the country (Naqshbandi 2015b), Muslims have made Great Britain their home and have brought to it a distinctive Islamic flavour; nowadays, 79 per cent of Muslims in the country are to be found in the inner-city conurbations of Greater London, the North West, Yorkshire and Humberside and the West Midlands (Ali 2015). However, as the recent *British Muslims in Numbers* report published by the Muslim Council of Britain (MCB) posits, 'Muslims [. . .] are to be found from Land's End to Stornoway' (Ali 2015: 16).

The diversity of the Muslim community in Great Britain, and across most European countries, makes it difficult to construct a single 'Muslim community' without incurring the risk of homogenising the experiences of individuals who differ along ethnic, theological, gender and age lines. While approximately 1.8 million British Muslims (68 per cent) are Asian (Pakistani, Bangladeshi, Indian, Chinese or other Asian), about 900,000 (32 per cent) belong to one of dozens of non-Asian ethno-national groups (Ali 2015). Theologically, Muslims in Great Britain affiliate with a range of Islamic denominations. Deobandi and Barelvi represent over two thirds of Muslim orientations, yet the Muslim community also includes members of various Shi'a, Salafi, Sufi, Ahmadiyya, Arabic or African mainstream groups (Naqshbandi 2015b).

There are, of course, differences in how religiosity is individually conceptualised and played out. The personalised aspect of religiosity is well described in the work of Volpi, who argues that 'unlike in recent history where religious experiences were mediated by collectivities in the form of institutionalized churches or national-based communities of beliefs, today religiosity is becoming personalized, while still retaining a highly visible public presence' (Volpi 2007: 463). Being Muslim in a Muslim minority context does not end with Islam and with a religious identity (Jeldtoft 2011). Instead, being Muslim is characterised by different expressions of minority identities and various types of individualised processes of religiosity that help Muslims to 'mak[e] sense of the world' (Jeldtoft 2011: 1147). The sociological complexities inherent in describing a group of people bound by faith, ethnicity and/or any other element of similarity should not be underestimated. Attaching a default religious identity to Muslim communities is particularly problematic:

The religious label accorded to Muslim citizens does now appear to have some problematic dimensions. Increasingly, Muslim identity is viewed as reified and exaggerated. A criminal is now a 'Muslim thief', the local GP is a 'Muslim doctor', and so on. The trouble with this is that Muslims cannot be seen simply as human beings: they have to be perceived mainly through the religious prism. Giving them a one-dimensional description, however important, undervalues the complexity of that person. (Hussain 2008: 40, cited in Gilliat-Ray 2010: xi)

But while scholars should not overlook the nuances that characterise any social aggregate, this book takes forward Gilliat-Ray's (2010: xii) proposal that 'a generally shared set of core religious beliefs' makes it 'meaningful to consider Muslims in [Great] Britain [and beyond] as constituting a distinctive social group' and not simply a discursive construction. While being very much aware of the permeability of groups' boundaries and subjective, strategic and context-dependent approaches to religiosity, Gilliat-Ray (2010: xiii) admits that 'Muslims in [Great] Britain arguably have sufficiently shared beliefs and practices to warrant their categorisation as a distinctive group'. This book supports Gilliat-Ray's position. The following chapters will highlight the distinctive and nuanced ways of being Muslim across ethnic, age and gender lines, but they will also describe wider social and cultural trends In order to provide a sufficiently generalisable assessment of the Scottish Muslim community as a single entity.

Muslims in Scotland: An Invisible Community

The events of 11 September 2001 mutated Western–Islamic relations forever. The increasing threat posed by violent jihadists, Western policies against terrorism, foreign interventions in the Muslim world, polarised social attitudes featuring either 'victimist' or 'alarmist' views (Joppke 2014) of Muslim integration and cultural suspicion of diversity have all emerged as a response to the killing of 3,000 people on American soil. The subsequent major terrorist attacks in Madrid in 2004, in London in 2005, in Paris in 2015 and in Brussels, Nice and Orlando in 2016 have left a deep wound in the relations between Muslims and non-Muslims in the West. Academic and non-academic researchers have naturally responded to the real and perceived threat of Islamist terrorism. While

2000, the year before the terrorist attacks on the United States, registered the publication of 150 books on terrorism, 2002 saw 1,767 titles being published and the following three years recorded well over 1,000 books every year (Silke 2008). As Silke (2008: 28) noted in 2008, 'the five years since 9/11 have probably seen more books published on terrorism than appeared in the previous 50 years'. Various aspects of Muslim life have also been studied, surveyed and analysed as never before. This has sparked much-needed research on the contemporary role of Islam in Western societies. Among several titles of dubious quality, a number of masterpieces have appeared on Western bookshelves. Today, academics and lay readers have no excuse to ignore the social history and settlement of Muslim communities in Ireland (Scharbrodt et al. 2015) and Western Europe (Nielsen 2004) or in countries as far away as the United States (Kabir 2012) and Australia (Kabir 2005).

In Great Britain, scholars have produced outstanding analyses of the Muslim communities living in England (Gilliat-Ray 2010; Kabir 2010). Regrettably, the experiences of Muslims living in Scotland have been relegated to the dimly lit corners of scholarly research. Hosting fewer than 77,000 (3 per cent) of the total 2.7 million Muslims living in Great Britain, Scotland has been largely invisible to academics studying Western Muslim communities. Most of the existing academic work on Muslims in Scotland relies on research conducted between the late 1980s and the early 2000s by three pioneering researchers: Ali Wardak (2000 and 2002), Karen Qureshi (2004, 2006 and 2007; also, with Shaun Moores, 1999) and, particularly, Peter Hopkins (2004a, 2004b, 2007a, 2007b and 2009). These three authors have offered important contributions to understanding Scottish Muslim identity, community, social control and cultural negotiations, albeit with an almost exclusive focus on the Pakistani element of the community.

While himself not an academic, Bashir Maan (1992, 2008 and 2014) has provided a unique historical insight into the early migration and settlement of South Asians in Scotland. However, none of the literature currently in circulation offers a specific perspective on Muslims *qua* Muslims in Scotland. In light of the increasingly significant role played by Islam within Muslim communities in Great Britain (more details throughout the book), a concurrently historical and holistic perspective on Muslim life in Scotland has long been overdue. The peculiarly Scottish stories recounted by several Muslim migrants in the Colourful Heritage (2016) project and the documentary material surviving in the Bashir Maan Archives at the Mitchell Library in Glasgow ought to be complemented with a thorough analysis of today's experiences of younger Muslim generations living in Scotland. In a country that has often been romanticised as a social justice paradise and where, however, both a history of discrimination and the more recent ramifications of the post-9/11 sociopolitical climate have left some scars, Muslims have encountered uniquely Scottish life experiences. This book gives a voice to these Muslims and to their experiences.

Aim of the Book

The absence of a scholarly book on Muslims *qua* Muslims in Scotland constitutes a significant gap in the growing body of academic literature exploring the development of Muslim communities in the Western world. The main aims of this book are to address this omission and to provide an updated account of the meanings attached to being a Muslim in contemporary Scotland. These meanings are both shaped by the global and national post-9/11 shift in public attitudes towards Muslims and infused by the social, cultural and political ways of dealing with minorities, diversity and integration that are peculiar to Scotland. This book offers a bird's eye view of the interactions between Muslims and Scottish society and the ways in which such interactions both colour Muslims' identities and community structures and redefine Scottish sociocultural boundaries. It locates the specific problems of discrimination that Muslims face within the Scottish context. Muslims' cultural adaptations include strategies of survival channelled by both a collective sense of global unity and a strong allegiance to Scottishness.

The book also aims to highlight the changes that have occurred within Muslim community structures and that move beyond ethno-cultural-centrism towards a Scottish experience of being Muslim. Such an experience brings together civic and social belonging to Scotland with a stronger religious and ideological commitment to Islam. Moreover, the book links to ongoing debates on the inclusive, open and tolerant nature of Scotland and explores the specific social, political and cultural aspects of the country (at times opposed to those of England) that colour Muslims' perceptions and standing in society. A novel analysis of Edinburgh demonstrates that the Scottish capital can serve as a model of Muslim integration within a cosmopolitan and economically prosperous city. Lastly, the book envisions a model of local pluralism based upon a community of diversity bound by a set of shared civic values. Such a model is a post-ethnic, transcultural society glued together by the recognition of human universals and naturally located within the Scottish tradition of social justice.

Methodologically, the book brings together empirical data collected by the author predominantly between 2011 and 2013 and an extensive range of secondary sources. Primary data consist of qualitative fieldwork conducted with Muslims living in Edinburgh. It involves in-depth interviews[1] with thirty-nine male and female Muslims of various ages, ethnic backgrounds and social classes and protracted participant observation in the capital city, including but not limited to conversations at mosques, attendance at *iftar*, charity, fundraising and interfaith events, participation in the meetings of a Muslim student society, observation of pro-Palestine, anti-Israel and anti-SDL (Scottish Defence League) demonstrations, and many more occasions during which the author immersed himself in local Muslim life. Readers should be aware that, due to a confidentiality agreement established with research participants in the course of data collection, pseudonyms are used instead of respondents' names and mosques are identified as 'Mosque A', 'Mosque B' and so on.

Secondary sources include existing academic research, policy documents, government reports, police statistics, censuses, surveys, racist incidents and newspaper articles. Edinburgh and Glasgow account for almost 60 per cent of the total Scottish Muslim population. Therefore, they represent the natural geographical focus of this book, given how important and different they are at the social, cultural, political and economic levels. By way of a brief example (more in Chapter 1), the relative affluence of Edinburgh contrasts with serious urban deprivation in Glasgow and this is also evident in the results of the independence referendum. But, thanks to various pieces of research that have surveyed different aspects of Muslim life beyond the Central Belt (see, for example, Homes et al. 2010; Kidd and Jamieson 2011; Colourful Heritage 2016; Shaikh and Bonino forthcoming), this book sets itself the goal of presenting a wider overview of Muslims in Scotland. While not every single Muslim reader will find his or her own experiences reflected in this book's accounts, the author aims to analyse broader social and cultural trends that cut across the experiences of the majority of the Scottish Muslim community.

Organisation of the Book

This book contains a short introduction and seven chapters, including the Epilogue. Chapter 1 covers the settlement and development of Muslims in Scotland, from the first contact between Scottish traders and people of Islamic faith in North Africa in the eighth century to the establishment of today's Muslim community living in the country. Chapter 2 explores the historical intersections of religion, ethnicity and nation in the construction of Muslim identities in Scotland. It highlights the ways in which Islam binds together an ethnically heterogeneous set of people who affiliate both globally and locally, and who resist the post-9/11 stigma through the shared destiny and the sense of belonging offered by religion. It also posits that the predominantly civically oriented nature of Scottish identity has facilitated Muslims' integration in Scotland. Chapter 3 is closely connected to Chapter 2 and explores the reshaping of Muslim community boundaries as a result of the increased affiliation to Islam and a strong sense of belonging to Scotland. Chapter 4 analyses Scottish Muslims' experiences of discrimination. It reflects on the lingering presence of a post-9/11 securitisation of Muslimness and forms of everyday discrimination that might be overshadowed by the romantic narrative of Scotland as a land of tolerance. Chapter 5 demonstrates the ways in which Muslims and non-Muslims together have challenged global stereotyping and local discrimination through acts of resilience, engagement and mutual interest. Chapter 6 further reflects on the Scottish inclusionary ethos and cultural history of tolerance, both real and perceived. It argues that Edinburgh is a successful place of inclusion, comfort and belonging, where Muslims can openly express their visible diversity. The concluding chapter, the Epilogue, discusses theories of integration and sketches a Scottish future as a model of local pluralism based upon a community of diversity bound by a set of shared civic values.

Note

1. Twenty-seven interviewees were male and twelve were female. Half of the interviewees were within the age group twenty to thirty-nine, while the other half were within the age group forty to sixty-plus. These were the age groups of interviewees at the time when the primary research was conducted (2011–13).

About two thirds of the interviewees were of South Asian background or heritage (Pakistani, Bangladeshi, Indian and Scottish or British Pakistani), while the remaining third were from a range of different ethnic backgrounds (African, Middle Eastern, British mixed, Scottish and so on). Half of the interviewees had lived in Edinburgh for over twenty years (some for their entire life), and the other half for less than twenty years. According to an educated guess mostly based on educational attainment and occupation, slightly more than half of the interviewees were from a middle or upper-middle social class (in particular, those within the age group twenty to thirty-nine), while the remaining section belonged to the working and lower classes.

1

MUSLIMS IN SCOTLAND: MIGRATION, SETTLEMENT AND DEVELOPMENT

Historical accounts of the settlement of Muslim communities in Scotland are scarce and patchy, thus creating an obvious problem for academics wishing to unearth the specific circumstances that led people of Islamic faith to put down roots in the country. Much research conducted until about twenty years ago tended to focus on South Asians. Therefore, it did not necessarily take into account the religious background of these people and, crucially, often conflated Pakistanis, Bangladeshis and Indians by placing them within the same ethno-cultural category. It is with this limitation in mind that any history of Muslims in Scotland, and Great Britain more generally, needs to be considered. While not an academic himself, Bashir Maan, the first Muslim person to hold public office in Great Britain and a key figure in the history of Muslims in Scotland, attempted to remedy this gap. His trilogy, *The New Scots: The Story of Asians in Scotland* (1992), *The Thistle and the Crescent* (2008) and *Muslims in Scotland* (2014), represents the most comprehensive source available on the history of Muslims living in Scotland.

In his work, Maan takes the reader through a journey from the first contact between Scottish traders and people of Islamic faith in North Africa in the eighth century to the establishment of today's Muslim community living in Scotland. Here, this history is not comprehensively narrated but accurately summarised in order to provide the reader with an understanding of the settlement of Muslim communities in Scotland that can help comprehend more recent developments. The last two Census surveys (2001 and 2011), which include a question on religion, are particularly useful for uncovering the demographic variation, the geographical distribution and the ethnic diversity of today's Scottish Muslims. Glasgow and Edinburgh, the cities hosting the two biggest Muslim communities, present several geographical, social and economic differences that explain the peculiar features and successes of the Scottish capital (see Chapter 6).

From the Eighteenth Century to the Mid-Twentieth Century

As evidenced in Maan's work, the eighth century marked the beginning of recorded contact between Scotland and Islam, particularly through trading links with North Africa, historical accounts in the *De Locis Sanctis* (a treatise written by the Irish abbot Adomnán and mostly based on the Gaulish monk Arculf's travels to the Holy Land) and pilgrimages that Scottish people conducted to the Holy Land. Between the ninth century and the twelfth century, Scotland was mentioned in the works of a couple of Muslim geographers, notably Masudi and Al Idrisi. However, it is unclear whether they simply had topographical knowledge of the geographies of Scotland or whether people of Muslim faith had actually travelled to the country.

In general, there are no recorded accounts of Muslims in Scotland throughout the Middle Ages. Instead, contact between Scotland and Islam was predominantly a one-way traffic with Scottish pilgrims, crusaders[1] and traders travelling to Muslim countries. In Maan's history there is some circumstantial evidence (for example, in entries in *The Lord High Treasurer's Accounts* 1505–8) of Black Moors[2] working as musicians and entertainers at the court of King James IV of Scotland and his successors in the sixteenth century. In 1679 six black trumpeters, presumably Muslim, were attached to the Scottish Life Guards. In the eighteenth and nineteenth centuries a number of black musicians were also attached to the Scottish regiments. Although they did not settle in Scotland, the skin colour of these early Muslims made them visibly different from the white Scottish majority, even if they reached a Scotland that, in medieval times, 'had evolved from a mix of ethnic groups of Gaels, Picts, Scandinavians, Britons and Angles' and that 'to a much greater extent than either Wales or Ireland [. . .] was [already] a heterogeneous society' (Devine 2012: 486).

According to Maan's historical account, the first officially recorded Muslim in Scotland was Ishmael Bashaw, a Turkish man who reached Great Britain in the late eighteenth century after escaping captivity in Spain and hiding in Lisbon for three years. He managed to obtain safe passage to Scotland through England and stayed in Scotland for a few months before going back to England. He was married to an English woman by a Scottish minister and later converted to Christianity. However, despite his conversion, he still suffered from humiliation, abuse and violence at the hands of the majority and never managed to fully integrate within society. Bashaw's experiences of discrimination are not unique but were shared by other migrants who reached Scotland after 1800, when a strong national identity had developed and when suspicion and hostility had been directed towards newcomers of different cultures, languages and religions (Devine 2012).

The British Empire's expansion to, and ruling of, India brought Scottish people and Indians[3] of Muslim (and non-Muslim) faith closer and increased opportunities for contact. This is especially true when considering that, by the mid-nineteenth century, 'when one in ten of the British population was Scottish, one third to a quarter of the civil service elite grade of the East India Company was Scottish' (Meer 2015a: 1487). Today, the Scottish tartan remains a feature in the formal regalia of the Indian military (Meer 2011). As noted by Miles and Dunlop (1987), the development of industrial capitalism in Scotland in the nineteenth century was grounded on the international activities of the Scottish merchant capital. Therefore, Glasgow became a commercial centre, was involved in world trading and partook in the colonial impetus. Scotland became greatly involved in the British territories in the Caribbean and in the British colonies in India and Africa.

Direct contact with colonised populations means that 'since the late eighteenth century there has been an awareness in Scotland of populations in different parts of the world and therefore an imagery of those people [including South Asian Muslims]' (Miles and Dunlop 1987: 122). Maan also recounts that, between the mid-eighteenth century and the mid-nineteenth century, a steady, although numerically unknown, flow of Indian seamen, also known as 'lascars', and servants reached Scotland for both short-term and permanent settlement. In the mid-nineteenth century a number of students from Muslim countries were recorded pursuing higher education in

Scotland. An inflow of middle- and upper-middle-class students coming from India to English and Scottish universities was recorded in the 1840s and 'Scottish universities were especially popular, perhaps because of the dispro-portionately large numbers of Scottish teachers in India' (Ansari 2004: 32). Larger numbers were recorded in the 1880s to the point that, by the begin-ning of the 1900s, the Edinburgh Indian Association, which had originally been set up by six students in 1883, reached 200 members (Ansari 2004).

At the end of the nineteenth century the expansion of the British mer-cantile favoured the employment of lascars on ships trading with the East due to (1) a need for additional workers to expand business and the idea that colonial workers were cheap and docile; and (2) the fact that new areas of employment emerging within the British shipping industry, as a result of structural and technological changes, were unpopular among white European workers and more desirable for South Asian workers (Dunlop 1990). By the end of the same century, Indian seamen had developed colonies in the main Scottish port cities, especially Glasgow and, to a lesser extent, Edinburgh and Dundee. Dundee's 'import of raw jute from Bengal and export of jute prod-ucts attracted Indian seamen from Bengal' (Ansari 2004: 36) and, later in the 1920s and early 1930s, would facilitate the penetration of Muslims into the north and north-east of Scotland (Maan 2014). The presence of Indian seamen was also recorded in Aberdeen, Dumbarton, Clydebank and Ben Lomond (Ansari 2004). While Ansari (2004: 36) defines it as 'the Second City of Empire' and a place where the production of heavy capital goods enticed Muslim seamen to congregate, Dunlop and Miles argue that the role of Glasgow as

> A major imperial port was therefore a principal determinant of the presence in the West of Scotland of a population of colonial origin (and especially from India) from the end of the nineteenth century. [. . .] A similar rela-tionship probably applies in the case of Edinburgh, the main port of which was Leith. (Dunlop and Miles 1990: 151)

The presence of Indian seamen in Glasgow is well evidenced in the books of the Glasgow Sailors' Home, which recorded about 5,500 lascars among its annual nightly boarders in 1903 (Ansari 2004). Although many of these Indian seamen did not permanently settle in Scotland, but congregated in docklands of major Scottish port cities and eventually returned home, they both provided an ongoing influx of Muslims to the country and prepared the way for more sustained settlement. The migration and gradual settlement of South Asians in Scotland throughout the nineteenth century and, later on, the twentieth century was contemporaneous with the migration of other foreign communities, especially those of English, Irish, Italian, Lithuanian, Jewish and Polish origin. These people moved to Scotland in what is believed to be 'the most concentrated phase of immigration since the Irish, Scandinavian and Britannic tribes had established themselves hundreds of years before' (Devine 2012: 486). The settlement of these minority ethnic groups, which over time would be known as the 'new Scots', sparked different social responses from the native Scottish majority. The establishment of the South Asian Muslim community shared some similarities with the experiences of other migrant groups and was met with a set of social responses that largely depended on both the position of migrants within the labour market and their efforts to integrate in wider Scottish society. The next few pages will draw on the research of Scotland's leading historian, Tom Devine (2012), to provide an overview of the settlement of some of these migrant groups.

Irish Catholics are a key immigrant group in modern Scottish history. As Devine (2012: 487) notes, 'already by the 1850s there were around a quarter of a million Irish-born in Scotland and the immigration continued on a significant scale until the 1920s, when it started to decline'. Predominantly originating from the historic Ulster province, Irish Catholics tended to concentrate in and around Glasgow, Dundee and the various mining districts of the Lothians. Their unskilled and semi-skilled labour made an important contribution to nineteenth-century Scotland's economy, although they received little credit from the Scottish majority. Often considered to be aliens due to their religion and culture, they struggled to affiliate with a Scottish national identity that was largely based on Presbyterianism – even if the preservation of religion was never married with a strong and distinctive Catholic politics (Bruce 1988). Religious and cultural diversity and poverty made Irish Catholics the victims of discrimination and the scapegoats for various socio-economic malaises afflicting Scotland, such as falling wages, epidemic diseases and drunkenness. The collective response of Irish Catholics aimed to advance a process of integration, for example by marrying native Scots and by becoming an invisible minority. Irish Catholic involvement in trade unions and radical movements helped the community to foster partnerships with Scottish workers that pursued common social, political and economic causes. This shared experience in the workplace also ensured that the Irish Catholic enclave mentality never became too strong. But it is true that, during the second half of the nineteenth century, with the arrival of the Famine immigrants and with the mobilisation of a strong Irish identity through the Home Rule Movement, Irish Catholics 'developed almost as a distinctive and introverted ethnic community' (Devine 2012: 495). The elasticity of this relationship between Irish Catholics and Scots would carry on during the first thirty or forty years of the twentieth century too. The positive shared experiences of fighting together in the First World War and the bringing of Catholic schools into the Scottish system through the 1918 Education (Scotland) Act went hand in hand with negative, anti-Catholic hostilities fuelled by a sectarian mentality, economic decline, mass unemployment and Scottish emigration. The ensuing economic recession in Catholic areas and the discrimination in the labour market left scars that would take time to heal and would allow Irish Catholics to fully integrate only in the latter part of the twentieth century.

Irish Protestants started migrating en masse to Scotland in the late eighteenth century when sectarian divisions in Northern Ireland were intensifying. This was also a period when Scotland was entering rapid industrialisation and could offer better economic opportunities to skilled tradesmen, labourers, weavers, bleachers and farmers than Northern Ireland could. Unlike Irish Catholics, in the nineteenth century Irish Protestants were well integrated within Scottish society thanks to both their religion and their employment in higher-skilled occupations, although some people also worked in unskilled and semi-skilled professions. Despite a relatively easy integration in Scotland, Irish Protestants maintained strong ties with Ulster. Their identity was reinforced by the Loyal Orange Order, an organisation which was based around lodges and had been 'founded in Armagh in 1795 to defend Protestants against the Catholic secret societies which were becoming aggressively active in the region' (Devine 2012: 504). Scotland hosted lodges in Glasgow, Galloway and Ayrshire in 1830 and there was a striking correlation 'between areas of Orange strength and Irish Protestant settlement' (Devine 2012: 504).

Orange parades on 12 July every year and faction fights created a confrontational relationship with Irish Catholics living in Scotland. Nevertheless, a decline in Ulster Protestant migration after the First World War and the absence of disturbances in Scotland during the 1968–98 Northern Irish conflict ('the Troubles') between the Protestant Unionist majority and the Catholic Republican minority in Northern Ireland point to a lessening of the Irish Protestant identity in a context of increasing integration within Scottish society.

Lithuanians, most of whom had reached Scotland between the 1860s and 1914, were predominantly employed in unskilled jobs in coal mining and in the manufacture of pig iron. They experienced hostility from the Scottish majority, which lessened when Lithuanians started visibly displaying their allegiance to Scotland, as epitomised by their active presence in the mining unions and in the national miners' strike in 1912. Yet, they led a rather secluded life, clustered as they were within certain areas of Central Scotland, and their colourful clothes turned them into a visible minority. The initial process of integration into Scottish society took a particular form, notably through the Anglicisation of Lithuanian surnames. A spike in interwar marriages, peer pressure, entrance in higher education, Scottish life experiences among the new generations, a halt in post-1920s migration, internal ethnic fracturing between the conservative majority and the socialist minority and the small size of the community eventually facilitated full integration and led Lithuanian ethnic identities to become invisible.

Many Italians migrated to Scotland between the 1880s and 1914, although it was towards the end of this phase, in the 1910s, that they became a distinct community. A good number of Italians lived in Glasgow and tended to be dispersed across working-class areas, unlike other minority communities, which tended to cluster around a few neighbourhoods. Italians offered a popular service in the catering sector, predominantly in ice cream parlours, fish and chip shops and cafes. The Italian entrepreneurial mentality and Italians' direct ownership of businesses, which avoided fuelling job or wage competition with the Scottish majority, drew much less hostility from Scottish people compared to the Irish Catholics and the Lithuanians. Although geographically dispersed, Italians maintained little contact with broader Scottish society outside working hours. They married within the community and, at home, they spoke Italian and ate Italian food. The Fascist regime in Italy (1922–43) strengthened a sense of patriotic, rather than ideological, identity[4] and instilled in people feelings of belonging to their home country, possibly playing on the emotions of a community that had originally been pushed into emigrating from their motherland but was still not fully integrated into Scotland. Strong anti-Italian hostility was excited by Benito Mussolini's declaration of war against Great Britain in 1940. In the post-war context, Italians integrated within Scottish society more visibly, for example by initiating naturalisation processes and marrying Scottish women, while still retaining strong intra-community business networks and family links with Italy.

Similar to the Italian community, Jews suffered prejudice but to a lesser degree than Irish Catholics and Lithuanians. Unlike the latter, who were employed as unskilled workers in the docks, mines and steel mills, Jews established a self-contained economy, setting up a community welfare system, owning their own businesses, working as butchers, bakers, grocers, tailors, pedlars, travellers and hawkers, and not competing with Scottish people in the labour market. The Jewish community reached significant numbers only in the 1870s. The nineteenth century's mass migration from Central and Eastern Europe drove the community to settle and concentrate in the Gorbals in Glasgow. These Jews were, for the most part, of Russian and Polish background and economically poor, speaking Yiddish and possessing little knowledge of English. However, they were not insulated from society: the Labour Party's interest in Zionism is a case is point. In the 1920s and 1930s, Jews started to integrate more obviously within Scottish society as Yiddish slowly gave way to English. They also entered and established themselves in the medical profession. Importantly, they experienced upward socio-economic mobility to become, later in the century, an affluent community populated by the professional and business classes and predominantly based in Giffnock in Glasgow.

In contrast to these migrant communities, the numbers of South Asians remained very low until after the Second World War. Nevertheless, South Asian migration to Scotland induced national fears about a cheap colonial workforce that was perceived to lower the rates of pay of white native sailors and this triggered opposition to the employment of Indian lascars within the industry (Dunlop 1990). This opposition, exclusionary and racist in nature, against Indian (and Chinese) seamen increased both before the outbreak of the First World War[5] in 1914 and after its end in 1918, when competition in the labour market intensified as a result of the global collapse of the shipping industry. Riots exploded in 1919 in many British ports, including Glasgow (Dunlop 1990). The late 1920s and the early 1930s saw the emergence of a 'colour problem' throughout Great Britain, including Scotland, and featured anti-'coloured'-labour campaigns promoted by the National Union of Seamen (Sherwood 2003).

During that period, 'there were accumulative movements to perceive Indian lascars and other Colonial seamen as a constant "threat" and a potential "problem" primarily on grounds of negative associations of skin colour' (Dunlop 1990: 46). Mixing fears of visible ethno-cultural diversity with local and national economic worries, the idea that Indian workers would take jobs from the white majority and favour wage reductions during periods of recession became socially widespread and put Indians in the same position as Irish Catholic, Lithuanian and Polish workers. Dunlop (1990) argues that hostility and resentment over the employment of Indian labour intensified and took on a further dimension – it now (1) questioned the morals of Indian workers; (2) assessed the threat that Indian workers posed to the population; and (3) racialised the issue of the employment of Indian workers.

Before and during the Second World War, Indian seamen in Scotland and, more broadly, Great Britain fought to achieve better wages, in labour conditions that were highly disadvantageous compared to white seamen, who earned about eight times more. Notably, Glasgow hosted a branch of the All-India Union of Seamen (AIUS), which opened in 1943 in Liverpool and also had a branch in London. Alongside other trade unions, such as the All-India Seamen's Federation (AISF), the AIUS helped colonial workers, predominantly people of Indian origin, to become more aware of their rights and to openly voice economic demands (Ansari 2004).

In the early and mid-1920s, alongside a minority of people who found jobs as wage labourers, mostly in iron and steel industries in Lanarkshire, many Indians worked as itinerant pedlars, 'selling mostly ladies', children's and gents' clothing' (Maan 2014: 20). While 'peddling was a trade directed towards the poorer sections of the Scottish population living in the poorer parts of the city [of Glasgow] and rural areas' (Maan 2014: 21), it soon became a decent source of income for those Indians who could not find work and had to create their own jobs. When others realised that peddling could be a profitable activity, the number of Indians increased and the market soon became saturated. This situation forced the community to disperse to Aberdeen, Dundee, Edinburgh and, during the economic depression of the early 1930s, also to remote villages across the country (Ansari 2004). From 1933 onwards, a modest economic recovery helped the community prosper, although Maan argues that it still lived a frugal life. However, the improved economic situation enticed more migrants to join forces towards the end of the 1930s. By 1940, the numbers of settlers had reached

> Over 400 [. . .] in Glasgow, especially in the Gorbals neighbourhood [and in later decades, when the numbers increased further, in Pollokshields, Govanhill, Woodlands, Garnethill and Maryhill (Maan 2014)], and also in other cities, as well as the more outlying areas such as the Highlands and Islands and the north-east. (Ansari 2004: 48)

The evolution of the Muslim community in Scotland during this period was particularly successful and,

> Despite state and trade union opposition to this presence, these migrants created the material basis for permanent settlement and so constituted themselves as pioneers of a process of migration and settlement that was to continue during and after the Second World War. (Dunlop 2009: 52)

Peddling was to become more significant during and after the Second World War with 30 per cent (that is, 190) of pedlar certificates in Glasgow being issued to South Asians in 1939 and 50 per cent (that is, 330) by the end of the 1950s (Maan 1992). Before the Second World War, a unique event marked the cultural and religious formal establishment of Muslims in Scotland. According to Maan's historical accounts, in 1933[6] the first Muslim-branded organisation in Scotland, a branch of the *Jamiat ul Muslimin* (the Muslim Association),[7] also providing space for Friday prayers, was established in Glasgow, the only Scottish city to have a local Muslim organisation. The organisation aimed 'to look after the religious, cultural and social interests of the Muslim community in [Great] Britain [, irrespective of the ethnicity, nationality and theological orientation of its members,] and to build a Mosque or Mosques wherever needed' (Maan 2014: 25). The efforts of the organisation and local community members helped to acquire a building at 27/29 Oxford Street (Gorbals) in Glasgow in 1944. This building would be converted into the first Scottish mosque later that year, around the same time as the first burial plot for the exclusive interment of Muslims was acquired in the Sandymount Cemetery in Glasgow. The first mosque and the first Muslim burial plot in Scotland were some of the primordial symbols of what would become a strongly visible Muslim settlement in the country.

After the Mid-Twentieth Century

In the post-Second World War context of labour shortage, a number of South Asian migrants moved to Scotland and brought with them their families, thus continuing the settlement of Muslim communities in the country. This was not an exclusively Scottish phenomenon. A similar pattern can be found in the South Asian migration to England narrated in Humayun Ansari's (2004) masterpiece *The Infidel Within: Muslims in Britain since 1800*. But the labour shortage in Scotland was not as serious as in England, as the Scottish economy had not grown and transformed as much as the English economy did in the 1950s and 1960s (Miles and Dunlop 1987). Nevertheless, the mid-1940s and the mid-1950s had brought historical changes to the welfare of Scottish people. The Marshall Plan, providing aid from the United States to Europe, which opened up new markets for exports from British and Scottish industry; strong socio-economic state intervention in agriculture and rural society; the nationalisation of coal, railways, electricity, iron and steel; the Beveridge Plan, requiring compulsory national insurance; the creation of the National Health Service; the mechanisation of agriculture; and growing availability of housing (especially council houses) are some of the factors behind the increased affluence, and the positive changes in employment, health and living standards, of Scottish people (Devine 2012).

According to Devine, better times and the difficulties in filling menial jobs, especially as Irish migration and the low-cost labour it brought with it had slowed down, brought in new South Asians. During this period, South Asians could be found working in unskilled and semi-skilled professions in jute mills, the building industry, transport departments and bakeries. Many South Asians who had migrated from the industrial areas in the Midlands and Yorkshire in England to Scotland helped to bring the total Scottish population to 4,000 in the 1960s. Many of these internal migrants ended up working as bus drivers and conductors in the transport departments of the main Scottish cities (Maan 2014). Curiously, Devine recounts how Glasgow fell into chaos when India and Pakistan went to war in 1965: Indians and Pakistanis, who comprised over half of the labour force in the Glasgow Corporation Transport Department, took leave from work to follow the war on radio and television. As the number of (mostly Pakistani) South Asians living in Scotland increased, community members realised that their interests differed from those of the white Scottish majority. Therefore, in 1955 a group of young Pakistanis founded the Pakistan Social and Cultural Society in Glasgow, which operated under the aegis of the *Jamiat* and catered for the social, cultural and recreational needs of the settled community. The Society and the *Jamiat* would later operate as the two wings of the Pakistan Association, which would be founded in 1962 (Maan 2014).

In the 1960s a large number of migrants arrived in Scotland from the Indian subcontinent. This happened both before and after the Commonwealth Immigrants Act 1962, which regulated unrestricted migration from the New Commonwealth countries to Great Britain. Many Pakistanis and Indians had moved to Great Britain in 1961, when the Act was already under consideration, as part of a 'beat the ban' strategy. After 1962 and throughout the 1960s and 1970s, dependants of previously migrated Pakistanis and Indians joined the developing community in Scotland in what is considered to be a 'chain migration' (Wardak 2000). During the 1960s, South Asian migrants and settlers started climbing the labour ladder by opening small businesses that would slowly replace peddling (Maan 1992). Pakistani grocery shops and newspaper shops appeared in Scottish cities and, in order to survive, often cut prices and stayed open after midnight. The Scottish population showed some initial prejudice towards the increased visible presence of Asians (also bolstered by people from China and Hong Kong), at a time when, by contrast, hostility towards descendants of Irish Catholic migrants was falling. However, 'racial tensions north of the border never reached the acute levels of some English cities, though this may have been mainly due to the relatively small number of coloured immigrants to Scotland in these years' (Devine 2012: 564). Instead, little by little, 'Pakistani corner-shops became as much a part of the Scottish retail scene as the Italian ice-cream parlour established many decades before' (Devine 2012: 564).

The spread of grocery shops followed a more general move to petit bourgeois activities among South Asians, mainly warehousing and restaurant ownership, which helped the community establish itself and penetrate the Scottish socio-economic system as small entrepreneurs (Miles and Dunlop 1987). This was facilitated by the fact that

> The Asian migration to Scotland was not as centrally related to the demands of the capitalist economy as in the instance of New Commonwealth migration to England in the same period and in the case of the Irish migration to Scotland in the nineteenth century. (Miles and Dunlop 1987: 125)

The 1960s also experienced a more visibly Muslim, and not simply South Asian, presence across the main Scottish cities. In 1962, the first mosque in Edinburgh, and the second one in Scotland, opened. Dundee followed the trend in the late 1960s. By the end of that decade, Scotland recorded important growth in the demographic, social and economic development of Muslim communities.

In 1970 Bashir Maan, who had arrived in Scotland from Pakistan in 1953 and had already been appointed as the first ever Muslim Justice of the Peace in Scotland in 1968, also became the first Muslim city councillor (Glasgow) to be elected in Great Britain.[8] This bestowed on Scotland a record in the formal involvement of Muslims in politics within a context of growing participation of British Muslims in national mainstream politics, often in support of the Labour Party, since the 1970s (Ansari 2004). This Scottish achievement would later be followed by the election of Mohammad Sarwar as Member of Parliament (MP) for Glasgow Govan in 1997 (the first Muslim MP in Great Britain) and further signalled the emergence of a visible Muslim presence within the Scottish political and public sphere.

The 1970s and 1980s also recorded the internal migration of a few hundred Muslim families from England to Scotland. According to Maan, such internal migration was driven not only by business opportunities, family connections and the relative prosperity of the Scottish Muslim community but also by the perception of a more tolerant and less prejudicial Scottish environment. There are historical and social reasons to believe that Scotland could have created a more welcoming cultural environment than England. While these reasons are discussed at length in Chapter 6 and in the Epilogue, here it will suffice to present as an example the meritocratic and egalitarian system of schooling and the wealth of opportunities for education available to the lower classes during the Victorian era in Scotland (Devine 2012). Devine goes as far as to call the parish school 'the cradle of the "democratic intellect"' and to talk about a context in which mixing classes produced 'a more egalitarian society than England and was a way of asserting distinctive Scottish values in the one area where the Scots believed themselves not simply the equal but the superiors of the English' (Devine 2012: 91).

Yet, there also exists evidence that in the 1970s South Asians in Scotland were victims of racism and that in the 1980s Glasgow suffered from widespread racial harassment (Bowes et al. 1990). Miles and Dunlop (1987) argue that in the 1980s racist attacks were regularly reported by South Asian and other minority groups, especially in Glasgow, in a context in which a lack of confidence in the authorities and the police and feelings that racial harassment would be underestimated had previously led many people not to report racism (Bowes et al. 1990). The same period records the emergence of the British National Party (BNP), the National Front and similar neo-fascist organisations, which were involved in printing neo-fascist newspapers and organising political rallies. In 1989, associates of the National Front killed two Somali refugees in Edinburgh (Croall and Frondigoun 2010). These political organisations 'link[ed] the much longer tradition of anti-Catholicism with a racism which focuses on the [South] Asian presence' (Miles and Dunlop 1987: 138). As a response aimed at 'seeking action to deal with racism and patterns of exclusion and calling for direct [South] Asian participation in decision-making' (Miles and Dunlop 1987: 138), South Asians started uniting in more self-conscious political organisations, such as the Scottish Asian Action Committee and the Minority Ethnic Teachers Association.

Maan maintains that by the early 1980s Scotland had about 25,000 Muslims and nine mosques (four in Glasgow, two in Edinburgh and one each in Aberdeen, Dundee and Motherwell). In 1982, the Scottish Pakistani Association was founded and sought to foster good relations between

Scottish and Pakistani people. The community started diversifying, dispersing, expanding its businesses and entering new sectors (motor repair, service industry, property, do-it-yourself shops, catering, computer technology and so on). At the same time, young, educated Scottish-born Muslims accessed a range of professions that allowed a certain degree of social mobility. In the early 1990s, about 35,000 Muslims were living all over Scotland and formed a visible presence in the main urban areas as shop, restaurant and takeaway owners, as well as through a growing global and local participation in political affairs.

Interestingly, on 20 October 1991, St Giles' Cathedral in Edinburgh hosted the Service of Repentance in memory of the victims of the First Gulf War, which represented a unique moment in Christian–Muslim relations in Scotland. As Maan recounts, at 6.15 p.m. the Minister of St Giles' Cathedral, Reverend Gilleasbuig Macmillan, stopped the service for a few minutes to allow Muslims to perform their evening prayer next to the altar of the Cathedral. In Maan's (2008: 206) words, 'the Muslim call for prayer was made from the pulpit of the Cathedral and the prayers were performed in the midst of a Christian congregation of over a thousand'. The author posits that 'such an unprecedented and noble gesture could only have come about in Scotland, where tolerance and benevolence in some quarters of society sometimes exceed expectations' (Maan 2008: 206).

Nevertheless, the 1990s and the period leading to 9/11 were not free of racist incidents, especially in Edinburgh (Wardak 2000) and Glasgow (Hopkins 2004a): the stabbing of a sixteen-year-old South Asian boy, Imran Khan, in 1998, as a result of a fight between young South Asians and whites, and racist events promoted by the British National Party in Scotland are notable examples. The shift from racially motivated to religiously motivated intolerance, abuse and attacks will be fully discussed in Chapter 5, as it is an issue at the core of the changing ascription and internalisation of Muslim identities.

While the tension between ongoing discrimination and improved integration will occupy a central role throughout this book, before ending this historical journey it is necessary to stop and explore the last fifteen years of Muslim settlement in Scotland, with particular attention to the two cities, Glasgow and Edinburgh, hosting the two largest Muslim communities.

The Demography of Muslims in Scotland Today

Thanks to the introduction of a question on religion in its previous iteration in 2001, the Scotland 2011 Census represents a very useful resource for
contextualising the contemporary presence of Muslims in Scotland (see also
Elshayyal 2016). The Scottish Muslim community accounts for about 1.4
per cent (76,737) of the total Scottish population (5,295,403), an increase
from 0.8 per cent (42,557) registered in the 2001 Census (Scottish Executive
2005). This is part of a wider process of growing ethnic diversification across
the four main Scottish cities – that is, Aberdeen, Dundee, Edinburgh and
Glasgow (Kelly and Ashe 2014b). When people of no religion (36.7 per cent)
are excluded, Muslims form the second-largest religious group in the country behind Christians, who account for 53.8 per cent of the total Scottish
population, provided that 'Church of Scotland', 'Roman Catholic' and 'other
Christian' are brought together under a single category (National Records of
Scotland 2013). Over a third of Muslims were born in Scotland (37 per cent),
while the majority were born in the Middle East and Asia (41 per cent). Of the
remaining Muslims, 10 per cent were born in Africa, 7 per cent in England
and 4 per cent in Europe, and 1 per cent trace their roots to Wales, Northern
Ireland, the Americas and the Caribbean, Antarctica, Oceania and other places.

The city that hosts the largest section of the Scottish Muslim community
is Glasgow (42 per cent), followed by Edinburgh (16 per cent): these two
cities together account for almost 60 per cent of the total Scottish Muslim
population. After adding to the count Aberdeen (6 per cent) and Dundee (5
per cent), the Census shows that almost 70 per cent of Muslims in Scotland
are concentrated in four main cities. Glasgow also has the highest concentration of Muslims living in any single city, followed by East Renfrewshire,
Edinburgh, Dundee and Aberdeen. Other major communities with more
than 1,000 Muslims, and making up over 20 per cent of the total Scottish
Muslim population, can be found in East Dunbartonshire, East Renfrewshire,
Falkirk, Fife, North Lanarkshire, Renfrewshire, South Lanarkshire and West
Lothian (Table 1.1). Another 10 per cent of Muslims are dispersed across
the twenty remaining Scottish council areas.[9] The Orkney Islands hosts the
smallest community with just twenty Muslims[10] out of a population of more
than 21,000 people. In percentage points, Muslims in the Orkney Islands

Table 1.1 Geographical distribution of Muslims in Scotland (council areas with 1,000+ Muslims)

	Number of Muslims	% of the total Scottish Muslim population	% of the total local population
Glasgow	32,117	41.8%	5.4%
Edinburgh	12,434	16.2%	2.6%
Aberdeen	4,293	5.6%	1.9%
Dundee	3,875	5.0%	2.6%
North Lanarkshire	3,315	4.3%	0.9%
East Renfrewshire	3,002	3.9%	3.3%
Fife	2,591	3.4%	0.7%
South Lanarkshire	2,514	3.3%	0.8%
West Lothian	1,746	2.3%	1.0%
Falkirk	1,415	1.8%	0.9%
Renfrewshire	1,313	1.7%	0.7%
East Dunbartonshire	1,044	1.4%	1.0%

Source: 2011 Census (National Records of Scotland 2013)

constitute a mere 0.03 per cent of the total Scottish Muslim population. The Orkney Islands also hosts the smallest concentration of Muslims (0.09 per cent) in any Scottish council area.

According to the online directory compiled by Naqshbandi (2015a and 2015b), there are seventy-six locations for prayer in Scotland,[11] consisting of mosques, *musallā*,[12] prayer rooms managed by university Islamic societies or Muslim community centres and so on. There are also many Pakistani (or other ethnic) cultural associations (Maan 2014). The four cities with the largest Muslim communities in the country host fifty-eight locations for prayer in total (76 per cent of the total locations for prayer in Scotland): Glasgow has twenty-eight (37 per cent), Edinburgh has twenty (26 per cent),[13] Dundee has six (8 per cent) and Aberdeen has four (5 per cent). The two most important mosques are Glasgow Central Mosque and Edinburgh Central Mosque. Glasgow Central Mosque is a Deobandi-oriented, Sunni mosque, which was largely funded with money from Saudi Arabia and opened as the first purpose-built mosque in Scotland in 1984 (Palmer and Palmer 2000). It can accommodate about 2,500 worshippers. Edinburgh Central Mosque is also a Sunni mosque funded through a donation from Saudi Arabia, specifically from the then King Fahd (who died in 2005), and was inaugurated by his son, Prince Abdul Aziz Bin Fahd, in 1998 (Maclean and Veitch 2006). It uses 'Scottish stones and slate to represent both modern-day Islam and Scottish nationhood' (Ansari 2004: 223) and can host about 1,300 worshippers.

Almost 60 per cent of Muslims living in Scotland are of Pakistani origin or heritage, thus demonstrating that the links between Scotland and Pakistan are extremely strong. This is well exemplified by the curious case of the Pakistani town of Sialkot, one of the world's top manufacturers of bagpipes (Tyab 2013). Another notable example is the parliamentary oath made in both Urdu and English by Scottish-born MSP Humza Yousaf in 2016 (Gilbert 2016). More than half of the Pakistanis[14] who live in Scotland were born in Great Britain. They are also the largest non-white ethnic group in Scotland, accounting for 0.9 per cent of the total population, an increase from 0.6 per cent in 2001. The second-largest Muslim ethnic community is that of Arabs,[15] who make up almost 10 per cent of the total Muslim population in Scotland. Among South Asians, Bangladeshis[16] are the second-largest Muslim ethnic community, making up about 4 per cent of the total Muslim population in Scotland. Other sizeable Muslim ethnic communities are Africans,[17] approximately 6 per cent of the total Muslim population in Scotland, and other Asians,[18] another 6 per cent of the total Muslim population in Scotland. Other large ethnic communities, comprising at least 1,000 people who identify themselves as Muslim, are white Scottish, other whites,[19] mixed or multiple ethnic groups,[20] Indians,[21] and other ethnic groups (Table 1.2).[22]

Table 1.2 Ethnicity of Muslims in Scotland (ethnic groups with 1,000+ Muslims)

	Self-identified as Muslim	% of the total Scottish Muslim population	% of the total ethnic group being Muslim
Pakistani	44,858	58.5%	90.8%
Arab	7,505	9.8%	80.1%
African	4,779	6.2%	16.4%
Other Asian	4,664	6.1%	22.1%
Bangladeshi	3,053	4.0%	80.6%
Other white	2,572	3.3%	2.5%
White Scottish	2,501	3.3%	0.1%
Indian	1,954	2.5%	6.0%
Other ethnicity	1,657	2.2%	33.4%
Mixed or multiple ethnicity	1,342	1.7%	6.8%

Source: 2011 Census (National Records of Scotland 2013)

Unlike Christians, Buddhists and Jews, Muslim males (54 per cent) out-number Muslim females (46 per cent). This occurrence is similar to both the other religious groups predominantly populated by South Asians (Hindus and Sikhs) and people who do not identify with any religion. Slightly less than a third of Muslims are aged below sixteen years, while almost 90 per cent are younger than fifty years of age. These two elements combined make Muslims (with Hindus) the youngest religious group in Scotland, a group that also boasts having full-time students as about a quarter of its members. In comparison, all other religious groups (that is, other than Muslims and Hindus), including people of no religion, have between 19 per cent (Sikhs) and 55 per cent (members of the Church of Scotland) of people being fifty or more years of age.

As far as the labour market is concerned, despite high rates of unemployment, a larger proportion of Muslims of Pakistani and Bangladeshi heritage work in higher-status occupations in Scotland compared to England. Moreover, Pakistanis in Scotland have higher employment rates than Pakistanis in London, north-west England and eastern England (Weedon et al. 2013). Notably, Pakistanis have the highest proportion of self-employed people among all minority ethnic groups in Scotland (National Records of Scotland 2013). The 2011 Census shows that most Muslims tend to work across four sectors: 'distribution, hotels and restaurants' (46 per cent); 'public administration, education and health' (20 per cent), 'financial, real estate, professional and administrative activities' (14 per cent); and 'transportation and communication' (9 per cent). The young age of a majority of community members and the fact that many women still maintain traditional gender roles can explain why Muslims are the least likely group to be economically active, have the least overall wealth compared to other religious groups (Kidd and Jamieson 2011) and have lower than average rates of house ownership, with 54 per cent of people living in an owned property against an average of 67 per cent across the total population (National Records of Scotland 2013).

Among the enduring problems that the community faces are very high levels of overcrowding, with 27 per cent of households being overcrowded against a Scottish average of 9 per cent (National Records of Scotland 2013), and lower than average educational attainment (Kidd and Jamieson 2011). However, the dynamic nature of such a young population offers hope for the future. The 2011 Census records 'very good' and 'good' self-reported health within the two largest Muslim ethnic groups – that is, Pakistanis (85 per cent) and Arabs (91 per cent) – at higher levels than white Scottish people (81 per cent). Yet again, this is a finding that must be interpreted in light of the young age of these two ethnic communities.

Younger generations are entering the educational system – to the extent that not only are young Muslims more educated than their parents (Hopkins 2004a) but, also, South Asians pursue further education more than indigenous Scottish people[23] (Hussain and Ishaq 2002; National Records of Scotland 2013) – and are moving up the socio-economic ladder at a steady pace. The baseline financial condition of Pakistanis, which is the largest Muslim ethnic community in Scotland, was originally more secure compared to the Muslim Pakistani community in England. This is largely due to the fact that the Pakistani community that migrated and settled in Scotland tended to originate from the relatively well-off area of Faisalabad in the Punjab, unlike fellow Pakistanis now residing south of the border. These latter migrants left rural Mirpur for Bradford, Birmingham and other major English conurbations to offer cheap guest labour to the post-Second World War, recovering British economy and after the displacement of over 100,000 people following the construction of the Mangla Dam in Pakistan.

The growing political participation of Scottish Muslims is exemplified by current MSPs Humza Yousaf (also Minister for Transport and the Islands) and Anas Sarwar and former MSPs Hanzala Malik and the late Bashir Ahmad (the first ethnic minority MSP, elected in 2007); the twelve Muslim local councillors;[24] Member of the British Parliament (MP) Tasmina Ahmed-Sheikh; and life peer in the House of Lords Nosheena Mobarik. The political success of these Scottish Muslims and the increasing engagement of younger generations in global, national and local Muslim politics have opened new avenues for the inclusion of Islam within Scottish society.

Muslims have contributed to all spheres of life in Scotland. Among the most prominent public Muslim figures are University of Edinburgh Professor of Islamic and Interreligious Studies Mona Siddiqui; ex-advisor to former Scottish First Minister Alex Salmond and the former Head of Communications of Al Jazeera Osama Saeed; founder of the Murabitun World Movement Abdalqadir as-Sufi; lawyer and human rights activist

Aamer Anwar; community leader and the first female Muslim Justice of the Peace in Scotland Farkhanda Chaudhry; author and dramatist Suhayl Saadi; entrepreneur Amar Latif; billionaire Mahdi al-Tajir; actor Atta Yaqub; and filmmaker Sana Bilgrami.

On the political, legal and policy sides, Scotland has put in place measures to better cater for its Muslim community. Meer and Rosie (2012) suggest that the Scottish Government has attempted to empower minorities. For example, Scottish race equality policies aim to (1) tackle religious discrimination, despite Kidd and Jamieson's (2011) argument that Muslim communities have not been sufficiently protected; (2) encourage skilled migrants to work in Scotland; (3) further integration; and (4) take forward the 'One Scotland Many Cultures' (today known as 'One Scotland') manifesto. In particular, Kidd and Jamieson (2011: 1) note that 'the Scottish Government Race Equality Statement published in 2008 committed the Scottish Government to improving the evidence base on issues of race and faith equality and discrimination to assist with policy development at both national and local level'. Meer (2016: 3) also posits that 'successive Scottish Acts tackling religious bigotry and incitement to religious hatred have adopted tariffs and sanctions that make the treatment of religious discrimination more symmetrical with racial discrimination than is the case in England and Wales'. Although Scotland's engagement with race equality (or alleged lack thereof) has received criticism (Hopkins 2016), the new Race Equality Framework for Scotland 2016–30 (Scottish Government 2016b) demonstrates that the country 'has retained a public commitment to race equality and explicitly sought to entrench its mainstreaming' (Meer 2016: 3). In this sense, asylum policies that align themselves with international covenants and dispersal policies that promote settlement (Meer 2014b) are yet another demonstration that Scotland has often tackled the 'minority question' in inclusionary, rather than exclusionary, terms.

The two cities hosting the two largest Muslim communities, Glasgow and Edinburgh, have taken dissimilar socio-economic trajectories (Scottish Government 2012). Glasgow scores very high levels of economic deprivation among its total population: 19 per cent of Glaswegians live in employment deprivation compared to 8.8 per cent of people in Aberdeen, 9.5 per cent in Edinburgh and 17 per cent in Dundee; 21.5 per cent of Glaswegians also live in income deprivation compared to 9 per cent of people in Aberdeen, 10.4 per cent in Edinburgh and 17.8 per cent in Dundee. Glasgow faces similar rates of challenge when all of the seven domains of the Scottish Index of Multiple Deprivation (SIMD) are taken together: (1) employment; (2) income; (3) health; (4) education, skills and training; (5) geographical access to services; (6) crime; and (7) housing. Similar to the patterns observed in the SIMD 2009, most datazones[25] in Glasgow, as well as in Dundee, are found in the most deprived deciles in the SIMD 2012 and 2016.

While numbers have been falling over time, 48 per cent of all datazones in Glasgow are within the most deprived 20 per cent in Scotland. Three of its datazones are also listed in the five most deprived datazones in Scotland. These are Possilpark (ranked second), Keppochhill (ranked third), and Parkhead West and Barrowfield area (ranked fifth). Moreover, Glasgow (and the wider West Central Scotland region) suffers from high levels of poor health and low life expectancy. These problems are often described as peculiar Glaswegian features, particularly when compared with similar industrial cities in Great Britain and Europe (Walsh et al. 2010a, 2010b). Excess mortality in Glasgow appears to result from various intertwined factors, including the lagged effects and the inadequate measurement of deprivation; post-war regional economic policies; the nature of urban change; and key vulnerabilities, notably the so-called 'democratic deficit' of the 1980s (Walsh et al. 2016). In contrast, compared to Glasgow and Dundee, Edinburgh and Aberdeen are in a much better socio-economic condition, with most datazones to be found in the least deprived deciles in the SIMD. Edinburgh also boasts the least deprived datazone in Scotland in the Craiglockhart area (Scottish Government 2012).

The composition of the Muslim communities in Glasgow and Edinburgh is different. The Scottish capital relies on its international appeal and attracts a much more ethnically diverse Muslim community compared to Glasgow (Figure 1.1). Two thirds (65 per cent) of the Glaswegian Muslim population is Pakistani, while the three other biggest, yet comparatively very small, communities are made up of Africans (9 per cent), Arabs (7 per cent) and other Asians (7 per cent). The Bangladeshi community is minute and accounts for just 1 per cent of the total Glaswegian Muslim community. In contrast, Edinburgh has a much larger Muslim Bangladeshi community (9 per cent)

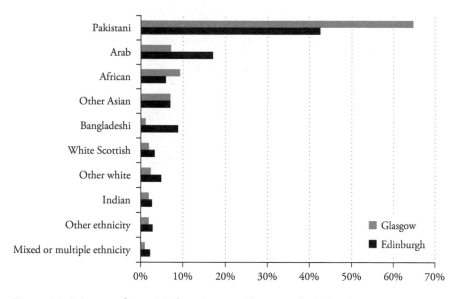

Figure 1.1 Ethnicity of main Muslim groups in Glasgow and Edinburgh (percentage)

Source: 2011 Census (National Records of Scotland 2013)

in a context of higher ethnic diversification that nonetheless retains a distinctive South Asian flavour. The Edinburgh Pakistani Muslim community is relatively large (43 per cent) but proportionally small compared to that of Glasgow and to the Scottish average. Instead, Edinburgh hosts a considerable Muslim Arab community (17 per cent). While two thirds of Glaswegian Muslims are Pakistani, Edinburgh needs to include Arabs and Bangladeshis in the count to reach the same figure. Other notable Muslim communities in Edinburgh are other Asians (7 per cent) and Africans (6 per cent). When all the six white subcategories are brought together in a single white category, Edinburgh (10 per cent) again shows a higher ethnic diversity compared to Glasgow (5 per cent).

Similar to Glasgow, East Dunbartonshire, East Renfrewshire, Falkirk, Fife, North Lanarkshire, Renfrewshire, South Lanarkshire and West Lothian, which are all main areas hosting at least 1,000 Muslims, have a strongly Pakistani component: between 61 per cent and 87 per cent of their Muslim populations are of Pakistani origin or heritage. In contrast, Aberdeen and Dundee, the cities hosting the two biggest Muslim communities after

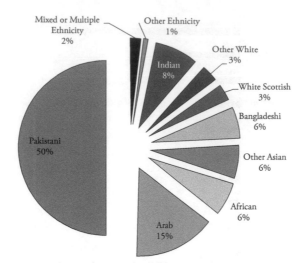

Figure 1.2 Ethnicity of main Muslim groups in Dundee (percentage)

Source: 2011 Census (National Records of Scotland 2013)

Glasgow and Edinburgh, boast highly ethnically heterogeneous Muslim populations similar to Edinburgh, although with some differences in their ethnic composition. Dundee (Figure 1.2) has slightly smaller Bangladeshi and white Muslim populations but a much larger Indian Muslim population compared to Edinburgh. Since the discovery of the North Sea oil in the 1970s, Aberdeen has been Great Britain's centre of the oil industry and has attracted numerous Muslim professionals and entrepreneurs (Maan 2014). Nowadays, Aberdeen (Figure 1.3) is more ethnically diverse than Edinburgh, and obviously much more heterogeneous than Glasgow, with five groups (Pakistani, Arab, Bangladeshi, African and other Asian) each consisting of between about 10 per cent and 20 per cent of the total Muslim population.

Not only do the Muslim communities living in Glasgow and Edinburgh have a dissimilar ethnic composition, they have also followed different trajectories. Glasgow hosted the initial settlement of South Asians in Scotland[26] and currently has the largest percentage (42 per cent) of Muslims in the country and the highest proportion (5.4 per cent) of all Scottish cities. These levels, however, are still not comparable to those of English cities, such as Bradford, Birmingham, Leicester, London and Manchester, which host Muslims in proportions of 10 per cent to 25 per cent of the total local populations (City

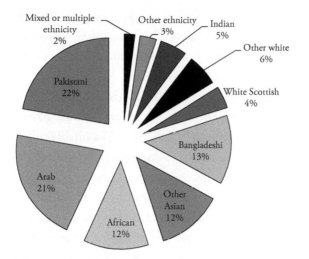

Figure 1.3 Ethnicity of main Muslim groups in Aberdeen (percentage)

Source: 2011 Census (National Records of Scotland 2013)

of Edinburgh Council 2013). Over 60 per cent of Glaswegian Muslims are concentrated in Glasgow South and more than 20 per cent live within two neighbourhoods alone: Govanhill, which hosts 3,700 Muslims out of a total population of 14,400, and East Pollokshields, which hosts 3,500 Muslims out of a total population of 8,100.[27] East Pollokshields is also the most ethnically segregated area in Scotland (Hopkins 2004a). The fact that most Muslims living in Govanhill and East Pollokshields are of Pakistani origin or heritage is not surprising, given that Glasgow hosts 45 per cent of the total Pakistani population in Scotland (Kelly and Ashe 2014b). Pakistani (and Bangladeshi) groups are also the most segregated groups in Glasgow. But their levels of segregation have been falling and are lower than in other main cities in England and Wales, for example Bradford (Carling 2012), Manchester and Cardiff (Kelly and Ashe 2014b).[28]

According to the 2011 Census, 53 per cent of the East Pollokshields population is from a minority ethnic group (an increase from 48 per cent in 2001), a very high figure compared to the Glaswegian average of 12 per cent and the Scottish average of 4 per cent (Understanding Glasgow n.d.). Forty-three per cent of these people are Muslim. Almost 35 per cent of residents speak a non-English main language against a Glaswegian average of less than 15 per cent and a Scottish average of much less than 10 per cent (Kelly and Ashe 2014a). The area suffers from overcrowding (Understanding Glasgow n.d.), is burdened with serious problems of discrimination and racism (Hopkins 2004a) and has become a distinctively Pakistani and Muslim place: shops have dual signs (English and Urdu), South Asian clothes shops display mannequins dressed in *shalvar kameez* and there are beauty salons that are for women only (Siraj 2011). Nevertheless, it remains a 'reasonably affluent area, with almost a third of the population belonging to the professional/managerial class' (Hopkins 2004a: 95). Compared to Glasgow, this population also has slightly higher than average rates of car ownership, educational qualifications, life expectancy and quality of health, and lower than average disability-related problems, although some of these factors might be influenced by a much larger than average young population (Understanding Glasgow n.d.). More generally, data from the SIMD 2012 demonstrate that only 2 per cent of Pakistanis and 3 per cent of Bangladeshis live in the most deprived 10 per cent of datazones in Glasgow. This is a percentage lower than any other group, including white Scottish people (11 per cent) (Kelly and Ashe 2014a).

Unlike in Glasgow and other main British conurbations, where ethnic communities tend to live clustered within particular city areas, the smaller Muslim community living in Edinburgh is widespread and scattered across the city. As Chapter 6 suggests, this could favour closer contact and better integration within wider society. Despite Wardak's (2000) warning that pockets of economic disadvantage exist and, in particular, that there remains ethnic clustering among older Pakistanis through mosques, community centres, sociocultural gatherings and family visits, there are no 'Muslim' or 'Pakistani' neighbourhoods in Edinburgh as there are in Glasgow. Edinburgh Pakistanis enjoy decent standards of living and financial security, often living in well-off areas of the city (Qureshi 2004). The fact that Edinburgh is small and that the Pakistani community is dispersed allows relatively high levels of interaction between young Pakistanis and Scottish people (Qureshi 2004). Many older members of the Pakistani migrant community – 90 per cent, according to Wardak's (2000) study conducted in the early 1990s – originate from the Faisalabad area in the Punjab and live in Leith (East Edinburgh), Gorgie (West Edinburgh) and Broughton (North Edinburgh).

The great majority of Edinburgh Muslims are of Sunni affiliation (Hanafi school of jurisprudence)[29] and in large part adhere to either the Barelvi movement, which is a traditionalist and populist version of Sunni Islam originating in the Indian subcontinent, or the Deobandi movement, which is a South Asian revivalist version of Sunni Islam influenced by Wahhabism. The remaining Muslims are Shi'a, adhering to either the Ja'afari school of jurisprudence or Isma'ilism (Wardak 2002). The main Edinburgh mosque is located in the city centre and within the University of Edinburgh campus, thus representing a visible urban sign of Muslimness within a very diverse geographical and social location that is highly populated with students and tourists. Edinburgh city centre is one of the few areas in Scotland where less than half of the total population in the area is white Scottish. This is part of a trend of increasing ethnic diversity, which 'is not creating polarised islands of different groups, but a mosaic of differently mixed areas' (Simpson 2014). Ten mosques cater for the majority Sunni Muslim community, while the smaller Shi'a Muslim community (estimated at around 500 people) holds prayers at two mosques. While being formally 'open' to all Muslims, these mosques in practice cater for different ethnic and cultural communities, such as Pakistanis, Scottish Pakistanis, Bangladeshis, Arabs, Turks and so on. Some of these mosques operate in 'partnership' with one another in terms of activities and core membership based upon similar ethnic and cultural affiliations, as well as theological understandings of Islamic principles. Being home to very diverse ethnic communities, these mosques represent different micro-social worlds that promote particular conceptualisations and representations of Muslimness in ethno-cultural and religious terms.

Edinburgh presents some unique and defining characteristics that make it an appealing city for people to live in. An analysis of the 2011 Census conducted by the Edinburgh Partnership (2014) reveals that the Scottish capital is a cosmopolitan, compact city that depends on the service sector rather than manufacturing. A city with areas of very high population density, Edinburgh offers sustainable travel and boasts a relatively healthy, well-educated, well-qualified and largely professional young population who enjoy high levels of full-time employment and live in small households, often flats and tenements. It is a city in which many Muslim respondents feel safe and in which they are happy to live and raise their families, in a context of social harmony.

Conclusion

Scotland and Islam have been developing social and cultural ties since as far back as the eighth century: at first sporadically, and particularly through the travels of Scots to Muslim lands; and subsequently in a more continuous and sustained fashion through the settlement of various peoples of Islamic faith in the country. As with England, the bulk of the Muslim diaspora to Scotland are South Asian migrants who came into contact with their former rulers in the British Empire. The settlement of South Asians should be understood in light of the experiences of other notable migrant communities, in particular Irish Catholics and Protestants, Lithuanians, Italians and Jews. There are commonalities with and differences from each of these communities. The experiences of discrimination and prejudice that South Asians shared with Irish Catholics and Lithuanians are particularly significant. The racial and cultural visible diversity of South Asians compared to the white Scottish majority certainly promoted a climate of hostility towards the community, which shifted to encompass religious grounds in more recent times (see Chapter 5). But despite these hurdles, which have a resonance with wider experiences in Great Britain, the settlement of South Asians, and of Muslims from other ethnic groups, in Scotland has been particularly successful.

Contemporary Muslims are entering education at a very steady pace, can be found working at the highest political levels and have offered important contributions to Scottish society, culture and economy. Today, Muslims represent an ethnically heterogeneous population, particularly in Aberdeen, Dundee and Edinburgh, where their diversity can sustain a sense of trans-ethnic Muslimness. Yet, it is important to consider that the largest Scottish Muslim community resides in Glasgow, which is not only a culturally thriving place but also a city suffering from poverty, unemployment, crime and discrimination. When coupled with a Muslim tendency to concentrate within a few specific Glaswegian neighbourhoods, this situation calls for caution when depicting Scotland as a flawless example of Muslim settlement. It is important to bear in mind that the experiences of Scottish Muslims are twofold. They include high levels of integration, social participation and tolerance, which are unique to Scotland and are epitomised by Edinburgh. But they also register more complex living conditions, which are typical of large British conurbations hosting large Muslim populations and which are exemplified by Glasgow.

Notes

1. Scotland's participation in the Crusades is a particularly important point to consider, also in light of the later deep involvement of Scotland in the British Empire, entailing a military, administrative and missionary presence in South Asia (Devine 2012). This exercise in historical awareness can also serve as a countervailing narrative to romanticised notions of Scotland as a land of extreme tolerance and unique egalitarianism.
2. While evidence of their religion is not available, it is likely that these Moors were Muslims from Morocco.
3. Here and further in the text, the term 'Indian' is used in its pre-1947 (Partition between India and Pakistan) meaning to include what today are better known as Indians, Pakistanis and Bangladeshis.
4. Fascist clubs were established across the main Scottish cities and, in 1933, 50 per cent of Italians living in Scotland were members of the Fascist Party (Devine 2012).
5. Western historiography often forgets the key role played by South Asians during the two world wars. India raised the world's largest volunteer armies, about 1.5 million people during the First World War and about 2.5 million people during the Second World War, and fought in all theatres of war alongside British troops (British Library n.d.; Sumner 2001; Ansari 2009; Khan 2015), as well as Scottish regiments (Hall 2014).
6. In the same year, Lady Evelyn Cobbold, a Scottish aristocrat and convert to Islam, became the first British woman to make the pilgrimage to Mecca (Maan 2014).
7. The *Jamiat ul Muslimin* and a splinter group set up in 1943 called the *Ittehadul ul Muslimin* (the Union of Muslims) later, in 1945, merged into a single organisation, the *Jamiat Ittehadul ul Muslimin* (the Muslim Mission) (Maan 2014).
8. Forty-four years later, in 2014, commenting on his unexpected election in a ward of 10,000 electors, only about thirty of whom were Muslim, Maan states that his success 'was a splendid example of the tolerance and friendliness of the Scottish people and indeed their recognition and acceptance of the recently arrived Muslims. The good behaviour of the Muslim community and their contribution to society played an important part in my unexpected victory' (Maan 2014: 62–3).

9. Aberdeenshire, Angus, Argyll and Bute, Clackmannanshire, Dumfries and Galloway, East Ayrshire, East Lothian, Eilean Siar, Highland, Inverclyde, Midlothian, Moray, North Ayrshire, Orkney Islands, Perth and Kinross, Scottish Borders, Shetland Islands, South Ayrshire, Stirling, West Dunbartonshire.

10. Fourteen Pakistanis, three Bangladeshis, one African, one Arab and one member of an unspecified ethnic group.

11. For a detailed description of the history of several of these mosques, see Maan (2014).

12. This is a non-designated, temporary space for ritualistic prayer, which does not meet the criteria for a mosque.

13. In other publications (Bonino 2015a and 2015b), the author indicated that Edinburgh hosts eleven known mosques, in line with the count provided by a Muslim respondent who is very involved in the social and institutional spheres of the Edinburgh Muslim community. The source claimed that eight mosques follow the Hanafi school of jurisprudence (six mosques under Pakistani management, one mosque under Bangladeshi management and one mosque under Turkish management), one mosque follows the Hanbali school of jurisprudence under Arab management and two mosques follow the Ja'afari school of jurisprudence under, respectively, Pakistani management and mixed Pakistani/Iranian management. This book indicates twelve mosques in order to follow Naqshbandi's directory and harmonise Edinburgh with the figures that he provides and that include eight other locations for prayer too. Yet, it should be pointed out that these numbers often vary as mosques open or close to cater for the needs of a changing Muslim population. It is true that Sunni jurisprudence (*fiqh*) establishes strict criteria for a mosque (*masjid*) to be considered as such, for example being a sanctified area where the rewards of prayer in congregation increase twenty-five to twenty-seven times, being permanently dedicated to Allah, being formally designated by the committee and so on. Often mosques evolve from ad hoc and largely private arrangements; the arrangement becomes regular and then it becomes institutionalised through the need to spend significant money, employ an imam and address planning and similar regulations. However, there can be contestation as to whether a mosque should effectively be considered a mosque or, instead, whether it should be considered a *musallā* – that is, a non-designated, temporary space for ritualistic prayer which does not meet the criteria for a mosque.

14. This group includes Pakistani, Pakistani Scottish and Pakistani British.

15. This group includes Arab, Arab Scottish and Arab British.

16. This group includes Bangladeshi, Bangladeshi Scottish and Bangladeshi British.

17. This group includes African, African Scottish and African British but not 'other African', which constitutes a separate category in the Census.
18. This is an unspecified category in the Census. It includes Asians who do not identify as Pakistani (Pakistani, Pakistani Scottish or Pakistani British), Bangladeshi (Bangladeshi, Bangladeshi Scottish or Bangladeshi British), Indian (Indian, Indian Scottish or Indian British) and Chinese (Chinese, Chinese Scottish or Chinese British).
19. This is an unspecified category in the Census. It includes white people who do not identify as Scottish, other British, Irish, Gypsy/Traveller or Polish.
20. This group is unspecified in the Census.
21. This group includes Indian, Indian Scottish and Indian British.
22. This group is unspecified in the Census.
23. This is part of a wider process that has also been identified in England and Wales, where the second and third generations of most minority ethnic groups have made significant progress and South Asians have an ambition to be university educated and to move up the social class ladder (Modood 2005).
24. Muslims are still under-represented among total elected Scottish councillors (Improvement Service 2013) and this is also true of black and minority ethnic (BME) councillors in Scotland (Meer and Peace 2015).
25. These are small areas, each consisting of around 350 households or 800 people.
26. According to some sources, Glasgow also invented the popular chicken tikka masala dish, thanks to the culinary skills of Ali Ahmed Aslam, the owner of the Shish Mahal restaurant in Park Road in the West End of the city (BBC News 2009b).
27. Other Glaswegian neighbourhoods hosting large Muslim populations (more than 1,000 people) are: Pollokshields West; Ibrox and Kingston; South Nitshill and Darnley; Hillhead and Woodlands; the city centre and Merchant City.
28. Overall, the levels of ethnic group concentration in England and Wales as measured via the 'Index of Similarity' are lower than popular perceptions might suggest. Research demonstrates that Muslim communities are rather evenly spread across England and Wales and that their Index of Similarity score is 54 per cent (Jivraj 2013). By comparison, the Index of Similarity scores for British Hindus, British Sikhs and British Jews are, respectively, 52 per cent, 61 per cent and 63 per cent (Meer 2014c).
29. For a quick and basic treatise on the theology, jurisprudence and social aspects of Islam, see Ruthven (2012).

2

SURVIVING THE CRISIS AND RESISTING THE STIGMA: THE POST-9/11 EMERGENCE OF A MUSLIM CONSCIOUSNESS

The life experiences of Muslims in Scotland are multifaceted and are coloured by the many complexities of a post-9/11 world. Muslims of different ethnic backgrounds have united under a common religious banner in the wake of the Rushdie Affair and, particularly, in the years after September 2001. Perceptions of being stigmatised a priori, for the very fact of being Muslim, have shaped the idea of a global 'Muslimness under siege'. Such an idea has reproduced culturally in a 'memic' fashion. While experiences of discrimination exist (more in Chapter 5), yet do so within a context of general positivity towards Muslims (more in Chapter 6), it is important to present a wider perspective and reflect on how globally and nationally informed perceptions of an unequal social standing have translated to the local Scottish level. At such a level, Muslims have resiliently challenged the alienation of visible diversity and have used Islam to construct a Muslim consciousness that goes beyond mere cultural defence. Instead, it serves as a tool of both social survival and group formation, despite the existence of fragmentations in individual and community understandings of cultural, religious, moral and social norms.

The Emergence of Religious Identities among South Asians in Great Britain

The presence of Muslim communities in Great Britain has gained great social and political visibility in the past thirty years, especially after the Honeyford Affair in 1984 and the Rushdie Affair in 1988–9 and, from 2001 onwards, following several Islamist terrorist attacks in the United States and Europe. The Honeyford Affair exploded in 1984, when Ray Honeyford, then headmaster of Drummond Middle School (a predominantly non-white majority school) in Bradford, published an article in the *Salisbury Review* that was harshly critical of the effects of multicultural policies and practices on British education. Honeyford received a storm of accusations of racism and was subsequently suspended from his post. He was reinstated after appealing to the High Court but, facing continuing hostility, he decided to retire in 1986.

The publication of Salman Rushdie's novel *The Satanic Verses* in 1988 was of much greater importance for the development of cohesive Muslim identities. The novel was considered by some Muslims to be blasphemous and gained world attention. By 1989 the book was banned in a number of countries, including India, Bangladesh, Kenya, Indonesia and Sudan. American and British bookshops were threatened and bombed. But the most notorious reactions to the publication of the book are the fatwa issued by Ayatollah Khomeini to kill Salman Rushdie and, notably, the public burning of copies of the book by Muslims in Bradford. The importance of the Rushdie Affair in the shaping of a sense of British Muslim collectivity cannot be stressed enough since it 'marked the end of local pan-Asianism and the emergence of a separate Muslim identity that did away with a particular idea of South Asian cultural heritage in favour of a number of brands of "authentic" Islam' (Bolognani 2012: 622). This gradual process has taken place in a context in which 'British discourse on racialised minorities has mutated from "colour" in the 1950s and 1960s to "race" in the 1960s–1980s, "ethnicity" in the 1990s and "religion" in the present period' (Peach 2005: 18).

The Rushdie Affair effectively marked the beginning of the history of British and European Muslim communities, signalling the emergence of a 'Muslim' (instead of ethnic, such as 'Asian' in Great Britain) social identification and categorisation that places religion at the core of broad discourses around the integration of people of Islamic faith within modern Western societies (Marranci 2008). A key distinction between 'religion' and 'ethnicity' started to take shape. In the early 1990s, Knott and Khokher (1993) demonstrated how young British Muslim women were rejecting their parents' subscription to traditions that were not aligned with their own goals. Jacobson (1997) later highlighted the appearance of Muslim identities that transcend ethno-national boundaries and, instead, indicate belonging to a global community. Similarly, in the Fourth National Survey of Ethnic Minorities in Britain, South Asians for the most part self-identified through religion (Modood et al. 1997). Research conducted by Archer (2001) in the late 1990s gives further credence to the thesis of a gradual shift from ethnic to religious identities. Young Muslims living in England who took part in Archer's study upheld predominantly religious, and not national or ethnic, identities. According to Archer, such a choice allowed Muslims to reject both whiteness and a wider British identity and to unite with people from different ethnic origins under the same religious identity banner. Yet, at the same time, ethnicity has not been entirely displaced by a shared religion. High levels of intra-Muslim ethnic segregation in London (Peach 2006) suggest that the British Muslim community remains divided across ethnic lines, despite a superficial religious, albeit not theological, homogeneity.

The events of 11 September 2001 and the related sociopolitical climate played a key role in further strengthening Muslims' religious affiliation. Peek (2005) draws important parallels between the emergence of hybrid Arab-American identities after the 1967 Arab–Israeli war and the solidification of Muslim American identities after 2001. In the author's own words:

> That catastrophe [9/11] led to an identity formed in response to crisis – an *identity of crisis* – as Islam came under intense scrutiny by non-Muslim Americans. Following September 11 [. . .] being Muslim American has new meanings, as religious identity has become even more central to their social and personal selves. [. . .] The interviewees' religious identities were shaped and further strengthened by the post-September 11 hostility as well as the perceived threat to both Islam and their individual identities. (Peek 2005: 237, emphasis in the original)

The emergence of public Muslim identities, which Meer (2010) calls 'Muslim consciousness', has not only taken place in American society. Current generations of British Muslims have also come much closer to Islam due to a better comprehension of the religion and as a consequence of racial hostilities (Abbas 2005). Within a sociocultural context in which adherence to Islam passes down from one generation to another with very high frequency (Scourfield et al. 2012), nowadays young, predominantly British-born, Muslims have sidelined regional identifications in favour of more prominent religious identities (Meer 2010). Notably, they have publicly reasserted their Muslim identities in the many acts that have brought together ethnically diverse communities under the banner of Islam, from marches in opposition to media depictions of the Prophet Muhammad that they consider offensive (*Guardian* 2015) to everyday display of Muslim symbols, such as long beards and the hijab. In Scotland, Hopkins (2007a) demonstrates that Muslims living in Glasgow and Edinburgh both affiliate with Islam and connect with Scottish society and culture. Saeed et al. (2001) also confirm this finding with regard to young Scottish Pakistanis, whose religious identities tend to go hand in hand with their national and ethnic identities. These findings generally follow broader British studies that assert that, while religion is a fundamental badge of identity (Nyiri 2007; Robinson 2009), Muslims hold multiple non-contradictory identities, usually premised upon *both* religion and nationality (Dwyer 1999a; Nyiri 2007).

While the interface between religious, ethnic and national identities will be discussed at length throughout this book, it is important to stress that being Muslim tends to be prioritised over other identities, even when dual identities are upheld. In line with a primacy of Islamic identification within locally born generations of Muslims in England (Archer 2001), numerous Scottish Muslim respondents proudly declare their Muslim-first identity. Babar, a Scottish-born Muslim of Pakistani heritage, clearly illustrates the power of Islam to connect ethnically diverse communities across the globe:

> The beauty of Islam and the Muslim community is that it is so global. We are so ethnically diverse and the one thing that we have in common is our religion. The pilgrimage to the Mecca is amazing. You literally see people from all over the world. You meet people from countries where you would not think there are any Muslims and it is incredible. It is really powerful.

That is why being a Muslim is more important to me than being Scottish,
British or Pakistani. (Babar, Scottish Pakistani man in his mid-twenties)

Muslims are not a monolithic group. They form diverse groups that play
out their Muslimness very differently (Field 2011). Importantly, Muslims
uphold dynamic and multilayered identities. British Muslims construct and
consolidate so-called 'and' identities (for example, British *and* Pakistani *and*
Muslim) which 'are evolving, heterogeneous entities that are shaped by a car-
ousel of identity choices around, *inter alia*, place, faith, nation and politics'
(Mythen 2012: 407, emphasis in the original). Three main elements characterise such identities: (1) 'solidity', in the form of strengthened religious
identities that positively resist and respond to suspicion, victimisation and
hostility (for example, questioned loyalty to Great Britain and experiences of
discrimination); (2) 'elasticity', as identities are geographically stretched to
connect together 'individual and collective, local and global, self and society'
(Mythen 2012: 400) and to cement the global Muslim community around a
politically transformative identification grounded in an attachment to Islam;
and (3) 'resilience' via strategies of circumnavigation, tactics of situational
avoidance (for example, not using rucksacks, not speaking foreign languages
in public places, wearing Western clothes and so on) and expressive resistance
in order to protect oneself, minimise negative labels and attenuate hostilities.

Muslimness becomes, therefore, entangled in a complicated network of
situational and contextual identity displays and performances. On the one
hand, national belonging can be defined in a way that delimits Muslim identity around discourses of practice and citizenship (Moorey and Yaqin 2010).
It follows that Muslims are required to both demonstrate allegiance to Great
Britain and their British identities and show active belonging to the global
Muslim community. On the other hand, young Muslims have had problems
reconciling ethnic and religious identities to the point that some decide to
give more emphasis to the religious aspect (for example, through liturgi-
cal languages, such as Arabic and Urdu) or the ethnic aspect (for example,
through their own native languages) of their identities based on the context
in which they find themselves (Jaspal 2011). Therefore, the context in which
Muslim identities are constructed is not linear but responds to internal and
external sociocultural tensions.

Developing Muslimness in Scotland: The Contested Nature of Visible Identities

The fact that the primary research informing this book was conducted about ten years after 2001 means that the initial reaction to, and the emotional impact of, 9/11 had reduced but had not vanished. Instead, the development of Muslim identity passes through a more settled post-9/11 process. This process operates at the interplay between wider social and political understandings of Muslimness and internal reflections of individual and community identity by Muslims themselves. This experience reaches higher intensity among younger Muslims and is fairly homogeneous across the ethnic and gender spectra. Consistent with the literature highlighted so far, Scottish Muslims address the uncertainties that have emerged from the sociopolitical response to 9/11 via a process of social identity construction premised upon collective membership and behaviour (Hogg 2000).

Cooley's (1922) 'looking-glass self' concept is particularly useful in understanding identity as a reflection of others' perceptions and judgments. Similarly, Jenkins' idea of selfhood as 'an ongoing and, in practice, simultaneous synthesis of (internal) self-definition and the (external) definitions of oneself offered by others' (Jenkins 2008: 40) fits squarely with the experiences of many Scottish Muslims. The transformative process of Muslim identities occurs at the interplay between both the global, post-9/11 sociopoliticisation of the meanings associated with being Muslim and a local, heightened awareness of being part of a very contested religious and ethno-cultural community. Being (at times negatively) categorised as a Muslim, or more broadly as someone different from the majority society, is experienced both by people who migrated to Scotland and still show visible signs of ethnic or cultural diversity other than skin colour (for example, accent, mannerisms, traditional clothes and so on) and by women who wear the hijab, a highly visible symbol of affiliation to Islam.

Some Scottish-born Muslims who possess many key 'Scottish identity markers' – in particular, birthplace, upbringing, residence and accent (Kiely et al. 2001; McCrone and Bechhofer 2008) – share similar perceptions too. Akhtar is a young man of Pakistani heritage who was born and socialised in Edinburgh. His only visible sign of difference from the white majority is his brown skin colour. Unlike some of his Muslim friends, he does not usually wear either a beard or traditional clothes that could make him stand out as 'alien' in society. Akhtar locates his identity within a multilayered ethnic, religious and national context and, very much in line with Cooley and Jenkins' social identity theories, argues that identity is deeply influenced by people's perception of, and engagement with, him. This young Scottish Pakistani man perceives that his 'otherness' might inform non-Muslims' specific attitudes towards him. While particular treatment and special attention are not always of a negative nature, these can nevertheless signal an out-group categorisation through which some non-Muslims place Akhtar on the outside by engaging with him differently from how they would with a white Scottish man:

> In practical terms my identity has not caused problems but it does very much affect things in terms of how people perceive me. I have seen situations in which I am studying or when I am doing similar things and people – the majority, the non-ethnic majority – would perceive me as someone of Pakistani background even though I have lived here all my life. But that is the way. At university, sometimes lecturers feel that they have got to tell me a little bit more because I am of Pakistani background. Of course, I do not tell them, 'Go to hell,' but I guess that it feels strange. [. . .] When I am with people from my own background then again I am perceived as of Pakistani background. So identity is very much affected by how people perceive you. [. . .] If someone asked me, 'What are you more?' I would probably say Muslim, although I do not know why it is like that. (Akhtar, Scottish Pakistani man in his early twenties)

Many interviewees uphold multiple identities (national, cultural/ethnic and religious) at the same time. These identities are integrated within a networked system in which no aspect of identity is fixed or completely separated from the others. Instead, they work in a dialogical and contextual fashion. Akhtar stresses the contextuality of identity – that is, the deployment of, or predominance given to, a particular aspect of identity in specific social occasions. Especially in Muslim places (for example, mosques and at events arranged by Islamic organisations) or highly cultural and ethnic spaces (for example, South Asian festivals and celebrations), Akhtar and his friends project and present identities that are better suited to the expected sociocultural rules. The shifting between the presentation of one aspect of identity and another is broadly based upon front stage techniques (Goffman 1990a [1959]) that allow the individual to navigate through different sociocultural expectations and ease interactions within different spaces. This process also follows Prokopiou et al.'s (2012) argument and other interviewees' idea of identity as fluid, fragmented, situational and contextual. Some aspects of identity might remain dormant in order to give prominence to those other elements that are more relevant to the immediate social situation in which one is placed.

Moreover, as Hopkins (2007a) found in his research in Scotland, the conceptualisation and representation of identity is extremely complex and becomes influenced by numerous elements, such as geography, time and social context. Many Scottish Muslims emphasise the concept of being a proper Muslim (namely, 'doing Islam' and adhering to the Five Pillars). However, some Islamic duties are difficult to fulfil in a Western society, for example because of educational or other everyday life commitments that make religious practices difficult to conduct (Hopkins 2007a). What remain at the core of Scottish Muslim identities are the feelings of shared religiosity and belonging to a global community of faith. Despite its many theological fragmentations, Islam has brought together very diverse ethnic elements of the community.

The Muslim Identity Shelter: Surviving the Stigma through Islam

The shaping of Muslim identities is a process influenced by externally ascribed categorisations that inform the ways in which individuals of Muslim faith are considered by others and, as a result, how they consider themselves. The developmental process of Muslim identity's formation has been underway since 9/11.[1] Crucial to this process is an idea, spread in a 'memic'[2] fashion, that Muslimness has been 'under siege' in the aftermath of the terrorist attacks on the United States. Publicly visible Muslim identities become reinforced as a consequence of both superimposed labels of outsiderness (Becker 1966) – that is, the idea that people take up the social labels and/or identities that are attached to them by others – and individual reactions to and reflections on such labels. A Pakistani interviewee, Saad, skilfully describes this process in the following terms:

A lot of Muslims will live their lives without knowing what a Muslim is. But as soon as people start calling them 'Muslim', 'Muslim', 'Muslim', they will start thinking about what being a Muslim means. Then, if they find that being Muslim is bad they might leave Islam. However, if they think that there is nothing wrong with being Muslim and that people accusing them are wrong, they will become stronger Muslims. This situation has helped Muslims wake up to their internal realities. That is why you now see a lot more people with beards, a lot more people wearing a hijab and a lot of people becoming Muslim. After 9/11 many people asked themselves, 'What is Islam?' because they did not know much about it before. People used to know me as Saad, but after 9/11 they started considering me as 'Muslim' Saad and having an interest in what Islam is. That is why many people started reading about Islam and becoming Muslim, because they understood that this is the right religion. (Saad, Pakistani man in his mid-thirties)

This extract is crucial in comprehending the constructed nature of Muslimness, whose conceptual foundations reject both universalist and culturalist approaches to identity (Marranci 2008). Muslim identities are negotiated and premised upon the inferences, expectations and ascriptions of behaviours that are attached to role signs. By way of example, a person wearing a turban is labelled a 'Sikh' and is expected to behave according to the ascriptions popularly accorded to a Sikh person. Some white people infer group identity based on non-phenotypical attributes, such as Muslim names, in such a way that this is categorised and understood as a racialised code of cultural belonging and influences white people's ways of dealing with the person in question (Virdee et al. 2006). Muslimness is shaped through an interactional process of external categorisation and internal self-reflection that has emerged since the Rushdie Affair but that has sped up within post-9/11 societies as a result of global events that have influenced the identities of Muslims. In Foucault's (1998 [1978]) *History of Sexuality*, homosexuals became a 'species' and a group as a consequence of the labels and definitions that were imposed on them. Similarly, the process of Muslimness has been promoted by the global categorisation and essentialisation that emerged from 9/11, particularly within mixophobic[3] 'communities of similarity' (Bauman 2007) coloured by social insecurities and fears of the 'Other'. Sartawi and Sammut (2012) posit that perceived threats to Muslimness cause identity pressures on Muslims. Such pressures are dealt with either by avoiding identification with the Muslim community or by emphasising it.

Informal conversations with people in positions of authority at local mosques seem to downplay the argument that Muslims have rejected Islam as a reaction to social labelling, although some Muslims might certainly have become more cautious about showing visible signs of Muslimness in public. On the contrary, several people, including Saad, argue that the external process of Muslim categorisation has determined a shift in the understanding of Muslimness and the awakening of internal religious identities. This is a finding that consistently runs through a number of interviews and informal conversations with Muslims and is particularly relevant to the younger generations: these are young Muslims who were born in Scotland, or who migrated to Scotland in the last ten or fifteen years, as opposed to the older migrants who arrived and settled in Scotland over thirty years ago and who have united mostly on the basis of cultural and ethnic similarity. While this is not necessarily a Scottish-related finding, it certainly confirms that Scottish Muslims have not been left behind in the emergence of a Muslim consciousness. Understandably, not all Muslims link a religious awakening to 9/11 per se. Alena, a Palestinian woman, finds in Islam a tool of cultural transition (Bruce 2011) – namely, a way to overcome her identity struggle and to adapt to a different social and cultural environment:

> The language, the culture and all the rest are so different here. I am from
> Palestine. I came from Gaza, which is such a closed environment, and all of
> a sudden I found myself in Edinburgh. So it was difficult and I think that
> it was also an identity struggle. [. . .] I was confused. I was Palestinian and
> different from others. I was Muslim as well. So I was kind of in between
> but gradually I built up strongly my Muslim identity. I just found myself
> doing that, especially in my early years of university. With time this became
> stronger and stronger – this Muslim part of me. I was always proud of my
> Palestinian part and still am. The British side took me ages to come round.
> [. . .] Being different was a major thing for me because people kept on

asking questions. [. . .] I was not wearing the hijab; that came a bit after that. I do not know. I felt that I found rest in my Muslim identity. (Alena, Palestinian woman in her late twenties)

While cultural transition is a reason for a heightened sense of belonging to the Muslim community, this does not happen in a vacuum. Instead, it is deeply embedded within a global context in which Muslims have been scrutinised and in which Islam serves as a ready-made shelter against real and perceived hostilities. Many Muslims consciously frame their identity changes as a response to the post-9/11 external social categorisation of Muslims *qua* Muslims. Zakir lived for just over twenty years in England before moving to Scotland in the late 1980s. He describes his identity transformation through the 1980s and, in its latest development, after 9/11:

> *Stefano*: What impact did 9/11 have on the relationship between Muslims and wider society?
> *Zakir*: After 9/11 things changed a bit. I had had my own post office for eight years. When 9/11 happened, customers that had known me for years would ask me, 'Are you a Muslim?' They started questioning my faith. I thought that it was a joke but it was not. So my identity changed as well. When I was born we were classified as 'Asian' or 'Pakistani' but mostly Asian. In the 1980s they started putting us into different boxes: 'Pakistani', 'Bangladeshi' and 'Indian'. They split the group. When I used to go to school we would just say 'an Asian meal'. I would call myself British Asian. Sure, British, but also Asian because I would never be fully accepted as part of the indigenous population. Now I have come to emphasise my Muslim identity more than my Asian identity.
> *Stefano*: When exactly did this happen?
> *Zakir*: I think that it happened after 9/11.
> *Stefano*: What was this due to?
> *Zakir*: Mostly because of people asking me if I was a Muslim. (Zakir, British Pakistani man in his mid-forties)

This view is taken forward by Munawar, a Yemeni man, who highlights how Muslim identities have not taken a passively ascribed but an active, expressive role that serves the purpose of surviving the post-9/11 social crisis that

Muslims are experiencing. This is what can be called a positive 'reaction formation' (Cohen 1955) to social exclusion and a form of secondary (social) 'deviance' that develops as a response to societal condemnation (Lemert 1951 and 1974):

> *Stefano*: How has 9/11 affected the ways in which Muslims go on with their lives here?
>
> *Munawar*: Muslims have a lot of problems to deal with. They have to clarify the difference between themselves and those people [namely, terrorists] and who did what. That is the point where identity became an essential thing to have, to show, to express and to tell people.
>
> *Stefano*: So Muslim identities have strengthened . . .
>
> *Munawar*: . . . as a response to what happened ten years ago. Actually, it was a response to the social response to what happened. (Munawar, Yemeni man in his early thirties)

The emergence of a religious and ideological Muslim shelter under which people of different ethnicities and cultures can find refuge and unite has speeded up as a response to the global sociopolitical focus on Islam and the real and perceived stigmatisation that has taken place since 2001. Stigmatisation operates in various forms, many of which are explored in Chapter 5. The most powerful, and one that is often cited during conversations with Muslims, relates to the negative media portrayals of Islam, which have the capacity to reproduce negative social attitudes towards Muslims. In the words of Zemar, an Afghani man in his mid-thirties, through the media 'the story [9/11] gets refreshed and then people think that Muslims are bad'. Scottish Muslims react by internalising an individually and collectively (re)constructed Muslim label that appropriates, resists and challenges perceived social stigmatisation through the development of a strong survival-oriented and proud allegiance to Islam. Such reinvigorated Muslim identities are formed to actively and consciously unite diverse ethnic constituencies, which might otherwise remain separate, through the religious and ideological tools offered by Islam. This idea is well captured by Adila, a Kenyan Pakistani woman, who argues that 9/11 spurred Edinburgh Muslims to look beyond their own cultural environment and to mobilise through shared social experiences:

> I think that 9/11 made us wake up. It made Muslims wake up. They were all in their family circles, in their clan circles, in their communities and then they realised that Islam had been insulted because the 9/11 terrorists were Muslims or so-called Muslims. They did something that was very wrong, that in Islam is very wrong. So now we have to tell people that what those people did was very wrong and this is what brought a lot of Muslims together. (Adila, Kenyan Pakistani woman in her mid-forties)

To sum up, Muslim identities have been formed through, and reacted to, the post-9/11 formative years, rather homogeneously among the ethnically diverse younger generations, despite obvious political, social and theological fragmentations in the ways in which these identities are played out on a daily basis. Furthermore, Islam has served as a tool of individual and collective survival through which Muslims can find a sense of in-groupness and shared social and moral identity in the face of threat and uncertainty. Lastly, Muslim identities have been visibly declared and expressed as a symbol of allegiance to a collective struggle for recognition and equality. This flows into a strong, quasi-metaphysical experience of global collectiveness that Babar describes as the power of Islam to unite ethnically diverse people, and into the related feeling, shared by many respondents, that 'being a Muslim is more important than being Scottish, British or Pakistani'. The individual and collective self-awakening and sense of unity that is subsequently projected externally via expressions of visible Muslimness follows on from a fifteen-year process of transformation in the ways in which Muslims actively think about themselves and interact with wider society:

> There have been occasions on which Muslims tried to show that they had nothing to do with terrorists. This was probably driven by a fear of being singled out or picked on by their neighbours, for example. On these occasions people think that they should live in a society of people like themselves and have a safe neighbourhood. (Munawar, Yemeni man in his early thirties)

This extract explains how Lemert's idea of secondary 'deviance' as a response to another social response and Cohen's 'reaction formation' work in practice within a religious community that has come to the foreground in public and political discussions on community cohesion and integration. During field-work, an opportunity arose to observe this pattern of reactive and expressive strengthening and cohesion of Islamic identity at the weekly meetings of a Muslim student society. During the weekly meetings, members of the society usually discussed news and issues of relevance to Muslims living in the West. A shared sense of victimhood, often related to the fates of fellow Muslims involved in conflicts abroad (in particular, Palestine, Iraq and Afghanistan) and the perceived negative portrayal of Muslims in the media, reinforced individual attachments to religious and ideological identities, irrespective of different ethnic and cultural backgrounds.

This situation traces its roots to a generational sociopolitical mobilisa-tion, faith-based activism (Hamid 2011) and (re)assertion of identity in an age of uncertainty and hostility that has seen Muslims across Scotland stand up and make their voices heard within wider society. During meetings of the student society, attendees often used the 'Muslim soft cushion' of religious similarity and commonality of mores to reinforce one another's ideas and beliefs about a number of issues of relevance to Muslims globally and locally.[4] These public occasions often prompt a united Muslim self-constructed 'con-sciousness *for* itself' (Meer 2010: 141, emphasis in the original). Visible signs of Muslimness are and will remain powerful tools to reassert public identities, and nothing encapsulates the complexities around symbols of Islam in the public sphere better than the hijab.

Uncovering Islamic Symbols

Throughout this book, the hijab will emerge as a contested symbol, one that can attract criticism, scorn, praise and interest from both the Muslim and the non-Muslim communities. While media reportage that use of the hijab is on the rise (Goldsmith and Harris 2014) needs more substantiated appraisals, anecdotal evidence and observation at the Muslim student society suggests that, at the very least, the veil publicly asserts strong Muslim identities that challenge the post-9/11 perceived stigma and displays people's pride in being Muslim. A number of interviewees started wearing the hijab only after 2001 or after moving to Scotland from abroad. Interestingly, during the period of fieldwork, a new committee led by a more conservative female president took over the Muslim student society and new members appeared at the weekly meetings.

The most notable element was that a much stronger religious atmosphere permeated the activities of the group compared to the previous year. The formal meetings were now preceded by seminars on the life of the Prophet Muhammad. Prayers were officially introduced and all members would break away from the meeting to go to the mosque (male members) or to an adjoining room (female members) to pray. The weekly topics for discussion were structured around religious or current affairs. Partly motivated by the attention that Western societies have placed on Muslims after 9/11, a sense of shared belonging to Islam manages to unite Muslims from different walks of life. The most significant change that occurred from one year to the next was the appearance of numerous hijabs to cover the hair of most female members of the student society, including several young women who had not worn the veil during the previous year. There are many individual and community purposes that are fulfilled by the hijab and these are outlined in Chapter 6. What is important for the current discussion is to understand the multiple functions of the hijab and the impact of 9/11 on the shaping of reactive and expressive public identities. These identities signal the belonging to a global community of faith even in Scotland, where Muslims have had more positive life experiences than their co-religionists south of the border.

However, not all Scottish Muslim women have adopted the hijab. Rules governing 'Muslim' social spaces also remain contradictory. A telling example is the case of Aisha, a British-born Muslim who actively helped run the Muslim student society, organised meetings and events and, essentially, maintained a role of leadership under the previous Muslim student committee. Aisha was in every sense a very successful member: she managed to bring in new people, both Muslims and non-Muslims, and planned several projects for the year ahead. She did not wear a hijab and dressed in typically Western clothes (jeans, pullovers and so on), a feature that distinguished her from several Muslim female members who preferred more traditional garments. Aisha's choice cost her the election at the end of the year, when a more socially conservative woman, who had not played any role and who had barely attended any meetings, won the contest to become the new president of the Muslim student society. Behind the scenes, speculations suggested that the society's 'old guard' – namely, students of Pakistani origin or heritage –

found Aisha's 'progressive' appearance and mannerisms to be religiously inappropriate. Aisha's style of leadership – standing at the centre of the room when addressing members of the society – coupled with her choice of clothing and her attempts to expand the society's gaze beyond its Pakistani membership is thought to have caused resentment among some members of the society. A more inwardly refocused orientation was very palpable under the new presidency and brought to light the contradictions of a community that is superficially united through faith yet remains divided along social, cultural and theological lines.

These contradictions are all the more evident in identities and practices that are still heavily shaped by religion and by ideas of masculinities premised upon an ethnic, patriarchal and hierarchical system that considers the man as the dominant element of the gender equation (Dwyer et al. 2008). Crucially, this case epitomises a cultural *and* religious dissonance in which dress is a symbol of two oppositional identities: one identity that conforms to South Asian (and Muslim) expectations and one identity that conforms to Western standards (Dwyer 1999b). While many Muslim women seem to be able to negotiate different cultural influences in a way that is acceptable to most fellow Muslims, some more conservative men might not appreciate that women express 'Westernised' and sexualised identities. When coupled with the fact that public Muslim identities have come to represent allegiance to a global set of expected religious, social and political beliefs, challenging such identities is all too problematic for women.

It is therefore not surprising that, as Chapter 4 further demonstrates, Scottish Muslim women search for ways to escape culturally mediated religious expectations via a series of navigation tools. In a context in which modesty is still an expected trait of Muslim femininity, women construct a series of layers that can help them survive different social and cultural environments. A key area that remains taboo within many Muslim communities, especially the more traditional ones, is dating. Muslim women who wish to enter the dating market tend to juggle identity performances in order to retain honour in the house and in the community while behaving very differently in bars, nightclubs and other sexualised spaces. What could be termed 'moral Muslim identities' are therefore utilised by, if not directly imposed on, women in order to reassert their desexualised, decent and modest femininity in front of their parents and other community members. Here, 'make or break' family approaches to thorny personal issues based on prescriptive rulings and customs (Suleiman 2012) certainly play a role in sustaining young Muslims' feelings of a detachment between home and the outside world. At the other end of the spectrum are 'sexualised Muslim identities', which are deployed during romantic relationships[5] and which remain in a limbo of false secrecy. That is, parents and community members are unaware of, or turn a blind eye to, such identities but sisters and close friends know what happens outside the cultural and spatial boundaries of the Muslim environment. 'Transitional Muslim identities' can mediate the two extremes and are often shown to those friends who act as confidants and psychological supporters. While formal social events still maintain a certain level of detachment, if not total spatial segregation, between the sexes, several young Muslim women socialise in mixed-gender environments. This is a testament that community dynamics are influenced by Western sociocultural practices and are played out in local negotiation with ethnic, cultural and religious mores.

A highly religiously and ideologically charged conference that took place in Edinburgh during Islam Awareness Week in 2013 is a telling example. The event recorded over 700, mostly Muslim, attendees coming from all over Scotland. Men sat on the left-hand side of the conference theatre, while women sat on the right-hand side of the room. But as soon as people broke for lunch, the gender segregation reality started to take on a new character. Several food stalls had been put in place in the hall outside the conference theatre, and many attendees decided to eat there. Although gender segregation could not be fully maintained in that context, there was still a visible physical and social detachment between men and women. Men were eating with other men while women were eating with other women. Meanwhile, at a local McDonald's, male and female conference attendees were freely socialising, enjoying their time together and eating non-halal meat. All the rituals associated with gender segregation had been left at the conference venue. Only a few hundred metres away, this group of Muslims freely enjoyed their lunch break in a mixed-gender environment. Islam still united this group of people but codes of behaviour and norms and religious performances became irrelevant, as a further reminder of the complexities and nuances of the Muslim community living in today's Scotland. Importantly, this event highlighted the key fact that 'a strong community is not airtight, but open, plural and flexible, and inclusive of creative energies and voices' (Suleiman 2012: 16). There are no better words to describe the Scottish Muslim community.

Conclusion

The changes brought into the relationship between Muslim and non-Muslim communities by 9/11 have shared many similarities across different Western countries. In Scotland, Muslims have followed the path taken by their counterparts south of the border and in other European countries: they have united under the banner of Islam. But what is peculiarly British and, by default, Scottish about the strengthening of religious identities is the process through which the formative years of the Rushdie Affair created a fertile ground for an intra-community cohesion that found its turning point in 9/11. Partly as a reaction to the increased public focus on Islam, and partly as the outcome of a more easily connected global community, Scottish people of Islamic faith place being a Muslim above other identities. Islam has come to play the role of a shelter identity through which Muslims survive the perceived post-9/11 stigma and reassert their sense of in-groupness. Clearly, there remain theological, cultural, moral and social fragmentations in the ways in which the Scottish Muslim community operates. This is true for any other Muslim community in Europe and, for that matter, for any ethnic and religious community in the world. Tensions between, on the one hand, family and community expectations and, on the other hand, wider social opportunities have shown the complexities and contradictions of being a Muslim in Scotland. Yet, Scottish Muslims do feel a strong sense of belonging to the country. Undoubtedly, Scotland sits at the core of many Muslims' self-identification.

Notes

1. Interestingly, most respondents glossed over the terrorist attack on Glasgow airport in 2007 and, instead, simply referred to September 11 and the post-9/11 context when commenting on the changes in personal and social understanding of Muslimness. The few interviewees who spontaneously talked about the Glasgow bombing argued that the event had not had a major effect on community relations.

2. The word 'meme' was coined by Richard Dawkins in his masterpiece *The Selfish Gene*, which was published in 1976. Dawkins considers 'memes' to be the cultural mirrors of 'genes' and describes them as culturally reproduced ideas, behaviours and styles that transmit from person to person.

3. Bauman defines mixophobia as the fear of mixing with different religious, social or economic groups.

4. By way of example, these issues included but were not limited to the following: the Israeli–Palestinian conflict; the Western military involvement in Iraq and Afghanistan; the perceived demonisation of Muslims in the media and its repercussions on social perceptions of Islam; and Western sexual relationships falling outside religious marriages.

5. While the degree of physical intimacy between Muslim partners outside marriage may vary among couples, the dynamics of such relationships do not differ much from typically Western relationships, except in some of the daily practicalities that need to be put in place to make them work, for example being discreet with family members, avoiding places of Muslim congregation and so on.

3

POST-ETHNIC SCOTTISH MUSLIM IDENTITIES AT THE NEXUS OF NATION AND RELIGION

The construction of Muslim identities in Scotland, within a global climate that has often contested Muslims' belonging to the Western countries where they live, operates at the intersection of religion, ethnicity and nation. While a shift from ethno-cultural to religious identities is not necessarily a uniquely Scottish experience, the marriage between national and religious identities, mostly among young Muslims, finds a particularly strong resonance in the Scottish context. In such a context, Islam binds together an ethnically heterogeneous set of people who affiliate globally and locally and resist the post-9/11 perceived stigma through the common destiny and the sense of belonging offered by religion. This goes hand in hand with strong Scottish identities, which are less ethnically fixed and more inclusionary than English identities, and which allow Muslims to integrate with people of other faiths and cultures under a national banner of civic unity, belief in social justice and a sense of tolerance. Islam as a religion, an ideology and a way of life and Scottish nationalism emerge as the bonds and the bridges that unite diverse Muslim constituencies with one another and with Scotland's non-Muslim majority. A Scottish experience of being Muslim is underway in twenty-first-century Scotland and is permanently changing the face of the Muslim community.

Scottishness: Between Inclusion and Exclusion

To comprehend in what ways and to what extent Muslims can make reasonable claims of being Scottish, it is crucial to unpack the nature and essence of Scottish identity. While Britishness has always maintained an important role in Scottish people's identities, sentiments of personal affiliation to Scotland have increased since the 1970s at the expense of British identities (Bond and Rosie 2002). In Bond and Rosie's examination of the period 1992–2001, 36 per cent of people reported holding an exclusively Scottish identity in 2001, as opposed to 19 per cent in 1992. At the same time, people holding dual Scottish and British identities declined from 33 per cent in 1992 to 24 per cent in 2001. The strengthening of Scottish identities is nowhere more evident than in the Scotland 2011 Census (National Records of Scotland 2013), which recorded that 62 per cent of people in Scotland feel 'Scottish only' against 8 per cent of people who feel 'British only'. Dual Scottish and British identities account for 18 per cent of the population. Scottish people are bound by national solidarity rather than class solidarity, in a context in which Scottish people feel closer to fellow Scots of different social classes than to English people from the same social class (Bond and Rosie 2002). Bond and Rosie's study demonstrates that, for slightly more than half of the population, national identity is central in making sense of oneself.

In a country that has witnessed the ascendancy of the independence movement, a strong national identity may well explain the increase in identification with Scotland at the expense of Great Britain. Nonetheless, a strong national identity alone does not necessarily equate with blind support for independence. The independence referendum, which took place on 18 September 2014 and was voted against by a majority of 55 per cent of people, is a case in point. In what would now appear to be prophetic words, back in 2002 Bond and Rosie (2002: 43) noted that

> Strong levels of 'Scottishness' as measured by asking people about their national identity do not correspond to other apparent indicators of strong Scottishness – support for the SNP [Scottish National Party] and for an independent Scotland – as neatly as a common sense understanding might lead us to suspect.

Similarly, in another study the two authors found a 'substantial "non-alignment" between identities and political preferences' (Rosie and Bond 2008: 63), although the ascent of the SNP has certainly transformed Scottish nationalism from a movement of symbolic political struggle into a cardinal, institutional feature of Scotland. With the exclusion of a dip to 23.8 per cent of preferences in the Scottish parliamentary election in 2003 compared to the 1999 elections (28.7 per cent of votes), the SNP has been on the rise. It collected 32.9 per cent of votes, and a minority government, in 2007 and 45.4 per cent of preferences, and the first majority Scottish government, in 2011. A landslide victory in the General Elections of 2015 further strengthened the position of power of the SNP in Scotland: an unprecedented 50 per cent of votes and fifty-six out of fifty-nine seats won. In 2016, the SNP won a historic third term in the Scottish Government with 42 per cent of preferences.

Muslims have been very much involved in writing the history of the SNP. While the appointment of Humza Yousaf as the first ever minister from an ethnic background in Scotland in 2012 is the most obvious example, the increasing support for the party by Muslims of Pakistani background has broken the traditional identification with the Labour Party. In 2003, many Muslims switched their support from Labour to the SNP and started advocating for full Scottish independence, possibly at even higher levels than the indigenous Scottish majority (McGarvey and Mulvey 2016; Hussain and Miller 2006; *Economist* 2009).

Strong sentiments of belonging to Scotland can well be explained within a context that has facilitated community cohesion across various ethno-cultural communities. Again, cultural identities and political separatist identities need to be distinguished, since 'it is quite compatible, for example, to define oneself as [culturally] Scottish, and yet be opposed to either Independence or Home Rule [as signs of a political separatist identity]' (McCrone 2001: 165). This position is reinforced by the idea that 'ascription to Scottish nationalism and national identity can be expressed within cultural and political terms but does not necessarily necessitate support for secession' (Mycock 2012: 64). While this book is not a comprehensive study of Scottish national identities, it is important to stress the fact that feeling Scottish and supporting independence are often linked but not necessarily coterminous. Statistical evidence pointing out that about 61 per cent of SNP supporters would still feel British even if Scotland became independent, due to common historical, cultural and geographical connections (McCrone and Bechhofer 2015), is a testament to the intricate layers of identity in a politically fragile multinational state.

The ways in which national identity plays out on a day-to-day basis vary. National identity can be taken for granted, to the point of seeming to some people to hold little pragmatic relevance for them (Kiely et al. 2001). Yet, it still plays a crucial role in the organisation of social and political action, such as sporting events and war (McCrone and Bechhofer 2008), and the latter has certainly constituted a mark of pride for Scottish politicians and citizens who vehemently opposed the Iraq War in 2003. It is true that Scotland fails to offer strong markers of national identity in the form of language and religion, although Calvinism has definitely imbued and shaped Scottish culture (McCrone 2001). But there exist clear markers (Kiely et al. 2000) that help Scottish people to support their national identity claims during social interactions.

As McCrone (2001) postulates, claims of Scottish identity are premised upon five key markers: (1) place of birth; (2) upbringing and education; (3) ancestry; (4) place of residence; and (5) length of residence. Secondary identity markers are represented by one's name, commitment to place, accent, physical appearance and dress. McCrone further maintains that such markers can be either 'easily accessible to others' – that is, they are immediately understandable – or 'less accessible to others' – that is, they cannot be understood at once. Accent, physical appearance and name (fixed, unchangeable markers) plus place of residence, commitment to place and dress (fluid, changeable markers) belong to the former category and can be established during the first encounter with an individual. In contrast, place of birth, ancestry and place of upbringing or education (fixed markers) and length of residence (fluid marker) belong to the second category and can be established only after having become acquainted and communicated with an individual.

The identity markers just described do not exist in a vacuum but are strictly connected to identity rules. Identity rules are 'probabilistic rules of thumb whereby under certain conditions and in particular contexts, identity markers are interpreted, combined or given precedence over others' (Kiely et al. 2001: 36). Kiely et al. list nine identity rules that regulate how an individual claims a national identity. Some of these rules are important in explaining claims of national identities per se but are even more important as they regulate how Muslims can claim a Scottish identity that wider society is likely to accept. First, a claim should be made upon a set of identity markers that undisputedly demonstrate a strong national identity that wider society will be unlikely to reject. Second, and strictly connected to the first point, place of birth, ancestry and upbringing and education, plus place and length of residence, are the strongest identity markers that sustain national identity claims. Place of birth is the strongest identity marker on its own, not surprisingly given that many people equate birth with nationality. Third, contradictory markers undermine any national identity claim. If an identity claim is likely to be challenged or received in a negative way, people tend to avoid making such an identity claim. Last but not least, these markers and rules are important yet are not infallible in regulating national identities:

> Markers in themselves do not explain how people will use them, and [. . .] are subject to a series of probabilistic rules of thumb concerning how they operate. [. . .] These markers and rules are used in and generated by social interaction. In other words, they are sustained in the day-to-day dialogues people have with each other, in the course of which they make judgments about who people are, and whether they 'belong' or not. (Kiely et al. 2001: 52)

Despite their intrinsic limitations, markers of Scottish national identity are crucially important in explaining how Scottish Muslims can successfully lay claim to belonging to Scotland. In many ways, for some Muslims, especially those who were not born in Scotland, claims to Scottish identity are endangered by the anticipation of a negative social response:

> Those who feel they do not possess the necessary attributes and markers of Scottishness [, and some Muslims may well be part of this category,] do not feel able (or perhaps simply do not want) to claim a Scottish identity, and hence feel that others – particularly those lacking the key marker of birthplace – should not be able or want to claim such an identity marker. (Bond 2006: 620)

While citizenship grants the basic form of national inclusion, Bond argues that holding British citizenship does not imply that the majority group will recognise minorities' national belonging. Bond (2006: 610) astutely notices that Scotland's '"stateless" nature means that formal citizenship cannot be used as a surrogate for national belonging' in a context in which 'to be born in Scotland enables people, both white and non-white, to claim to be Scottish with little fear that the person receiving this claim will not accept it' (McCrone and Bechhofer 2008: 1259). But even Scottish-born Muslims face hurdles in successfully claiming a Scottish identity. Numerous studies (Bond 2006; McCrone and Bechhofer 2008; McCollum et al. 2014) have shown that ethnicity remains important in drawing national boundaries to the extent that accent, which would normally demarcate Scottish from non-Scottish people, cannot be used as a national identity marker by non-white people as successfully as by white people. Yet, the picture is more complex than just described.

It is true that 'the overwhelming importance of place of birth suggests that being Scottish still has a strong "ethnic" rather than a "civic" basis' (McCrone and Bechhofer 2008: 1259). However, it is equally true that 'Scottishness is less ethnically fixed than Englishness' (Kyriakides et al. 2009: 297) and offers a fertile ground for the thriving of hybrid, ethnic and national identities (McCrone 2002). Moreover, even those who were not born in Scotland and/ or do not have Scottish ancestors can rely on very long-term residence (over thirty years) to sustain the process of 'becoming' Scottish. But again, ethnicity may get in the way to the extent that there is a general reluctance to 'whole-heartedly accept the Scottishness of those from "visible" minority ethnic groups, even when they may have other identity markers (such as residence and accent) important to being Scottish' (Bond 2006: 623). Surprisingly, it is political elites who have a more inclusive sense of Scottishness, considering it a matter of individual choice or belonging (Kiely et al. 2005), compared to the more exclusionary masses (Leith and Sim 2016), who frame the idea of being Scottish around birthplace (Leith 2012). The same political context is also, at least in words, accepting of religious pluralism, with limitations on the spheres of multilingualism and institutional multifaithism (Meer 2015a).

There are suitable ways for Muslims to negotiate ethnic diversity within the Scottish landscape. Cultural syncretism can break the racialised connection between Scottish Asian Muslims and non-Scottish Asian Muslims

(Virdee et al. 2006). In other words, according to Virdee et al., those who have not internalised neighbourhood codes and have not adopted a 'syncretic' identity are at a higher risk of exclusion. On the other hand, hybridised codes of cultural belonging can reverse the ways in which phenotypical categorisations of non-whites, including Muslims from ethnic minorities, are evaluated. For example, a Scottish accent helps, to some extent, Muslims to break the perceived connection between skin colour and behaviour and the related racist response by the non-Muslim majority. This process de-racialises Scottishness, destabilises exclusion based on phenotype and allows Muslim to partake in the public sphere on a more equal basis. There is a different national discourse in place here, maintain Virdee et al., which employs alternative hybridised codes of cultural belonging to challenge the historical racialisation of national identity and offers a viable route towards the integration of minorities into Scottish society.

Other studies have also highlighted that hybridised codes of identity and validation from wider society are important aspects of ethno-religious minorities' integration and sociopolitical mobilisation. Research conducted with Somalis in Ealing, England, demonstrates that their political mobilisation in local elections is mediated by identification with the wider polity (Scuzzarello 2015). The validation of such identification by British institutions, which can manifest in Muslim freedoms to build mosques and celebrate Eid, is key to political mobilisation. In Scuzzarello's (2015: 1229) own words, Somalis' 'dual identification grants them a sense of entitlement of their rights and can make them more likely to voice their political opinions than other groups who do not feel equally part of the recipient society'. Scottish Muslims have come to uphold exactly this type of dual identification in a context that registers an ongoing Muslim involvement in the social and political affairs of the country.

Being Scottish *and* being Muslim

Since as far back as the early 2000s, Scottish Muslims have reported upholding multiple identities that mix religion, nation and ethnicity and remind us of the 'unsatisfactoriness of unitary definitions of Muslim or Pakistani identity in [Great] Britain' (Saeed et al. 2001: 839). An early study conducted by Saeed et al. (2001) collected data via a modified Twenty Statement

Test[1] from sixty-three young Scottish Pakistanis aged fourteen to seventeen. When people were not provided with any bicultural labels – namely, when they were free to choose a single identity – 41 per cent of responses in the study clustered around Scottish Pakistani (22 per cent) and Scottish Muslim (19 per cent), followed by Pakistani (17 per cent) and Muslim (16 per cent). While the figures for a combination of Scottish national identity with either Pakistani or Muslim identity were therefore already pretty high, when respondents were given a choice of dual identity labels, 63 per cent of people identified as Scottish Pakistani. To explain these results through a sociological lens, the authors employed Hutnik's (1991) quadric-polar model of ethnic identity strategy. This model proposes that ethnic minority identity choices produce four different possible outcomes:

1. Dissociation: high identity for the minority ethnic group (Pakistani) and low identity for the majority group (Scottish).
2. Assimilation: high identity for the majority group (Scottish) and low identity for the minority ethnic group (Pakistani).
3. Acculturation: high identities for both the minority ethnic group (Pakistani) and the majority group (Scottish).
4. Marginality: low identities for both the minority ethnic group (Pakistani) and the majority group (Scottish).

When people were not provided with any specific label to choose from, Saeed et al.'s (2001) study shows that 54 per cent of respondents fitted within the acculturation category (strong Scottish identity and strong Pakistani identity), while 46 per cent of respondents fell within the dissociation category (strong Pakistani identity and weak Scottish identity). However, when respondents were provided with a specific set of ethnic labels, the number of those in the acculturation category soared to 88 per cent, leaving only the remaining 12 per cent of respondents in the dissociation category. In both cases, no respondent fitted into either the assimilation category (strong Scottish identity and weak Pakistani identity) or the marginality category (weak Scottish identity and weak Pakistani identity). Saeed et al.'s (2001) work certainly suffers from the limitations of a small-scale study. Nonetheless, the strongly acculturative forms of affiliation to both national and ethnic identities are a notable finding that points to some of the integration successes of Muslims (in this case, Pakistanis) in Scotland.

The post-9/11 development of Muslim identities in the Scottish context has been largely overlooked, because of both the small size of the Scottish Muslim community and the invisibility of the Scottish dimension in what remains a largely English-dominated field of academic enquiry. However, a few recent studies have confirmed that Scottish Muslims manage to uphold multiple identities and successfully negotiate their place in society despite their ethno-cultural and religious diversity. Hopkins's (2004a) study of Scottish Muslim identities in the early 2000s demonstrates that generational changes (Robinson 2009) have brought young Muslims closer to Scotland than their parents are and have led them to develop novel forms of identification and integration strategies.

The 2011 Census has become the key tool for ascertaining Muslims' national identities and feelings of belonging to Scotland (Bond 2016). While it demonstrates that Scottish Muslims are less likely than non-Muslims to report feeling Scottish, this result should not mislead readers. In fact, other countries with more sizeable Muslim populations, for example France, register a correlation between increased religiosity and lower national identification among religious groups, including Christians (Maxwell and Bleich 2014). What matters for the analysis of Muslims' belonging to the country is that, in the long term, they will be 'one group among others for whom religiosity marginally decreases national identification, but for whom the passage of time and generational change will foster integration into the nation in this important respect' (Maxwell and Bleich 2014: 171).

Of more immediate relevance are findings that Scottish Muslims feel more Scottish (24 per cent) than English Muslims feel English (14 per cent). Affiliation to Scottishness can partly explain Muslims' alleged support for the independence referendum (Duffy 2014). The independence debate also spurred young people across the ethno-religious spectrum to reflect on the meanings of being Scottish and 'many [, including Muslims,] felt that Scotland was a "fair society" that was "diverse" and "friendly"' (Hopkins et al. 2015: 21). Unsurprisingly, Scottish Muslims feel much less British (29 per cent) than Muslims south of the border do (57 per cent). Once all of the relevant combinations of identities are taken into consideration, over two

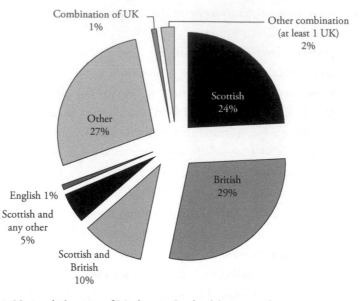

Figure 3.1 National identities of Muslims in Scotland (percentage)

Source: 2011 Census (National Records of Scotland 2013)

thirds (73 per cent) of Muslims express affiliation to the United Kingdom in one way or another and about one third (27 per cent marked as 'other') express an affiliation to a different ethnic identity (Figure 3.1).

As much as Muslim ethnic communities vary across Scotland, so does the distribution of their national identities. Muslims in Glasgow and Dundee, two cities where Pakistanis make up 50 per cent or more of the local Muslim population, record higher feelings of belonging to Scotland and lower affiliations to their non-UK ethnic identities compared to Muslims in Edinburgh and Aberdeen (Table 3.1). These results are not too surprising, given that Glasgow and Dundee are two of the only four Scottish local authorities (out of thirty-two in total) where the Scottish population as a whole voted in favour of independence in 2014.

Lower levels of affiliation to Scotland and higher levels of affiliation to non-UK ethnic identities in Edinburgh (34 per cent) and, particularly, Aberdeen (53 per cent) can be explained by two main factors: a sizeable Arab population, making up 15 per cent or more of the local Muslim population in each of the two cities, and the likely turnover of people that these two

Table 3.1 National identities of Muslims in Glasgow, Edinburgh, Aberdeen and Dundee (percentage)

	Glasgow	Edinburgh	Aberdeen	Dundee
Scottish	25%	19%	11%	24%
British	29%	30%	19%	27%
Other	25%	34%	53%	31%
Scottish and British	11%	7%	4%	9%
Scottish and any other	6%	5%	6%	5%
English	1%	1%	1%	1%
Combination of UK	1%	1%	1%	1%
Other combination (at least 1 UK)	2%	3%	5%	2%

Source: 2011 Census (National Records of Scotland 2013)

key economic Scottish centres experience. With regard to the former factor, Arabs in Scotland tend to identify with their own ethnic identity of origin (47 per cent) over and beyond any other identity, such as Scottish (18 per cent) or British (17 per cent). On the other hand, only 13 per cent of Pakistanis affiliate with their Pakistani identity only, and prefer to emphasise Scottish (31 per cent) or British (34 per cent) identities (Figure 3.2). With regard to the latter factor, Edinburgh's vibrant economy and cosmopolitan nature and

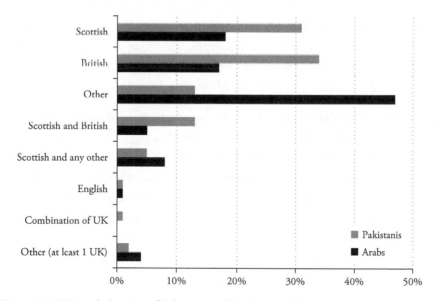

Figure 3.2 National identities of Pakistanis and Arabs in Scotland (percentage)

Source: 2011 Census (National Records of Scotland 2013)

Aberdeen's powerful oil industry may well attract a more mobile, educated and qualified population of Muslims 'on the go' who retain their own minority ethnic identities during their stays of varying length in Scotland.

While the 2011 Census provides a very useful picture of national identities among Scottish Muslims, it is by no means the most accurate methodological tool. Notably, it fails to measure how people rank their own identities, particularly when respondents uphold dual and/or multiple identities. The 'Moreno question' tool would be more useful insofar as it requires respondents to rank their identities in a hierarchy from 'Scottish, not British' to 'British, not Scottish'. Although this methodology says little about what people mean by these identities (Weber n.d.), it certainly provides a more nuanced understanding of identity, which takes into consideration the multiple effects that today's global and inter-ethnic world exerts on its citizens. In this sense, affiliations to Scotland or, more broadly, Great Britain are certainly not expressed in isolation from strong religious identities; in the case of Muslims, geographical boundaries are often disrupted in the conceptualisation of a global Muslim community.

Hopkins' (2007a) study clearly shows that Muslims manage to affiliate with Islam while, at the same time, connecting with Scottish society and culture (see also Hopkins et al. 2015). Scottish and Muslim identities are therefore cast as non-contradictory and are skilfully captured by a Muslim man interviewed by Hopkins during his fieldwork. The metaphor of a 'blue square' illustrates the idea that, as much as a square can be both a square and blue at the same time, a Muslim can be both Muslim and Scottish at the same time:

> A blue square, it's blue and it's a square. Its being a square doesn't interfere with it being blue. Its being blue doesn't interfere with it being a square. They're just nothing to do with each other but they complement each other and they make a complete blue square. If it wasn't blue it wouldn't be a blue square, if you see what I mean. So being a Scottish Muslim, you know, both of them go together and they make me who I am. They're part of what I am. They're not even completely what I am because it doesn't describe my character or personality but they don't contradict each other in any way. (Interview with Kabir, see Hopkins 2007a: 68)

Being Scottish or, for some people, British and being Muslim are not two contradictory states of being. They are simply two different aspects of identity that certainly need accommodation but are not mutually exclusive. A similar way of thinking was expressed by Babar during research conducted in Edinburgh:

> If people asked me, 'Are you British or are you Muslim?' I would answer that it is as if I were asked, 'Are you a father or are you a son?' I answer that I am a father because I have children but I am a son too because I have still got parents. Which one are you going to choose? It would be stupid if you had to choose one. For me being a father is equally important as being a son. My duty to my children is very important because they depend on me, but likewise my parents are very old so I have a duty to take care of them. Both are very important. (Babar, Scottish Pakistani man in his mid-twenties)

Ali, a British Pakistani academic who is well-known in the community and has previous experience in the MCB,[2] develops and expands this line of thought by noting that identity is highly contextual, grounded on multiple aspects, fluid and expansive:

> Context is an important shaping factor for identity. But I do not find different dimensions of identity juxtaposing against each other. Most of the time I am comfortable wearing different aspects of my identity. Identity is fluid and, if anything, expansive rather than restrictive. (Ali, British Pakistani man in his mid-forties)

These findings confirm wider British literature, in which religion emerges as a fundamental badge of identity for British Muslims (Nyiri 2007; Robinson 2009) but in a context where multiple identities can be accommodated at the same time (Dwyer 1999a; McVic and Nyiri 2007; Wiltshire 2010). As Karlsen and Nazroo (2015: 773) posit, 'many Muslims, and those with other minority ethnicities and religions, do not see a contradiction between being British and maintaining a separate cultural or religious identity'. In terms of national identity, Hopkins claims that young Scottish Muslims employ some of the markers previously mentioned – namely, place of birth, upbringing and accent – to lay claims of belonging to Scotland. As already highlighted, the white majority may not necessarily accept these claims, at least not at all times. Muslims' 'exclusion by force', due to their ethnic diversity, becomes even more serious when combined with 'exclusion by choice', which kicks in whenever Muslims 'choose to distance themselves from being completely Scottish through their linkages with other countries [that is, their countries of origin and/or heritage]' (Hopkins 2007a: 73). This is not at all surprising. Other research (Kidd and Jamieson 2011) stresses the key role played by ethnicity and religion in steering young Scottish Muslims' decisions to create or join a peer group. As Hopkins (2004b) demonstrates and as Chapter 4 confirms, Scottish Muslims' self-exclusion and detachment from mainstream social spaces and cultural norms operate via other approaches too, for example by growing long beards, dressing in particular ways or refusing to visit pubs and clubs. These processes of exclusion and inclusion are mediated through national, ethnic and religious traits.

Scottishness is both inclusive and exclusive. On the one hand, 'proof of Scottishness', such as birth, upbringing and accent, receiving education from Scottish institutions and living in Scotland, can help some Muslims to lay a claim of belonging to the country. On the other hand, certain cultural traditions, such as drinking and socialising in clubs, exclude some other Muslims on the basis of their religious principles (Hopkins 2004b). It is therefore logical that Scottish Muslims have resorted to multiple, hybrid identities as a way to fit into the different social and cultural environments with which they associate in their everyday lives; these could be spaces predominantly populated by indigenous white Scottish people (for example, schools, workplaces and so on) or ethno-religious spaces (for example, mosques, peer groups and so on). In the diasporic Scottish arena and especially in the metropolitan meeting place of Edinburgh, the identities of Scottish Pakistanis have turned into a 'remix' – that is,

> A musical form which combines Bombay film songs with a range of modern electronic rhythms. Sounds from 'the East' are thereby translated or 'rerouted' via the codes of western youth culture, which is itself hybridized, and that collision of styles may serve to symbolize broader patterns of social change among the young women and men in [Great] Britain's South Asian diaspora. (Qureshi and Moores 1999: 312)

Qureshi and Moores pin down the influences that are exerted in different spheres of Muslim lives and that play out at the community level: family and community via ethno-religious expectations and practices; and education and the media via mainstream norms and behaviours. In their study, clothing represents a telling example of this tension. For girls, traditional South Asian clothes can both bolster proud cultural identities and hamper acceptance from broader society. The same issue emerges for boys, with the caveat that, according to the authors, they draw their cultural inspiration from North American black culture (for example, jewellery, film and music), rather than South Asian culture. It is disputable whether this analysis remains correct nowadays. Walking through the main Scottish cities brings sightings of Pakistani and Arab garments rather than shiny golden chains. But the key point is to understand that Muslims, especially the young section of the community, present different identities to different audiences in order to deal with different social and cultural environments (Qureshi 2004).

The Relationship between National and Ethnic Identities

The conceptualisation and operationalisation of Muslim identity since the Rushdie Affair, and especially after 9/11, has been formed at the interplay between religion, ethnicity and nation. This process has not been homogeneous but has been played out differently across different Muslim constituencies. While most of the first generation of migrants maintain a primarily ethnic and cultural identity, a minority has combined it with a strong affiliation to Scotland. Nadeem, a Pakistani man in his late seventies, has lived in Edinburgh for over forty years. He speaks fluent English, is very involved in interfaith and intercommunity activities and has made an effort to integrate into wider society. He does present unusual traits of identity, unusual experiences of socialisation and unusual outcomes of integration that do not necessarily reflect those of the other older-generation Pakistani Muslims who also attend Nadeem's mosque of choice ('Mosque B'). While recognising the importance of his ethnic roots, Nadeem has developed a very strong identification with, and sense of belonging to, Scotland stemming from his positive experiences of life in the country:

> It is difficult to cut off from your original nation. You might look like a Scottish person. However, if somebody said to you, 'Are you Scottish?' you would say, 'No, I am Italian.' [Note: the author is a dual British–Italian citizen.] But if someone said to me, 'Who are you?' I would say, 'I am originally

from Pakistan but I have been living here more than I lived in that country.' The reality is that I am Scottish. Scotland gave me respect and I have lived here for so long, so peacefully. I mean, you just go to the area where I live, ask anybody, 'Do you know Nadeem?' and they will tell you where I live straight away. (Nadeem, Pakistani man in his late seventies)

Nadeem represents a particular case of a Pakistani migrant who has had his national identity reshaped by his lifelong experience in Scotland. In this sense, Nadeem challenges Jenkins' (2008) concept of identities as deeply rooted in primary socialisation – that is, established in the first years of life and very resistant to change. Instead, he supports Kabir's (2010: 93) argument that 'the longer an immigrant lives in their new "home" and obtains equal opportunities and recognition from the wider society, the more they are likely to feel connected to their new place'. But it would be naïve to generalise this situation to the whole community of first-generation migrants. On the contrary, elderly Muslims often live in a world of nostalgia (Bolognani 2007) that is ameliorated by the reproduction of ethnic and cultural values and practices within the boundaries of tight-knit subcommunities based on regional and tribal affiliations. These values and practices are not necessarily religious per se, if ethnicity is understood as 'an attachment to tradition and custom intertwined with cultural practice [that is] non-religious in origin' (Meer 2010: 82). However, older members of the community often think about these cultural values in religious terms.

Across the Scottish-born Muslim community, many people profess strong affiliation to Scotland – and the many oral histories gathered in the Colourful Heritage (2016) project confirm this finding. Nasir, a young Scottish Pakistani man who is very involved in the religious and social activities of 'Mosque C', represents the perfect example of a proudly Scottish Muslim who does not need to reject his family connections to Pakistan to claim a Scottish identity:

My Scottish identity is important to me because I was born here. Even though I go to Pakistan, which is where my parents are from, I do have relatives that live there and I do have a blood affiliation that matters to me, Scotland is my country. One of the things that I am happy about is that in Scotland we say: 'One Scotland Many Cultures'. So everybody can have their own culture or their own religion without any issues, but when it comes to Scotland we are all united and we do all act for the betterment of our country. (Nasir, Scottish Pakistani man in his early thirties)

Many young Muslims express pride in being not only Scottish but, more broadly, British citizens, often due to the range of freedoms and rights that they enjoy in everyday life and the ways in which these freedoms can be made to coexist with Islam and can boost one's loyalty to the country:

> For me being a good Muslim means that I am going to be a good citizen, because that is what Islam teaches me. Islam teaches me to obey the law of the country I am in, as long as I am not breaking any Islamic rule. Here I am not forced to eat pork, I am not forced to drink. To be honest, I think that I am very fortunate to be Muslim in [Great] Britain. In this country I have rights and freedoms that you cannot find even in Muslim countries. So I am very grateful to have lived and been brought up in Scotland and the United Kingdom. I am very loyal, I have a strong loyalty to Scotland. If it comes to the old Scotland–UK issue, maybe I am a bit on the defensive about independence. But *Braveheart* is one of my favourite movies! Every time that I watch *Braveheart* I think I am going to cry. It is a great movie. I feel really impassioned about that. And, to be honest, I really like the royal family too. I have a lot of friends, even Scottish friends, who do not like them but I got really excited about the royal wedding! (Babar, Scottish Pakistani man in his mid-twenties)

While feelings of belonging to Scotland and Great Britain vary across the ethnic and age spectra, several research participants shared at least a basic social commitment to Scotland. Similar to Babar, Bilel emphasises the freedoms that Muslims are able to enjoy in Great Britain, and the positive life conditions available in Scotland, as opposed to most Muslim countries:

> It is much easier to live in Scotland! To tell you the truth, consider that when I go anywhere in Europe or I go to Tunisia, especially before the revolution, I find that it is always easier for me to practise my religion in Scotland than in any of those places, especially Tunisia since there is [was] a dictatorship. I always tell people back home that I practise my religion better in the United Kingdom than anywhere else in the world. Better than in Italy for sure. In Italy there is no freedom. There is no freedom to express

yourself and your beliefs because in Italy there are no human rights in place. There are no human rights in Italy. I have lived in Italy and I have seen how the police beat people for nothing. There is no other country in the world like the United Kingdom or Scotland where you can express yourself and have human rights and freedoms. (Bilel, Tunisian man in his mid-fifties)

There are certainly important differences between the primarily ethnic and cultural identities of the older section of the Muslim community and the more religious and national-oriented identities of Scottish-born Muslims and some younger migrants. Yet, a few elements tend to be shared by the community as a whole, notably: (1) a sense of belonging to Scotland as a sociocultural space that allows freedom of expression and religion; (2) the maintenance of cultural connections to the country of origin or heritage; and (3) increasingly conscious aspirations to play out public Muslim identities that are religious and/or ideological in nature.

The young Scottish-born Muslim community is particularly interesting, not least because it will be the core of the Scottish Muslim community for years to come. A few traits are shared by young Scottish Muslims, notably: (1) a heightened sense of being Muslim that finds support in a sustained theological engagement with the Qur'an and Islamic scholars, either on an individual basis or during Islamic studies programmes such as iSyllabus (Bowen 2014) and small study circles;[3] (2) very strong and proud Scottish identities, often expressed in opposition to English identities; and (3) a renewed outlook towards ethnic identities that is filtered of emotional bonds but that continues to constitute an important component of self-identification as shaped through socialisation with family and friends (Jenkins 2008).

The younger section of the Muslim community is nevertheless not homogeneous. Some of the younger Pakistani migrants distance themselves from Pakistanis born in Great Britain (including Scottish Pakistanis) by referring to them with the pejorative term 'British-Born Confused Desi'.[4] Zemar, an Afghani man, takes this argument further. He maintains that Scottish-born Pakistani Muslims 'live on two boats' and fail to realise that they can be neither fully Scottish nor fully Pakistani due to the alleged intrinsic incompatibility of these two identities and ways of life. While this may well be an overgeneralisation, the fact that social identities are shaped in a dialectic fashion means that it is not only non-Muslims who provide an identity label to which Muslims ascribe. Other Muslims are involved in the same process, by pointing out the apparent contradictions in how Scottish Pakistanis attempt to uphold dual national and ethnic identities. The complex nature of self-identification and its elaboration in interaction with a wide range of entities, such as power, authority, religion, practice, occupation, neighbourhood, clothes, music and so on (Jenkins 2008), highlights the impossible task that scholars face when attempting to fully comprehend and explain all of the possible facets of human identity.

Conclusion

While Muslims strongly affiliate with Islam both individually and collectively, Scotland represents a key identity label for many of them. As argued elsewhere, Muslims hold a uniquely favourable position in Scottish society: 'they express strong feelings of belonging to Scotland. They can be found at the highest levels of government. They contribute to business and culture' (Bonino 2015c). This is as much a reflection of the inclusive and rather tolerant nature of Scottish people as it is a consequence of the efforts made by Muslim communities to foster successful integration strategies. These strategies have allowed religious and national identities to originate an 'Islamic tartanised' way of life that can reconcile Scottish culture with Islamic principles. The extent to which Islam has entered and directly shaped Scottish culture should not be overestimated. Nevertheless, it is certainly true that Muslim identities have been influenced by a national narrative of Scottish trans-ethnic unity.

Often devised in opposition to Englishness, the idea of Scottishness has acquired particular salience since the rise in power of the SNP. A nationalist party in Great Britain would normally attract protest voters who support right-wing, anti-immigration parties that often have an explicit or implicit anti-Islamic agenda. The SNP, on the other hand, navigates between Scottish nationalism and a pluralistic and diverse public sphere at the same time. When married with a progressive politics and a civic nationalism, Scotland's egalitarian nature garners much admiration from Muslim communities. As noted elsewhere, 'political messages close to traditionally Muslim positions, such as opposition to the Iraq War and a less vociferous take on anti-extremism policies, have earned the government Muslim support' (Bonino 2015c). A complex relationship of love and political convenience has brought together two actors that have historically felt socially, culturally and politically oppressed: the Scots, who have a history of grieving English dominance, and Muslims, who have traditionally felt humiliated by the 'imperialist West'. The ways in which Islam and Scotland have interacted at the communal level are about to put this relationship to the test.

Notes

1. The Twenty Statement Test is a psychological test used to explore people's self-identity.
2. The MCB was established in 1997 to act as an umbrella institution, including around 400 organisations, mosques and schools, and to give voice to Muslim communities. However, the MCB has incurred criticism from traditional, conservative and apolitical Muslim groups that do not affiliate to it. A poll conducted in 2007 shows that only 6 per cent of Muslims felt represented by the MCB (Archer 2009). These results can be explained by the dominance of ideologies springing from the Middle Eastern and South Asian sections of anti-colonial political Islam within the MCB. After 9/11, the British government started to find new ways to govern British Muslims and distanced itself from the MCB (Modood and Salt 2011).
3. Many mosques have provision for Islamic study circles that normally meet once a week.
4. 'Desi' refers to people of South Asian origin or heritage and culture.

4

THE NEW MUSLIM COMMUNITY: CHILDREN OF ISLAM AND SCOTLAND

The marriage between nation and religion in defining Scottish Muslims takes a distinctive form in changing notions and practices of community. As so far examined, ethnicity and heritage culture are being sidelined in contemporary definitions of Muslimness. Today, being a Muslim is no longer coterminous with being Pakistani or Bangladeshi or Tunisian or Somali. The fact that younger generations are widely departing from their parents' and other relatives' experiences of migration to Scotland is not in itself a major discovery. Migrants tend to reproduce their sociocultural patterns in the new setting, in order to preserve their identities and sense of nationhood (Laliótou 2004). Moreover, family subcultures, as instilled by first-generation Muslims, sometimes problematically relate to mainstream society and can aggravate the social exclusion experienced by second- and third-generation Muslims (Hellyer 2007b). In this regard, intergenerational changes and transformations are an obvious consequence of the deeply Scottish experiences of Scottish-born Muslims and of some younger migrants. Scottish Muslims' life perspectives and social practices are dressed up in tartan and play the music of Islam. Nowadays, being Muslim in Scotland is coterminous with being religiously and ideologically Muslim and being nationally and civically Scottish. And herein lies the novelty, as this has consequences for the dynamics of that collective aggregate of people of various ages, ethnicities and social classes who affiliate with Islam, live in Scotland and come together to form what is called a 'Muslim community'. Better, this should be called a *new Muslim community*. The new Muslim community equally gravitates around Islam and Scotland in ways that have never happened before. Undoubtedly, the marriage between Islam and Scotland is not free from obstacles. Yet, it feeds into powerful narratives of belonging to, and unity with, religion *and* nation which colour the practices of the community of its children – the children of Islam and Scotland. Ultimately, despite the perils that it encounters and will continued to encounter, this marriage has the potential to succeed. In the end, it will pave the way to a truly Scottish Muslim community, which will eventually contribute to shaping a new Scottish society (see Epilogue).

South Asian Transplant Rejected: Muslims at the Court of Scotland

Notions and practices of tribalism, parochialism and kinship still colour predominantly ethno-cultural understandings of community among older migrant Muslims, especially those of South Asian origin. Close local and transnational bonds of solidarity with members of the extended family and people from the same region or village are symbolically represented by 'Mosque B', a Pakistani mosque and cultural centre in Edinburgh that epitomises the tendency of South Asian Muslims to attend a place of worship with people who share the same ethnic origin (Sunak and Rajeswaran 2014). This mosque promotes a very ethnically and culturally focused sense of community, which centres on a lost Pakistan – a nostalgic sense of Pakistaniness that is kept alive by the practised memories of its attendees. These men (women at this particular mosque have been out of the reach of the author) share not only the same ethnic and cultural roots but also a language and similar experiences of functional migration and partition[1] from a land that they left in the 1950s and 1960s but still consider home. They quarrel over trivial committee matters and they discuss murky Pakistani politics in Urdu. They talk about a Pakistan that is long gone but is still as fresh in their mind as it was fifty/sixty years ago. They enjoy *gulab jamun*, a popular South Asian dessert, during their ritual gathering in a tiny office after Friday prayer. They envision their daughters and sons being married to good Pakistani men and women from within their own clan. They keep in constant touch and visit their families in Pakistan. They form business partnerships and they share community activities, often at the mosque. Effectively, they are reliving Pakistani experiences within Scottish geographies.

Although not all of them necessarily reach out to broader society, they neither live in complete segregation nor represent the wider Muslim community. Certainly, they do not represent the experiences of the younger section of the community, especially those who are Scottish-born. The strong sociopolitical links with Pakistan that are maintained by the older Pakistani community across Scotland (see, for example, Colourful Heritage 2016), for example by paying homage to highly influential Pakistani political members who come to Scotland, are not displayed by the younger section of the community. In fact, younger Scottish Pakistanis consider recognition of notable Pakistani politicians to be of little importance, unless these politicians demonstrate concrete forms of engagement with their local Scottish Pakistani community (Qureshi 2006). Moreover, tribal, clan and kin-based community structures and norms problematise the social choices of some younger Muslims who, while still placing the extended family at the core of their everyday life, are relatively culturally disengaged from South Asian mores. Effectively, they distance themselves from their parents' cultural and ethnic identities (Archambault 2007) and take up a stronger national and civic affiliation.

Research has shown tensions between the first generation of South Asians in Great Britain and subsequent generations, who are often considered to be 'caught between two cultures': the ethnic culture of their families and wider British culture (Bolognani 2007 and 2009). The cultural battle between orthodox and liberal sections of the Scottish Pakistani community at Glasgow Central Mosque is a case in point (see Epilogue). Parental values and the role of the family as the sole provider of moral education are now considered to be out of step with the life experiences of second- and third-generation Muslims. Similarly, community leaders and mosques (Bolognani 2007) are often deemed inadequate for the needs of new Muslim generations in a context of intergenerational instability and contested conformity to ethnic values (Wardak 2000).

However, the outlook of the older community members should not be pathologised but understood as the natural outcome of a strengthened ingroupness that helped them cope with a new cultural and social setting. Research respondents were well aware of this side of the story:

There are nuances here that need to be deconstructed and are unique to British life and do not emerge in the subcontinent. In some ways, it is a boiling pot that is unique only in [Great] Britain and you do not find it anywhere else, because the Bangladeshi community is not a routine Bangladeshi community here. Here, around 80 or 90 per cent of the Bangladeshi population is from Sylhet, which is the third-largest city in Bangladesh. For Sylheti people here in Great Britain, to marry a Bangladeshi, one first needs to be a Sylheti. It does not mean that the person cannot be from somewhere else, but the fact that one is not from Sylhet would be viewed as if the person were Pakistani or Indian. So here in [Great] Britain the Bangladeshi community is much more a unique society than the one that you would find there. (Arif, Canadian Bangladeshi man in his early thirties)

Arranged and forced marriages are a prime example of how cultural and tribal norms work in practice at the expense of the younger generations' more nuanced life views, opportunities and choices. For some scholars (Macey 1999), arranged marriages are pernicious because they function as a tool that legitimises the ongoing oppression of women under patriarchal structures through the alleged mandate of Islam. A more culturally aware analysis recognises that

> The politics of marriage [is] embedded in customary notions of honour and shame, which surround the right to control the sexuality and reproductive powers of young people, particularly younger women's bodies, specifically by men and more generally by an older generation of migrants. (Werbner 2012: 108)

Arranged marriages, especially with a family member, constitute one of the most powerful ways of maintaining a connection with, and perpetuating the legacy of, the extended kin and tribal network or *biraderi* (Qureshi 2006). A testament to the persisting importance of intra-family marriages are the findings that about half of British-born Pakistanis marry an indigenous Pakistani spouse, often a cousin, and usually within a conventionally arranged marriage[2] (Shaw 2001). Forced marriages are of a more legally and culturally problematic nature as, unlike arranged marriages, they entail coercion and/ or lack of consent. The Forced Marriage Unit (2016) recorded 539 cases of possible forced marriages out of 1,220 as involving people travelling to/ from Pakistan (44 per cent), and a further 89 involving people going to/ from Bangladesh (7 per cent), in the United Kingdom in 2015. Scotland accounted for 22 (2 per cent) of all cases. While forced marriages are not necessarily a Scottish-specific issue, they continue to be an under-reported practice and the real numbers are unknown (Bonino 2016a).

Ae Fond Kiss (2004), directed by Ken Loach, is a cinematographic representation of young Scottish South Asians' cultural dilemma – should they pursue their passions when these betray family norms and expectations or should they bow to tradition? A masterpiece of social realism, the movie narrates the story of a young Scottish Pakistani man who brings his family to the brink of destruction when he defies an arranged marriage in the name of love – his love for an Irish Catholic woman (she herself also has a significant set of problems with the strict management of the Catholic school where she teaches). Looking back to reality, one of the film's leads, Glaswegian actor Atta Yaqub, confirmed at a post-screening panel discussion during Islam Awareness Week in Edinburgh the cultural pressures that young – both male and female – Scottish Muslims face. For the majority Pakistani community, these pressures can be traced back to expectations of moral and behavioural conformity at home and outside the domestic arena under the forces of individual and family honour or *izzat*[3] (Qureshi and Moores 1999).

Such pressures are well described by the stories of two Muslims living in Edinburgh, which are by no means isolated experiences in Scotland (see, for example, Carroll 1998; Sarwar 2016). After reaching legal age, Parveen, a Scottish Pakistani woman now in her mid-thirties, was sent to Pakistan by her parents to marry a cousin whom she had never met before. Leaving aside whether technically this was an arranged or a forced marriage – Parveen had to reluctantly consent to her parents' decision – this move can be seen as a means to reinforce cultural connections between 'home' and Scotland and bolster honour within the community of provenance. A couple of years later, Parveen returned to Edinburgh with her husband. The man obtained British citizenship a few years afterwards and subsequently divorced her. Similarly, Zakir, a British-born Pakistani man in his mid-forties, and his brother were both married off to Pakistani women. Zakir divorced years later and is still suffering from the financial and psychological costs of his parents' choice. His brother broke off relations with his family after what was, upon Zakir's admission, a forced marriage. The rationale behind Pakistani parents' decision to marry off their children to women from home is best left to Zakir to describe:

> They say Pakistani women will be more obedient, know more about Islam, are more docile and look after children, while they think that British women might not be so obedient. But Pakistani ones would bring their culture and language in to keep the tradition going. The British would be quite liberal in their ideas so they want to keep the traditions with Pakistani women. The practices are not changing. (Zakir, British Pakistani man in his mid-forties)

Therefore, transnational marriages feed into the older generations' manifestation of bonds to their homeland, since 'they improve the economic conditions of a further member of the *biraderi* (extended kin network) and reinforce the bridge with back home' (Bolognani 2007: 62). This system follows the Pakistani rural structure of life that was organised locally by tribes and not centrally by the state, and

> One consequence was that people could not just marry whoever they wanted to. If they did, then over time tribal lands would be broken up by the rules of inheritance, and the economic base of the tribe, or *biraderi* (brotherhood), would be destroyed. This was one reason why children in rural Pakistan were often treated as the property of their elders and encouraged, or forced, to marry within the *biraderi*. (Kabir 2010: 43)

Obviously, transnational marriages do not exist in a cultural vacuum. Rather, they connect with broader *biraderi*-related norms within a hierarchical class-based social system that has been transplanted from South Asia into Scotland:

> There is a very huge clan system within the Pakistani community. In amongst that system they divide themselves and look down on other people, which is a totally wrong thing. So if they are looking down at their own people, you can imagine that they must be looking even further down on someone who is not Pakistani. There are people who came from Mirpur and those people were farmers. Another group were all landlords. All landlords. Of course those people look down on the farmers. Even now this kind of thing is in

their mind and they pass it on to their children. But now the third generations do not bother about these things because it is too much hassle. (Adila, Kenyan Pakistani woman in her mid-forties)

Despite the fact that tribal connections tend to matter mostly to older migrants, according to Lewis (2007) there has been an increase in first-cousin marriages among younger British Pakistanis with the aim of reaffirming *biraderi* loyalties. For Lewis, this is an emanation of the more conservative attitudes of young British Muslims (aged sixteen to twenty-four) compared to their parents and grandparents. While some have certainly come closer to forms of orthodox Islam, younger Scottish Muslims have also shown diverse ways of being Muslim, which depart from strictly conservative religious or cultural principles and mores. Furthermore, Lewis recognises that younger people's attitudes towards *biraderi* are at least ambivalent:

> The Pakistani community in [Great] Britain has been established here for over forty years. Now in their third generation, they face a crisis which threatens to undermine their future. At the heart of the problem lies the *biradari*, the extended clan network that governs all families and gives values and a sense of identity. Invisible to the outside world, a battle is taking place between *biradari* diehards and those who believe it has no place in modern British society. The youth are the casualties. (Lewis 2007: 46)

Arguably, retaining ethno-cultural mores within a sociocultural context that younger Scottish-born Muslims equate with Scotland rather than Pakistan/Bangladesh is uneasy. Such mores are often out of touch with young Muslims' daily experiences of Scottish life and might promote avoidance of, and seclusion from, cultural and ethnic intrusions within the fabric of the tight-knit tribal system. According to Hellyer (2007b), second- and third-generation British Muslims have experienced an aggravated sense of isolation and alienation as a consequence of the contrasting requirements set by family subcultures and mainstream values, the lack of British religious authorities and sociopolitical discrimination. At the same time, shared norms and values passed down by families can take the form of a positive 'ethnic capital' and serve as an important tool through which one can overcome social class and/or economic disparities and achieve upward social mobility (Modood 2004;

Shah et al. 2010). The system of *biraderi* is organised hierarchically, is influenced by caste and performs a controlling and normative role (Bolognani 2009). Furthermore, it offers a sense of cultural and social belonging within community boundaries (Wardak 2000). Lastly, South Asians' intergenerational continuity in the form of social, emotional and economic family ties, cultural enclosure and self-sufficiency help maintain positive control of anti-social behaviour (Smith 2005). It is known that the family offers protection and guardianship and proves to be an antidote against crime and deviance (Sampson and Wilson 1995), along with other institutions of social control at various stages of life – school and peer groups during childhood; higher education, work and marriage during young adulthood; and work, marriage, parenthood and commitment to community in later adulthood (Sampson and Laub 1990). To sum up, rather than being an abnormality of the new Muslim community, traditional ethno-cultural norms and mores behave like electrons. They can occupy two different places at the same time, being both antidotes and cures for social illnesses, and obstacles to changing ways of being Muslim in Scotland.

The Reality of Representation

When *Citizen Khan* was first aired on BBC1 on 27 August 2012, one could only sit and wait for a storm of criticism to hit its creator and co-writer, British-born Muslim Adil Ray, and the British Broadcasting Corporation (BBC). In a climate of legitimate heightened sensitivities around post-9/11 media representations of Muslims, this first BBC South Asian sitcom (Adewunmi 2012), parodying a Pakistani family, might have felt unnecessary. Allegations of stereotyping South Asians, making fun of Muslims (Revoir 2012) and ridiculing and insulting (BBC News 2012b) Islam ran high. In particular, a scene in which Mr Khan's younger daughter, Alia, who is wearing heavy make-up and has long hair, rushes to cover her hair with a hijab and pretends to be reading the Qur'an when her father enters the house, generated considerable heat (Revoir 2012; Huq 2013).

While the sitcom clearly built upon some cultural generalisations and essentialisations for the sake of entertainment, in the end it was 'British Muslims mocking their own communities, and how they're perceived by society [. . ., particularly by challenging] a myopic, indeed, racialist view of the Muslim family' (Saha 2013: 4). Abbas's (2013) concerns about Pakistanis being unduly stereotyped in the sitcom should not be dismissed. However, upper-middle-class Americans could have claimed similar grievances in the 1990s when *Beverly Hills, 90210* depicted them as a group of insecure (Brenda), cocky (Kelly), troubled (Dylan), clownish (Steve), lazy, alcoholic and unfaithful (all of them) privileged kids. Obviously, the concerns about the representation of Pakistanis and Muslims in *Citizen Khan* need to be located within the delicate post-9/11 sociopolitical context, which has augmented experiences, feelings and perceptions of victimhood. Yet, paradoxically the sitcom may have promoted normalised social views towards Pakistanis by portraying them as ordinary citizens who conduct ordinary lives with a flavour of cultural and religious distinctiveness.

Going beyond the satire and the potential underlying cultural 'subversiveness' of the comedy, *Citizen Khan* highlights some of the tensions that ongoing developments in identity, family and forms of community have brought into the lives of British and Scottish Muslims. The character of Mr Khan, in his proud and rather patriarchal form, resembles some of the older members of the Scottish Pakistani community. This is especially evident in the ways in which ethnic and cultural memories shape ideas, beliefs and practices of community in the Scottish context. Mr Khan also represents the typical Muslim migrant who comes from a country and a region where Islam is a taken-for-granted cultural, political, social and economic component of society (Lewis 2007) with little space for discussion, change or transformation.

Like many Scottish-born Muslim women, Shazia, Mr Khan's older daughter, places marriage and family at the core of her life. However, she maintains an independent vision of life, which considers the broader context through negotiated British and Pakistani practices. Finally, Alia, the most interesting and controversial character, features deeply intricate psychosocial elements that lead her to live a 'double life'. In front of her father she portrays herself as – to use Mr Khan's words – 'a very good Muslim girl'. She covers her hair with a hijab and pretends to read the Qur'an or do her homework whenever her father is in close proximity. She presents herself as a morally irreproachable Muslim girl to be in her father's good books and obtain his permission to engage in social activities that are astutely covered under religious pretexts – for example, when she asks for money to go on a study trip to Turkey, which turns out to be a party holiday. When her father is away or when she is shielded by the secrecy of her mobile phone, Alia reveals her inner self: a 'Westernised' young girl who wears heavy make-up, tight jeans and bright tops and craves mainstream entertainment, such as going out in mixed environments, partying or dating boys. Alia represents the more liberal, 'Westernised', 'rebellious' and sexualised Muslim girl that has a counterpart in Scottish-born Parveen.

A prime example of a 'Scottished' Muslim, Parveen has lived a life juggling family mores, community expectations and wider social opportunities. In many ways, Parveen, her sister and many of her friends conduct 'double lives' and refine cultural navigation skills (Qureshi 2006) that allow them to save face within their (extended) family and enjoy Scottish social life at the same time. While they maintain a facade of moral and religious purity in front of their families (especially their fathers),[4] Parveen and her friends do not refrain from entering the 'forbidden' spaces of clubbing, gambling, drinking and casual relationships. Parveen's nights out clubbing and her trips down to England to see one of her previous boyfriends were covered up through white lies that would prevent any family interference. Modern technologies and the far-reaching possibilities that the new social media offer in expanding human interaction outside the physicality of traditional face-to-face communication provide opportunities to redefine individual lives and the boundaries of community structures through negotiations and the integration of Scottish influences. While these cultural negotiations might not be part and parcel of all younger Muslims' experience of social life, surely they signal an internal awakening and the acceptance of Scottish elements that lead to the shaping of a forward-thinking Scottish sense of Muslim community.

Some Scottish Muslims try to escape parental restrictions on movement, which limit young women's friendships with white people (Qureshi and Moores 1999). In this sense, they are not immune from external social 'temptations' and might explore deeply sexualised spaces, such as nightclubs, where gendered relations are often based on the intoxication of the senses, a loss of personal control and high physical contact. As both informal conversations and, particularly, personal acquaintanceship with younger Muslims in town suggest, several members of the community can now be found mixing in social activities with non-Muslim people and enjoying 'forbidden pleasures'[5] that would be stigmatised by many in the Muslim community. It is hard to quantify the extent of this trend as not all young Muslims partake in, or condone, these behaviours. Yet, the new Muslim community is being reshaped around Scottish patterns of acculturation and mixed socialisation that defy traditional understandings of Muslimness through the morally pristine and ethno-culturally coloured lenses of the migrant community.

More broadly, this reflects changing patterns of socialisation, life opportunities and choices available to Scottish-born Muslims as opposed to their parents and the ways in which the former have managed to doubly cross ethno-cultural boundaries by extending their own networks to both different Muslim ethnic constituencies and Scottish society at large:

> In the Pakistani community and in the Arab community you will see that older people tend to stay among themselves because there is no such common ground to meet. I see that things are changing now, because kids are growing up and they want to meet with different Muslims, not only with the Pakistanis. When I came here the logic was more about which part of Pakistan you come from and then people would meet with each other accordingly. Now the kids are growing up and meeting with each other at university, college or school. That is why, when they grow up, they are more Scottish than they are Pakistani. (Muna, Pakistani woman in her early forties)

This changing sociocultural landscape will continue to intensify generational differences and to paint Muslims' experiences in tartan colours. In particular, it will provide further evidence for the argument that intergenerational changes have broken the traditional family system due to a much lower commitment to the preservation of the clan's bloodline, prestige and honour (Lewis 2007). The constraints of *biraderi* and community-related pressures still exist. Yet, the new Muslim community is quickly sidelining ethno-cultural values to embrace a wider commitment to both Islam and Scotland.

From Local Life Choices to Global Belonging

As the sociocultural landscape of Great Britain developed and registered an increase in young students' participation in higher education of over 20 per cent from the mid-1990s to the late 2000s (Higher Education Funding Council for England 2010), Scotland was not left behind in this process of educational massification. A recent study shows that Muslim families in Scotland (and England) have quite high educational aspirations for their children[6] (Weedon et al. 2013), who tend to have ambitions other than the mere pursuit of money. However, despite Weedon et al.'s optimistic findings, there exist tensions with family members who still prioritise financial stability over purely educational achievements:

> Younger people are a bit more ambitious. Older generations are much less ambitious and not even encouraging the younger generations to move ahead. At best what they would say is, 'Do what you want – if you want to become successful, go for it', but I have never seen them saying from a child's young age, 'You can be a doctor, you can be an engineer'. [. . .] People would not go that far if it means that they were going to affect their family bonds. The idea is that you should do what you want for your fulfilment – social happiness is good – but there is also a certain element of financial security that needs to be there to impress your parents and your family. It is a balance between the two. (Arif, Canadian Bangladeshi man in his early thirties)

Other Muslims have similar stories. One such person is Zakir. While his sisters were withdrawn from school at the ages of fourteen and fifteen, his dreams of going to college and becoming a lawyer were shattered by his parents' hostility. First, he was pushed to work as a repairman and then he was bought a post office to placate his intellectual aspirations. Zakir, now in his mid-forties, is finally studying for a university degree while teaching English. He reflected on his experience and on younger Muslims' changing experiences over a cup of tea at his rented flat:

> My parents did this because they had a village mentality. However, nowadays most parents would let their children be educated. I was the first one in my extended family to go to university. Now my nephew goes to university. Another nephew is an accountant in London. The other one is a teacher. Even my niece went to do business studies. This is because they saw someone do it. Otherwise they would have no aspiration to do it. I did it and

inspired people in my family. People of my generation are pushing children to get a good education. (Zakir, British Pakistani man in his mid-forties)

While family pressures may hamper the full realisation of young Muslims' goals, it is true that a number of Muslim families, and non-Muslim families alike, have an understanding of life goals that differ from those of their own children. This is substantiated by research on minority ethnic enterprise in Scotland (Deakins et al. 2005), which found that some members of the younger generation, especially South Asians, tend to be reluctant to continue their family businesses because they wish to choose career paths of their own. The life choices of the older members of their families are not only restricted by a different view of educational and career prospects. These choices also influence their reduced participation in Scottish society and in global politics, in which, by contrast, younger Muslims have been immersing themselves:

> If there is a protest in town run by Muslims, in order to join it, they have to close their business. You will not see a shop run by a Muslim close a single day. Even if it is the biggest celebration for Muslims, for example Eid, they do not even shut their business on that day, thinking that they might lose revenue. [. . .] It is only from my generation onwards that we have different perspectives, because the elders are mostly concentrated on their financial issues. They decided to bring up their children in the best way and they had a lot of hard times in their life. You can see some of the corner shops opening at 6 a.m. and not closing until 10 p.m. The money that they make is nothing compared to an educated person who has an office job. But they worked hard to raise their family. This is the reason why they came to [Great] Britain. The people that you will see in protests are Muslims who are mostly educated and are aware of right and wrong. (Yasir, Pakistani man in his mid-twenties)

Undoubtedly, younger Scottish Muslims have developed different survival skills and life goals from those of their families. With money not necessarily being their primary goal, education and career prospects have become the benchmark by which they compare their success to that of the wider non-Muslim population. While this may not apply to all of them, the aspirations of many young Scottish Muslims partially override core, traditional community values and expectations, such as gaining immediate financial stability, raising a family at an early age and reproducing kinship connections. Instead, they gravitate around Western goals of climbing the socio-economic ladder through middle-class means, such as education and hard work.

Young Scottish Muslims are engaging with the global world and are becoming more sociopolitically aware and active than their parents. This links with the formation and the development of a mix of religious, ideological and political Muslim identities that have been shaped through the Rushdie Affair and the more recent global, political reaction to 9/11 (see Chapter 2) and that have local ramifications in everyday Muslim lives. Yasir's belief that those Muslims who join protests are predominantly those who are educated and aware of social justice and ethical issues is not just a sweeping generalisation. Instead, it is supported by the evidence of an increase in civic and political engagement of the British Muslim elite – that is, 'a group of people – young students and professionals – who have or potentially have access to symbolic and economic capital conferred through entry into higher educational institutions and professions' (Edmunds 2010: 218; see also Peace 2015c).

In Edinburgh a considerable proportion of Muslims who join local anti-war protests, pro-Palestine campaigns and charitable causes are young, middle-class, educated and sociopolitically aware. This refutes the assertion made by Hopkins (2007b) that young Muslims are detached from politics partly as a result of conformity to a narrative of masculinity[7] that conceives of politics as feminine, and therefore soft. Instead, a global sense of Muslimness, which has been shaped by international events and feelings of both unity and victimhood, is played out locally through the display and deployment of a trans-ethnic and socially cohesive community. Arguably, the political mobilisation of Scottish Muslims *qua* Scottish Muslims predates 9/11.[8] Community responses both to the Rushdie Affair in 1988–9 and in opposition to the involvement of the United States and the coalition forces in the First Gulf War in 1990 (Maan 2014) are telling examples. However, 9/11 has increased the political activity and confidence of Scottish Muslims who, less than two months after the attacks on the Twin Towers, on 30 October 2001, could be seen taking to the streets of Glasgow, alongside the Campaign for Nuclear Disarmament and the

Stop the War Coalition, to protest against the invasion of Afghanistan by American, British and allied forces (Maan 2014).

Islam is the social glue that keeps together different cultural, ethnic and generational constituencies within a model of unity and relative homogeneity, not only of religious affiliation but also of ideas of social justice, human rights and ethics. Therefore, while single individuals play out their religiosity differently, Muslims' group identity is predicated on, and maintained through, Islam:

> There are many different Muslims in the world and we are not going to have the same goals in life, we are not going to have the same interests but there is one thing that draws us together and it is that we believe in the one God and the Prophet Muhammad (Peace Be Upon Him) as the last messenger. So we have got that in common. So I like when I am going out with my Muslim friends, I like that we all make the effort to make sure that we pray, and if we are fasting we all know that we are fasting. (Rabab, Scottish Pakistani woman in her late twenties)

'Charity Week', organised by Islamic Relief UK across Great Britain, is testimony to both the power of Islam to bring together different Muslims and the ideological and solidaristic nature of 'doing Muslim community' in practice. When Muslims gather in Edinburgh for the closing dinner and auction, one can normally see over 100 people, mostly Pakistanis in their twenties, thirties and forties, some children and a small number of elderly people in attendance. This broadly reflects the demographics of Muslims in Scotland but also the increased sociopolitical mobilisation of younger generations. The event is normally gender segregated, although towards the end barriers tend to break down and some men and women engage with one another. Attendees are dressed formally and elegantly, as one would expect at such an event, but even more so given the important role that honour plays within a South Asian majority community.

Requests for donations not only leverage Muslims' sense of social responsibility for those in conditions of disadvantage but also reinforce a publicly projected sense of performative morality and solidarity. In a post-9/11 context of heightened feelings of global victimhood (see Chapter 2), Scottish Muslims may well enjoy their 'privileged' life but do not completely forget the needs of fellow Pakistanis. Over the three-course dinner, touching videos capture people's emotions, while an eloquent imam plays on Islamic teachings to urge Muslims to empathise with the suffering of orphans. This has the double effect of reiterating one's religious and moral duties to donate (*zakat*) and appealing to one's feelings of empathy, diasporic guilt[9] and global connectedness. This is not only a performative display of active belonging to the imagined – or, as Roy (2007) would say, 'virtual' – global Muslim community (*umma*), whose increased affiliation has been promoted by global events, such as the wars in Afghanistan and Iraq[10] (Hussain and Bagguley 2012). It is also a direct manifestation of a 'glocal' community which is conceived globally through ideas of who a Muslim is and should be but is played out locally through practices that bind individuals to one another. To put it in Roy's (2004) words, it is a two-level community: the universal, global and ideal community of all Muslims as based on the notion of *umma*, and the local or national congregations of Muslims framed within the social and legal structure of a given society.

As the Syrian civil war had brought fear and destruction for about a year, the Edinburgh Muslim student society decided to organise a solidarity event open to the public in 2012. Unlike the relief activities in support of those affected by the Kashmir earthquake in 2005 (Archambault 2007) and the Pakistan flood of 2010 (Sarwar 2016), or even earlier solidarity events organised in support of Pakistan in the 1970s (Maan 2014), there was no sense of a community gathering based on shared ethnicity or personal connections with Syria. Instead, the Syrian solidarity event evidenced the commitment of predominantly younger Muslims to unite and demonstrate support for Muslims abroad by linking through their shared sense of global identity. It was a symbolic demonstration of what 'a global Islamic consciousness unbounded by geography' (Kundnani 2014: 38) looks like. Furthermore, this event displayed the Scottish Muslim community's potential for global and local mobilisation and unification in the face of world political events and conflicts.

Emotions, ideology, religion and solidarity mix together to shape and project an image of local and global Muslim homogeneity that goes beyond different geographies, ethnicities and cultures. This partly rejects the argument that Muslims in the West have paid lip service to the *umma* but have committed to communities in a Western and secular manner (Roy 2004). It also partly refutes the idea that 'much of the negotiation of difference occurs at the very local level, through everyday experiences and encounters' (Amin 2002: 959, quoted in Hopkins 2007b: 1129). Instead, Scottish Muslims are deeply committed to the ideas and practices of the *umma* and connect with fellow Muslims across the globe. Often in the absence of a shared language, heritage and culture, it is Islam as a religion, and sometimes as a political ideology, that brings together such distinct Muslim communities. This does not discount the fact that Scottish Muslims can *also* be equally committed to the Scottish nation, given that their group identity is a direct emanation of their individual identities (see Chapter 3). In fact, while being Muslim at heart, these men and women are also strongly and proudly Scottish (see Chapter 3). When these events are over, Muslims live ordinary lives as ordinary Scottish citizens. Here the joys but also the pains begin to emerge.

Negotiating Social Bridges

While embracing Scottishness as a marker of belonging offers Muslims a sense of place and a badge of cross-cultural unity, the negotiation of diversity in daily social life is not always free of obstacles. Arguably, the socialisation of young Scottish-born or 'Westernised', recently migrated Muslims into the daily Scottish system of education, entertainment and wider collective social spheres has broken cultural understandings of community boundaries as defined by the practices, mores and norms of its older, ethnic (predominantly South Asian) section. As other studies (Lewis 2007; Kabir 2010) have highlighted, migrant communities tend to colour their religious understandings and practices with ethnic and cultural traditions. In itself, this is a mutable process, as today's older generations, who castigate Scottish-born Muslims for engaging in unorthodox activities such as drinking and premarital sex, were guilty of similar 'sins' during their settlement in Scotland. Zakir highlights this moral shift:

> My father used to be a heavy drinker. But Ramadan was observed. He used to go to the Friday prayers. Most of the precepts were followed, like eating halal meat and so on. Wear a hat! [. . .] These are people from the old guard, very intolerant of the younger ones because they think that they are not doing things right, like playing football or snooker. They think that this is

corrupt Islam or not pure Islam because it is not their school of thought. You will see the old people wearing hats in the front rows during Friday prayers! (Zakir, British Pakistani man in his mid-forties)

Visiting 'Mosque B' on a Friday afternoon corroborates Zakir's points. At 'Mosque B', or at any other traditionally Pakistani mosque in Scotland, a curious visitor could spot a good number of Muslims who are each sporting a *topi*, the typical South Asian cap, in a climate strongly infused with Pakistani culture. This ranges from traditional clothes to heated discussions in Urdu, pictures of breathtaking Pakistani landscapes hanging on the office walls, and the ritual of eating traditional sweets after prayer. Undoubtedly, visiting this small mosque is a powerful cultural experience, which draws attention to a section of the Muslim community that remains united through a nostalgic sense of Pakistaniness suspended in space and time. At the same time, it acts as a reminder of the barriers that older generations still face in taking full part in public life. A generalised lack of language fluency and low levels of inter-est in becoming part of the broader Scottish community, compared to their younger counterparts, once again point at both their functional migration and their strong, romantic attachment to their home country (Bolognani 2007). This follows Lewis's (2007) argument that Muslim migration to Great Britain not only encompassed the need to adapt and live in equality and fraternity within a non-Muslim country but also included a major shift from a rural society to an urban society where diaspora communities attempted to recreate a clan-based organisation.

Turning back to Zakir's words on the ongoing shift of moral under-standings of Islam along cultural lines, documentary sources (BBC2 1966) demonstrate that South Asian Muslim migrants in Bradford had already started incorporating some adaptive approaches and British tools of socialisa-tion, including moderate drinking, within their own weekly social routines in the 1960s. Equally, a film representation of a mixed English family led by a Pakistani migrant (Mr Khan) in Salford, *East is East* (1999), directed by Damien O'Donnell, shows some of the English-born sons having already incorporated similar British tools of socialisation, including drinking, club-bing and quite relaxed sexual attitudes, in the early 1970. In this context, 'the film highlights the paradoxical nature of identity inevitably slipping away between two worlds [that is, the fixed world of the Pakistani father and the fluid world of his English-born Pakistani sons]' (Zapata 2010: 185). In Scotland, research (Shaikh and Bonino forthcoming) demonstrates that Pakistani migrants in the 1960s adopted Western clothing. It is therefore peculiar that older Scottish Muslim migrants project a highly moral and ethno-culturally grounded vision of personal development and social integration, which employs traditional understandings of Islam, as a tool for establishing norms of behaviours and practices.

This is even harder to reconcile with the more nuanced and complex social experiences of the younger section of the community. Such experiences mix nation, religion and culture in defining the fuzzy contours of Muslimness. Yet, while rejecting some of their home cultural norms, younger Scottish Muslims do not take up all Scottish socialisation practices by default. The 'clash of two cultures' thesis is less black and white than one might believe and involves a degree of personal and collective choice and sorting. In a way, the number of freedoms that Muslims believe Scotland and, more extensively, Great Britain (see Suleiman 2009) offer allows a pick-and-choose approach to national, ethnic and religious elements, selecting those that marry with one's hierarchy of norms and values:

> I do not have to adopt Scottish culture. Let's say that drinking is part of the Scottish culture. I do not have to do it. Ceilidh dance is part of the Scottish culture. I do not have to do it. They do clash with Islam. It is a big clash but I do not have to do it. But with regard to Pakistani culture, I live in a Pakistani family and my family is very open-minded but still when it comes to rituals, there is a hard-core Pakistani culture in there. We have a really big extended family. Just on Eid day we can have sixty people. I wear proper hijab for those occasions. On these days when all the cousins come together we have problems because my family has not adopted a culture of segregation and we have a very mixed get-together. But when my cousins are there I have to cover myself. (Nasha, Pakistani woman in her mid-twenties)

There is leeway for negotiation of community arrangements, as there are tensions between some aspects of Scottish social culture and some South Asian and Islamic mores and principles. Notably, Muslims lament that drinking is one of the main barriers to integration in Scottish social life (Homes et al.

2010). A powerful tool of bonding and networking, drinking plays a more important social role than one may think. In fact, about one in five Scottish people (20 per cent) finds it strange if someone refuses an alcoholic drink and considers getting drunk to be a perfectly acceptable thing to do at weekends. These figures go up to over 30 per cent (refusing a drink) and to 40 per cent (getting drunk) among eighteen- to twenty-nine-year-olds (Sharp et al. 2014). Deciding not to partake in social events in which alcohol is involved can backfire on educational and career prospects, as drinks receptions and dinners are typical spaces where job and personal connections can be nurtured. This may particularly affect those Muslims who are climbing the professional ladder rather than those who are already at the top:

> Deciding not to drink is clearly more difficult for some people. For example, professionally, for meetings I will not choose to have them in a pub. That said, when we do have dinner, a professional dinner or whatever, it is part of British culture that people are used to partaking in that [drinking] and I do not. It is fine. I think that it is their choice. I think that where it is more difficult is if you are not part of that process, if you do not progress up that social ladder or professional ladder. So for me it does not really arise as an issue. But I understand that for others this can be an issue because this is where decisions and key discussions take place and it can compromise people. (Ali, British Pakistani man in his mid-forties)

Rigid or fluid mechanisms of cultural openness often depend on the influences and expectations of one's extended family and closest community, whether friends, mosque members or others. In the case of Nasha and other Muslims, family influences and her own understanding of Muslimness and adherence to cultural community expectations allow the negotiation of her own self-presentation, such as wearing a hijab or not, in front of members of her family. The same family and community influences and understandings of Muslimness enforce strict moral and social norms in ruling out contested Western practices, such as drinking, which clash with traditional conceptions of a Muslim life.

Choosing not to drink and, extensively, not to attend social spaces that revolve around a drinking culture, such as nightclubs, is not easy. For many Muslims, it means adopting a policy of self-exclusion from a key sphere of socialisation. Nevertheless, there are growing feelings, particularly among the younger Scottish-born cohort, that nurturing a healthy detachment from the most problematic tools of socialisation can be achieved through appropriate social skills:

> Drinking is the biggest thing. Also, Muslims try not to go to nightclubs. Those who go do so because they are not educated about their religion or do not practise enough but, apart from that, social mixing and relationships outside marriage are probably the most problematic aspects. These are the areas that are probably the hardest to deal with for young people. It does not matter whether one is a Muslim or not, they are all the same – young people who want to enjoy life! Enjoy those things that you can, and with regard to the kind of things that you cannot, you can still go out together but you do not have to go to a club. You go to a restaurant, have food, go to a cinema, watch a movie, these kind of things that people can do while respecting each other. (Nasir, Scottish Pakistani man in his early thirties)

There is a rather orthodox undertone in the words of Nasir, a local imam, that several young Scottish Muslims do not necessarily agree with, although the view that certain elements of Scottish and Western culture cannot be incorporated within the normative boundaries of the Muslim community is shared by some younger and many older Muslims. A performed display of 'moral' Muslimness – avoiding drinking, clubbing, male/female physical contact and so on – certainly defines a number of Muslims' public attitudes. Broadly speaking, it ties in with wider research that found British Muslims to be more socially conservative than both non-Muslim Britons (Lewis and Kashyap 2013) and French and German Muslims (Gallup 2009). Whether this hampers a process of cultural cross-fertilisation and exchange with the Scottish community remains to be established. Certainly, drinking is a very sensitive issue and, possibly, a lose–lose situation. If Muslims decide to drink, they will be stigmatised by fellow Muslims; if they decide not to drink, they will be stigmatised by broader society (Fletcher and Spracklen 2013).

Arguably, fixed stances on both sides do not ease tensions. While one may chastise young Muslims for not 'trying' to be less Muslim and enjoying a pint at the pub, one may also reprimand young Scottish people for not 'trying' to be less Scottish and sipping a much healthier orange juice on a

Saturday night. The key point here is that some social barriers might be slow to break, and it might take generations until being Scottish is as coterminous with being Muslim as it is with being Christian or being atheist or being all or none of them at the same time.

Leisure activities in a broader sense impact on Muslims' sensitivities and demonstrate the changing face of the Muslim community living in Scotland. While many older Muslims were baffled by the idea that younger members of the community date 'like Westerners', a disgruntled Mustafa, an elderly Pakistani man, expressed all his disappointment when the author (a white non-Muslim man) told him that Muslim women had agreed to participate in his research. Mustafa's views, as bizarre as they may seem, are not too uncommon among the older cohort of Muslims. In fact, they represent 'traditional views of *purdah* – a need to "curtain" women away from non-related Muslims, especially in a Western society routinely dismissed as Godless, and marked by drunkenness, sexual promiscuity and lack of respect for elders' (Lewis 2007: 27–8). From this perspective, one may understand the dilemma that young Muslims face when approaching members of the opposite gender with whom they come into contact and who are rarely non-Muslim:

> Leisure activities are a big issue for Muslims in Scotland. Let's say that you have a nine-to-five job. What do you do outside your job? You go for a beer with your mates? No, you cannot do that, so at the workplace there are closer bonds among those who have gone to the pub after work. [. . .] Leisure in England is a lot more optimistic. Even the dating scene . . . Here it is really hard to date someone. Okay, dating is forbidden in Islam! [Laughs.] Okay, let's just say meeting members of the opposite gender. It is impossible to do it in Scotland. (Arif, Canadian Bangladeshi man in his early thirties)

These are just a few of the problems that Scottish Muslims face in their day-to-day socialisation. These constitute pragmatic considerations on how to go about one's life as a minority within a non-Muslim majority country. But they also raise a more general question of post-migration integration, which is going to be briefly introduced here but will be met with empirical evidence in Chapter 6 and will be theoretically developed in the Epilogue. Such a question asks how society should deal with cultural diversity in racially and ethnically mixed polities (Meer 2014a). Still a contentious topic, integration usually refers to two notions: one-way assimilation and two-way adaptation (Castles et al. 2002). Assimilation is essentially a one-way process of integration into the majority society, which requires minority groups to adopt the dominant values, beliefs and norms. Here, society remains impermeable to, and instead seeks to homogenise, the cultural diversity of minorities. Such a process presupposes that failure to assimilate should not be a reason to complain over exclusion and discrimination (Parekh 2000a). A system of integration typical of French and Italian societies, this is far from both the ideals and the realities of minorities living in Scotland.

Scotland follows a 'two-speed' integration process. Some aspects of day-to-day social life take a 'partial assimilation' orientation – that is, a less intense form of the assimilationist approach, which limits its scope to public life. Partial assimilation expects minorities to blend into the dominant political culture but allows them to retain cultural diversity within their families and in parts of civil society (Meer 2014a). This is evidenced by ongoing tensions between visible aspects of Muslimness and more orthodox Western norms, which pop in and out of existence depending on the circumstances. Chapter 5 shows how wearing a hijab, looking 'foreign' and practising Islam are met with suspicion, if not outright discrimination, on the street, at work, in schools and in other spaces by a small section of the Scottish community. The socialisation problems covered earlier demonstrate that Scotland is yet to achieve mutual integration, as non-Muslims do not want to give up their traditional social life to the same extent that a number of Muslims have given up their traditional values to join a more 'Westernised' way of life. Arif touches upon the possibilities for intercultural integration yet highlights the problems that still persist in building social bridges between different communities in Scotland:

> I think that the drinking culture separates people. My cousin here married a white Scottish person. However, he does not drink, his family does not drink – they had something in common. (Arif, Canadian Bangladeshi man in his early thirties)

Partial assimilation is normally associated with integration policies aimed at promoting social cohesion and fostering a national identity and value system, a common language, ceremonies of naturalisation and other public displays of sociocultural homogeneity and unity (Kostakopoulou 2010). While the

Scottish nationalist impetus is strong, it does not aim to impose its own features on minorities. Moreover, its political aspirations are inclusive rather than exclusive. This has historically characterised a careful Scottish nationalist approach of 'cultivat[ing] a sense of Scottish identity that [. . . is] not based on any narrow or exclusivist definition' (McConaghy 2015: 11). Therefore, Scotland confines partial assimilation to some aspects of social life, such as socialisation, leisure and so on, that are in the process of being transformed through a slow, generational adaptation to the globalisation of cultures. This connects to European scholarship (Roy 2004) that illustrates that Islam in the West has the capacity to malleably adapt to Western frameworks and has gone through a 'Westernisation' of some of its values' expression. The Islamic adaptation to the Western concept of the nuclear family, as opposed to the traditional Islamic polygamous extended family, is a notable example.

The ideals and the political aspirations of Scotland match with a limited or half-baked two-way process of adaptation, which conceives of its social and cultural landscapes as porous and open to diversity of values, beliefs and lifestyles and values integration for its potential to fulfil equal opportunities (Brighton 2007). Scotland has so far limited its two-way process of adaptation to the least contested areas of social life, which range from the promotion of Islam at public events, through geographical non-segregation, to general openness to Muslims' diversity. It is yet to be established how Scotland would react if its Muslim community, feeling empowered within a nation that promotes its 'many cultures and faiths', demanded Muslim faith schools or shari'a councils. Given Scotland's increasingly non-religious and secular connotations (National Records of Scotland 2013), the romantic idea of infinite friendliness and total inclusiveness would likely start to crumble. There are of course a number of spheres in which integration is measured and it is not the aim of this book to touch upon all of them. It will suffice to say that, while the focus here is predominantly on social connections, access to housing, employment, education and health are also crucial, as are so-called 'facilitators', such as language and cultural knowledge, and safety and stability (Ager and Strang 2008).

Muslim Belonging to 'Big Tent' Scotland

To further understand the contours and the meanings of people's belonging to Scotland, one must draw on the historical, social, cultural and political dimensions of the country. Along with historian Tom Devine, the most authoritative voice in this respect is David McCrone (2001), whose book *Understanding Scotland: The Sociology of a Nation* represents a sociological masterpiece on the formation of Scotland and Scottish national identity. After having played a major role in the emergence of the Enlightenment throughout the eighteenth century (Herman 2003),[11] Scotland has undergone recent developments, which McCrone breaks down into three main historical periods:

1. The 1900s, when Scotland was a very modern and industrial country driven by an imperialist politics, had an ethically and religiously Protestant outlook and was dominated by local capital.
2. The 1950s, when the previous locally based system of power lost ground to a central state power and patriotism took off, mainly through the symbolic role that the First and Second World Wars played in shaping a strong British identity.
3. The 2000s, in which the centrality of the family eroded in favour of strong individualism, the Scottish economy opened up to world markets, and access to higher education expanded to allow social mobility, although unequal distribution of social opportunities meant that class and gender barriers impeded equitable access to top jobs.

Nowadays, Scotland 'has a degree of statehood (a devolved parliament [established through the Scotland Act 1998], a governing bureaucracy), but it is still best described as a stateless nation, an imagined community, with considerable institutional autonomy and, at least as yet, no sovereign parliament' (McCrone 2001: 6). McCrone maintains that Scotland has built up a strong national identity since the 1960s, following the discovery of the North Sea oil and the rise in the SNP's popularity. While being a rather elusive term, the concept of nation in McCrone takes both the shape of a moral conscience based on collective solidarity and an imagined common history (Renan 1939) and the connotation of a socially constructed community characterised by a vertical (time) and horizontal (space) sense of belonging (Anderson 1996 [1983]). Moreover, McCrone adds, nationalism brings together a variety of elements that are sociological, political and psychological in nature. The historical continuity of Scotland, as a mutable yet enduring national artefact, is captured by McCrone (2001: 49) when he argues that

> There can be little doubt of the ideological power of 'Scotland' as a nation in these terms. It implies that Scotland is not simply a collection of rocks, earth and water, but a transcendent idea which runs through history, reinterpreting that history to fit the concerns of each present.

Elsewhere also considered a political ideology (Kyriakides et al. 2009), nationalism in McCrone's work emerges as a powerful force that mobilises culture to achieve goals such as avenging previous exploitation and discrimination, offering a voice in the political sphere and meeting social needs for a shared, individual and collective identity. Built upon strong anti-racist connotations and grounded in the idea of an 'oppressed Scottish identity' (possibly perpetuating the alleged inferiorisation of Scottish people (Cusick 1994)), postwar Scottishness has contrasted with English nationalism, which is thought to be based on oppressive imperialism (Kyriakides et al. 2009). The core of Scottish nationalism is 'firmly embedded in a "sense of place" rather than a "sense of tribe" [. . . which] derives from medieval *realpolitik* rather than moral superiority on the part of the Scots' (McCrone 2001: 155, emphasis in the original).

In the Scottish Muslim community, such a sense of place is played out in two ways. On the one hand, it serves the purpose of expressing a clear cultural and ideological demarcation between the boundaries of Scottishness and Englishness. A sense of belonging to Scotland and a feeling of being Scottish relative to one's non-belonging to England is part and parcel of the experiences of many of those Muslims who openly declare their emotional and cultural allegiance to the country, at times even in the absence of direct experience of life in England. Other research also demonstrates that Scottish Muslims have stronger national sentiments towards Scotland than English Muslims have towards England (Kidd and Jamieson 2011). On the other hand, Muslims' feelings of Scottishness are also played out in absolute terms through declarations of proud belonging to Scotland per se. Scotland is perceived to be a place where freedom of expression is valued, multiculturalism is promoted (for example, through the social enactment of the 'One Scotland' political manifesto), and ethnicity, while not unimportant, is not necessarily an ultimate barrier to inclusion. This is captured by McCrone and Bechhofer (2010), who argue that Scotland offers a low entry tariff to national claims of Scottishness, and is partly restated by Meer (2015a) in a study locating Scottish political elites' aspirational pluralism within a context that steers away from ethnically fixed barriers to one's belonging to the country. Muslims' active engagement with the notion of Scotland, and claims of belonging through markers of Scottish identity (see Chapter 3), help sustain ideas of nation as an intersubjective reality, which exists in collective imaginations yet plays a powerful role in binding people together (Harari 2014).

Many Muslims share the narrative, whether real or perceived, of Scotland as a relatively open and porous sociocultural space, which possesses almost spiritual capacities to absorb and integrate human elements and products of diversity. A measure of Scottish egalitarianism can be found in the study of Hussain and Miller (2006). The study consists of a large-scale survey of both Pakistani and English minorities living in Scotland and the majority populations living in both Scotland and England, and compares perceptions of discriminatory attitudes in Scotland and England. Despite the fact that Scottish people score higher on Islamophobia than Anglophobia in relative terms, only 42 per cent of Scottish people consider conflicts between Muslims and non-Muslims to be at least fairly serious, as opposed to 61 per cent of English people living in England. More broadly, Scotland is perceived to be less Islamophobic than England. Among the explanations proposed by Hussain and Miller are factors related to the particular settlement and development of Muslim communities in Scotland (see also Chapter 1) and the specific features of Scottish geographies and sociopolitical attitudes towards diversity:

- The smaller Muslim population in Scotland.
- The fact that many Muslims in Scotland are self-employed and work in business, while a good number of Muslims in England are unskilled labourers.
- Higher levels of segregation within English Muslim communities.
- Higher levels of racism in England, possibly due to the fact that Islamophobia is 'much more closely tied to English nationalism within

England than Scottish nationalism within Scotland' (Hussain and Miller 2006: 65).

Other research (Homes et al. 2010) has also found that the process of integrating Muslims into society is easier in Scotland than England due to lower fear of terrorism, lower settlement numbers and the positive features of Scotland, such as friendliness, sociability and a welcoming disposition. This furthers the political idea of Scotland as 'an inclusive club with a low entry tariff [. . . and characterised by a] "big tent" Scottishness, such that everyone living in the country has a claim' (McCrone and Bechhofer 2010: 926). Moreover, it builds upon the notion of the Scottish egalitarian society, which works as a social ethos and 'a celebration of sacred beliefs about what it is to be Scottish [. . . and functions as] an ideological device for marking off the Scots from the English' (McCrone 2001: 102–3). On the ground, this translates into Muslims' generally positive social and cultural experiences (see Chapter 6 and Colourful Heritage 2016), in a context in which discrimination exists (see Chapter 5) but is not a specific function of Scotland per se. Instead, it simply perpetuates a post-9/11 national and global perceived stigmatisation of Muslimness (Bonino 2012 and 2013) within the Scottish context.

However, while it is probably true that, for various reasons, Scotland offers a more open sociocultural environment, the myth of Scottish egalitarianism rests on a more nuanced reality. There is some truth in the romantic notion of Scots' historical friendliness towards South Asian subjects (Maan 1992). Similarly, in the context of a Scottish nationalism deemed to be a progressive force, 'the Empire was consequently represented either as the triumphant moment of British nationalism, or as a historical impediment to the ultimate triumph of Scottish nationalism' (Condor and Abell 2006: 469–70). But it would be historically amnesiac to forget that the Scots were deeply involved in all the aspects of the British Raj (Devine 2012), possibly through a larger contribution than that of England, and were proud of what 'they and their kinsfolk had accomplished' (Glass 2014: 147). Yet, a lack of historical memory seems to affect many young Muslims who still attach themselves to the Scottish narrative of tolerance. This narrative, their strong Scottish identities (see Chapter 3) and their generally positive experiences of everyday life are making it a Scottish experience to be Muslim.

A Scottish Experience to be Muslim

It has been highlighted that the sociocultural context that many Scottish Muslims inhabit differs in many ways from their parents' experience of Scotland. Whether they were born and raised in Scotland, whether they moved to Scotland at an early age and were partially socialised within Scottish culture or whether they spent their childhood and early adulthood in their home countries and then migrated to Scotland, the traditional, ethno-cultural migrant sense of community is giving way to a cross-bred Scottish Muslim community. Ali posits that Muslims in Scotland are going through a historical process of ethnic identity dilution. Instead, they embrace both national/civic Scottish and religious Muslim experiences, the latter at times being underpinned by ideological and political connotations:

> Historically here, being a Muslim has always been synonymous with being Pakistani or Bangladeshi. That is a historical perspective and if you look at it now, it is no longer true anymore. In time, people of South Asian origin will be the minority. It will be predominantly a British experience to be a Muslim in the UK context. It has already begun to happen. It will be like in the United States, where it is predominantly an Afro-American experience. English will reduce some of the barriers to entering into Islam. (Ali, British Pakistani man in his mid-forties)

As for the epitome of the current endurance of ethno-cultural modalities of Muslimness, especially within the older generations, some Muslims pick language as the main 'culprit'. The command of a *lingua franca* not only allows basic communication but also facilitates participation in civil society. Furthermore, it buys Muslims into a project of Scottishness that may not be normatively built upon language, but pragmatically rests upon cross-ethnic tools of unity. As many believe, it is becoming more and more of a Scottish experience to be Muslim:

> One benefit of being Muslim here is that you can come from any corner and mix up. Only sometimes, language barriers are a problem to interaction. There are Arabs and I am from Pakistan. There are people from India, Bangladesh, Iran, Indonesia, Malaysia and so on. So you need a *lingua*

franca. English is the language that fills the gap. [. . .] If people know English, then there is no problem. Otherwise, people need to acquire different languages for different interactions. (Sarmad, Pakistani man in his early fifties)

There are definitely micro-communities but one of the things to remember is that these issues will fade with the next generations. Take for example Urdu-speaking mosques. Whoever is not Urdu-speaking, even a Pakistani who is not Urdu-speaking – for example, my kids – is completely out of place in that context. But it is a matter of time because that is not going to persist when new generations will not speak Urdu anymore. (Ali, British Pakistani man in his mid-forties)

The transition from an ethno-cultural to a national and religious community is certainly a natural generational and environmental evolution that touches upon ideas of migration, settlement and development. It is also an environmental adaptation to maximise group survival. The advantages of sharing a common language in order to take an active part in Scottish cultural and political life are obvious. Similarly, as identified in Chapter 3, upholding two of the main 'markers of Scottish identity' (Kiely et al. 2001) – that is, place of birth and education – facilitates claims of Scottish identity and recognition from wider society.

What might go unnoticed are the benefits of actively engaging with the ideas, even if not the practices, whatever these might be, of the Scottish nation in ways that allow some detachment from ethno-culturalist understandings of nationhood towards the partial embracing of civic nationalism in the form of 'allegiance to a particular social system and constitution' (Weber n.d.: 5). This is particularly visible in declarations of allegiance to Scotland *as opposed to* England,[12] the elevation of Edinburgh to status of 'promised land' and the overall identification with the Scottish narrative of relative openness and tolerance (see Chapter 6). Declared belonging and active engagement with Scottish nationalism function as a solution to the problem of competitive exclusion posed by Gause's law (Gause 1934), which posits that when 'two populations are complete competitors and one is dominant over the entire niche, the less efficient competitor will be eliminated from the arena of competition' (Abruzzi 1993: 56). By avoiding competition with the definition of the main framework of Scottishness, which is premised upon an inclusive and civic, rather than exclusive and ethnic, identity (McConaghy 2015), and by underplaying ethnicity and culture in identity and community claims, Scottish Muslims achieve two results.

First, they retain an ecologically equal position within Scottish society by avoiding challenging the terms of reference of a Scottish civic nationalism. These terms are, at least in the public imagination (Leith and Soule 2012), based on an inclusive identity, and thus do not threaten Muslims' multiple identities as the ethnically fixed (Fenton and Mann 2011) and closed character of Englishness would. Muslims attach themselves to an aspirational, inclusive sense of civil nationalism. At the same time, they manage to retain ethno-cultural elements, such as family traditions, clothing, food and music, as side features of their identities. Second, they shape a cross-ethnic, religiously cohesive notion of Muslim community, an ecology in which both Muslimness and Scottishness can coexist. This also solves the English multicultural 'problem', which emerges from an ethnically fixed idea of Britishness that feels threatened by a myriad of cultural claims that are considered to be too distinct to be reconciled.

Building on very wide and strongly inclusive social categories of group identity ('Scottish' and 'Muslim') that contain, restrain and dilute ethnic differences, a rather vague yet malleable and marketable concept of unity takes centre stage and plays upon the combined strengths that Scottishness and Muslimness can offer to Muslims' claims of belonging. In the end, Muslims maximise individual and group survival by giving up some of their ethno-cultural distinctiveness, taking up the Scottish national narrative and building a cross-ethnic Muslim collectivity. In other words, Muslims maintain differences at the individual level but dilute them at the group level to the benefit of both. The interplay of Scottishness and Muslimness is nowhere better symbolised than in the creation of a halal haggis, by a butcher in Edinburgh (*Scotsman* 2003), and the Islamic tartan, blue for the Saltire and green for Islam, by Scottish Muslim entrepreneur Azeem Ibrahim (Marshall 2012).

The 'new Muslims' do not belong to the community structures of 'Mosque B', in which 'society and Islamic "community" are coterminous' (Lewis 2007: 9) insofar as individuals claim belonging to the ethnic community and maintain relationships with God at the same time. Instead, they fit within the fuzzier boundaries of 'Mosque A' and 'Mosque C', which come to represent places of worship, education and socialisation all at the same time. 'Mosque A' brings together Muslims from very diverse backgrounds, whether Pakistanis, Somalis or Tunisians, whether young or old, whether migrant or Scottish-born, and promotes sentiments of sharedness based on group commitment to the same set of beliefs, morals and practices. It is a Muslim community that is grounded on broad religious homogeneity, though infused with Saudi theological influences, relative cultural similarity and variable ethnic diversity. In Roy's (2004) terms, 'Mosque A' represents a 'parochial level' form of community – that is, a faith institution which employs religion as a symbol of unity and common identity, which is usually formed around mosques, spiritual congregations and student associations.

'Mosque C' targets predominantly Scottish-born Muslims with a view to furnishing them with Scottish sociocultural tools of survival. It tackles the perceived inadequateness of religious personnel (imams and ulama), who are normally brought from home countries, have little contextual knowledge of British and Scottish issues (Lewis 2007) and deliver sermons in their own native language (often Urdu; see Maan 2014), by training Scottish and British-born imams. It holds prayers in English and organises open days and interfaith events for non-Muslims. Furthermore, the experiences of its attendees are deeply embedded in Scottish life:

> Young Muslims do not really care about cultural views. They are here living the culture of Scotland as long as it is still compatible with their religion. That is what they want. They do not want it to be compatible with Pakistani culture, because Pakistani culture is not their culture. They do not call themselves Pakistani. They do not sign the ethnicity form saying 'Pakistani'. They want to be Scottish, but they want to be Muslim too. Scottish Muslims: that is what they want to be. (Nasir, Scottish Pakistani man in his early thirties)

This mosque actively encourages intercommunity contact and takes a proactive role in training local religious personnel who can speak English and can be attuned to the needs of Scottish Muslims. This is a direction supported and encouraged by the Muslim Council of Scotland (MCS) (*Herald Scotland* 2015a), an organisation representing Muslim associations, mosques and institutions across the country. It is also a direction that has been partly taken by Glasgow Central Mosque, a place of worship that features large panels of glass typical of Glaswegian public buildings and that hosts Muslims who marry in kilts to the sound of bagpipes (*Economist* 2015b). It is true that the Muslim community and Scottish mosques are often ethnically fragmented and theologically divided (Archambault 2007), to the point that different mosques have different timetables for Ramadan and different days for the celebration of Eid (Maan 2014). Glasgow Central Mosque has also been at the centre of cultural tensions between orthodox and liberal Muslims, mixed with issues of governance and institutional development (see Epilogue). Ethno-cultural and theological factionalisms are part and parcel not only of mosques in Glasgow and Edinburgh, but also of places of worship in other Scottish cities, for example Dundee (Caraballo-Resto 2010).

However, intercommunity contact remains crucially important in informing Muslims and non-Muslims' reciprocal views, since familiarity with minority groups helps reduce levels of prejudice (Field 2007: 465). As a Muslim woman, Nasha, puts it, the goal of Scottish Muslims should not be to intensify the 'Muslim factor' in their day-to-day way of 'doing community'. Instead, the possibly utopian goal should be to leave aside 'the Islamic factor', 'the Christian factor', 'the Jewish factor' and 'the atheist factor' to make Scotland feel much more like a super-community that values, yet transcends, diversity. This will be the path sketched in the Epilogue of this book: a Scottish community in which diversity and universal human values can meet and mutually thrive.

Conclusion

The reshaping of Muslim community boundaries as a result of increased individual affiliation to Islam and a strong sense of belonging to Scotland is well underway and is changing old concepts of Muslims as mere migrants with strong ethnic identities and an evergreen nostalgia for their countries of origin. The traditional ethno-cultural, predominantly South Asian, Muslim community bound by kinship, honour and tribal affiliation has given way to a more ethnically transversal aggregate of globally loosely affiliated and locally physically connected people. These people find a common ground in their belonging to Islam and in an externally scrutinised yet proudly internalised sense of Muslimness. The Scottish ethos of tolerance; peaceful, democratic and civic nationalism (McConaghy 2015); vivid and popular cultural iconographies exemplified by the poetry of Robert Burns and by traditional bagpipe music (*Economist* 2009); low entry tariff; sense of oppressed identity; and active detachment from a perceived 'imperialist' England have shaped emotions of belonging and unity among young Muslims. These young people channel their proud Scottish identities into an ongoing Scottish sense of being Muslim that, while not free from cultural tensions, contains the seeds of success. Young Scottish Muslims have survived the post-9/11 stage of real and perceived global stigmatisation. Locally, they have both formed ties within their own changing community and built bridges with the non-Muslim majority. It is in the hands of these new generations of Muslims, with their ability to both retain some of their parents' tools of community cohesion and, at the same time, develop a sense of collective identity more attuned to Scottish society and the contemporary world, that the future of the Scottish Muslim community rests.

There is little doubt that the intermingling of Scottishness and Muslimness in the construction of a cross-bred Scottish Muslim community will eventually contribute to building a new Scottish society (see Epilogue). But it would be inaccurate and misleading to depict the future and, in particular, the present through rose-tinted glasses and to gloss over the discrimination that Muslims have historically faced and continue to face. Moving on from the old cultural and racial hostility to contemporary experiences of religious prejudice, the lingering presence of a post-9/11 securitisation of Muslimness and forms of everyday discrimination must not be overshadowed by romantic narratives of Scotland as a land of tolerance. The ghost of 9/11 is out and about and is ready both to threaten generally positive experiences and to undermine the pathway towards full recognition of Muslims in Scotland.

Notes

1. The older migrant generation left Pakistan for Great Britain mainly for financial reasons. In fact, in the 1960s, a Pakistani migrant could earn a salary thirty times higher in Great Britain than in Pakistan and, thus, send good remittances back home (Ansari 2004).

2. This differs from a self-arranged marriage in which 'the girl and boy have courted secretly and have managed either to persuade or manipulate parents into arranging their wedding match for them' (Qureshi and Moores 1999: 324).

3. *Izzat* formally rests on the male members of the family but effectively depends on how female members, as transmitters of cultural values and identity, are perceived by the community (Qureshi 2004). *Izzat* plays a crucial role in family and community cohesion and is enhanced by a variety of elements including high caste, a large number of male family members, being able to exert sociopolitical influence in Scotland and/or Pakistan, good educational and professional achievements, and a range of other factors such as generosity, honesty, wealth and religiosity (Wardak 2000).

4. Whether families consciously or unconsciously decide to turn a blind eye to the social experiences of their children is unclear, although informal conversations with some older members of the community suggest that they are at least aware of the younger generations' redefinition of acceptable social practices and engagement in culturally 'reproachable' activities.

5. While some drink, Muslims are still the least likely religious group (2 per cent as opposed to 14 per cent of Hindus, 16 per cent of Buddhists and 32–40 per cent of the various Christian faith groups) to drink (or admit to doing so) at hazardous or harmful levels (Whybrow et al. 2012).

6. This resonates with research on South Asians in England and Wales, according to which migrant families instil in their sons and daughters a sense that education is important and that academic success should take precedence over youth recreational culture and other similar pursuits (Modood 2005).

7. While the author remains unconvinced by these arguments, readers may wish to refer to other work by Hopkins (2009) on the alleged crisis of masculinity among young Scottish Muslims.

8. For an analysis of British Muslims' political mobilisation and activism, see the work of Peace (2015a and 2015c).

9. This refers to the economic conditions of migrants being better off than those of their fellow countrymen who decided to remain in their home country.

10. British Muslims have historically been involved in the anti-war movement from the original foundation of the Stop the War Coalition (StWC) and through and after the invasion of Afghanistan and Iraq. On 15 February 2003, the StWC march in London against the war in Iraq featured many British Muslims in what has been their largest mobilisation so far (Peace 2015b).

11. The Scottish opposition to slavery during the Enlightenment is particularly interesting and was shared by David Hume, Robert Wallace and James Steuart (Webster 2003).
12. According to Weber (n.d.), Scotland's civic attitude in contrast to England's demonstrates that civic nationalism, and not only ethnic nationalism, can also be exclusive.

5

INTEGRATED YET DISCRIMINATED AGAINST: THE GHOST OF 9/11 IN EVERYDAY MUSLIM LIFE

The Scottish context has been characterised as an easier environment for Muslims to integrate into compared to England (Homes et al. 2010). Furthermore, the relationship between the Muslim and non-Muslim populations in Scotland has benefited from the specific socio-historical settlement of South Asian communities in the country, who did not compete for jobs with the majority Scottish people when working as pedlars in the mid-1920s and later when entering education and moving into self-employment,[1] who privileged house ownership and private renting and, therefore, avoided competition for public services in the 1950s and 1960s, who have so far not created major troubles and whose involvement in business has helped promote a positive public image (Maan 1992). Moreover, in Scotland Anglophobia may displace Islamophobia (Hussain and Miller 2006), in a context in which English people encounter barriers to belonging due to their national identities (McIntosh et al. 2008) and feed anxieties and insecurities among Scottish people (Bond et al. 2010). Lastly, the policy messages emerging from Holyrood, and particularly from the governing SNP, in support of immigration as a way to address demographic challenges and achieve sustainable economic growth in Scotland resonate in stark opposition to Westminster's measures to restrict immigration (McCollum et al. 2014).

Nevertheless, the daily realities in which Scottish Muslims live are diverse, fluid and complex. In fact, such realities also include prejudice and are coloured by the insecurities that sustain the cultural barriers between Muslims and non-Muslims, in a context in which the former might perceive the latter to hold more negative views of them than they do (Homes et al. 2010). The differences between the two constituencies that host the two largest Muslim communities – Glasgow and Edinburgh (see Chapter 1) – are a reminder of the rather inhomogeneous and patchy experiences of being a Muslim in Scotland. On the one hand, Glasgow hosts the most ethnically segregated area in Scotland, namely, East Pollokshields. On the other hand, Edinburgh presents itself as a socio-economically and culturally distinctive city. Unlike Glasgow, Edinburgh's smaller, ethnically diverse – albeit of majority Pakistani origin or heritage – Muslim population is scattered throughout the town, a socio-spatial factor which might favour integration, if contact theory (Allport 1954) – 'the greater the familiarity, the lower the level of prejudice' (Field 2007: 465) – holds true. The community gathers around twelve official mosques, which tend to serve different ethno-cultural and theological orientations of the Muslim population, although many people attend the main city mosque, which is located in the central, student area and is a symbolic reminder of the key role that Islam plays in the social geography of contemporary Western societies.

The next pages will elaborate on the history of discriminatory attitudes towards visible minorities and Muslims in Scotland, which was traced in Chapter 1, including a much-needed detour on the broader situation across Great Britain, and will subsequently focus on Muslims' specific day-to-day experiences in the fragile sociopolitical climate that has followed 9/11. In this sense, the increased visibility of Muslim religious identities will be posited to be a driver for real and perceived stigmatisation during interactions with non-Muslims in everyday life, but particularly at loci of security, such as airports, where Muslims feel an acute sense of social inequality, powerlessness and humiliation.

Prejudice and Discrimination against British and Scottish Muslims

As highlighted in Chapter 1, exclusionary practices based on racialised stereotypes against 'coloured' people have been reproduced in Scotland for centuries, at least since the eighteenth and nineteenth centuries: once fostered by tales of missionaries and Scottish soldiers returning from India and

Africa; then exemplified by colour bans in dancing halls in the 1920s; and, more recently, expressed through direct or indirect discrimination in various spheres of life, for example employment, housing and sociocultural entertainments (Wardak 2000). The post-9/11 discrimination against Muslims represents the consolidation of a shift from primarily racial to ethno-religious prejudice dating back to the Rushdie Affair in 1988–9, when Muslims across Great Britain, including Scotland (Maan 2014), started mobilising, being recognised and being targeted not only as an ethnic group, but also, and especially, as a religious group (Marranci 2008; Bolognani 2009).

In the wake of 9/11, Scottish Muslims became the main 'representatives' of religious diversity within the Scottish landscape, a fate that they share with Muslims south of the border. Clegg and Rosie argue that 'the attack on the World Trade Center in September 2001 marked a turning point from predominantly racial intolerance and abuse towards more religiously motivated attacks. People wearing distinctive religious dress or symbols are a particular target' (Clegg and Rosie 2005: 1–2). In the same study, all faith groups perceived Muslims to be the community most under pressure, especially after 2001. Among the targets of the post-9/11 retaliation are also members of other ethnic and religious minority groups (for example, Sikh) who might mistakenly be considered Muslim (Qureshi 2007) and who have also been stopped and searched by the police based on the belief that they are Muslim (Parmar 2011).

Discriminatory and racist attacks on Muslim people and symbols sharply increased after 9/11 (Hopkins 2007b). For example, in Edinburgh a mosque was vandalised less than a month after the terrorist attacks on the United States and damages were valued at £20,000. In Glasgow, eggs were thrown at a mosque and a Muslim woman was spat at on the street (Hopkins and Smith 2008). In Lanarkshire, the contractor working on Central Lanarkshire Mosque received death threats and had to resign from the job in late 2002[2] (Maan 2014). In 2003, a group of young white people attacked a young South Asian man who was walking to his local mosque in a Muslim community in Glasgow. Soon afterwards, gang problems and violent clashes between South Asians and white people erupted in Pollokshields, including 'tit-for-tat fire bombings of shops and cars' (Sarwar 2016: 8). After the London attack in 2005, Edinburgh experienced vandalism directed against one of its mosques and a serious attack on a young Scottish Pakistani man (Qureshi

2007), in a context in which Scotland as a whole suffered from increasing discriminatory treatment towards Muslims in schools and on the street (Maan 2014). Similarly, following a series of Islamic State-inspired terrorist attacks that killed 129 people and injured 433 in Paris on 13 November 2015, the Scottish Muslim community suffered from increased racially and religiously motivated crimes. Police Scotland reportedly recorded over sixty religiously motivated crimes in the weeks after the attack (Leask 2016c). Strathclyde University Muslim Student Association received death threats (Brooks 2015). A cultural centre used by Muslims in Glasgow was firebombed (Gray 2015). The owner of a takeaway in Fife was assaulted and a Scottish Asian woman and her child were physically attacked (Duffy 2015). After the UK's decision to leave the EU in June 2016, National Action, a neo-Nazi youth movement, placed racist stickers on lamp posts around Glasgow (McGuire 2016).

Several Scottish people believe that the attempted bombing of Glasgow Airport in July 2007 increased intolerance towards Muslims (Homes et al. 2010). Moreover, about 40 per cent of Scottish people seem to believe that Scotland would lose its identity if the Muslim population increased, while 37 per cent consider Islam to be incompatible with Scottish life (Homes et al. 2010). Approximately one in five (20 per cent) and one in eight (13 per cent) Scottish people, respectively, would be unhappy if a family member formed a relationship with a Muslim and consider Muslims to be unsuitable as primary school teachers (Scottish Governemnt 2016d). Research conducted by Kidd and Jamieson (2011) confirms the fact that global events have instigated racial and religious discrimination. This is considered to be 'a double burden' since 'Muslims experience unfair treatment and discrimination on the grounds of ethnicity and race, as well as in relation to their religious identity' (Kidd and Jamieson 2011: 31). Kidd and Jamieson also notice that unfriendliness and hostility towards Muslims have been fairly common in Muslim areas of residence and on the street, while women have reported intrusive attention from men or sexual harassment. The 2007 protests against the provision of a plot of land for a new Muslim cemetery at Windlaw Farm near Carmunnock, a village in the suburb of Glasgow (Maan 2014), demonstrate the ongoing prejudice against visible Islamic symbols.

The social context is nonetheless not too gloomy and hope rests on the large percentage of Scottish people, 77 per cent, who consider themselves not to be racist at all (Scottish Executive 2006), and the 66 per cent who have positive views of Muslims (Homes et al. 2010). Overall, racism in Scotland is declining, while prejudicial attitudes have fallen in Great Britain since the 1980s (Ford 2008) and over seven in ten British people hold positive views towards Muslims (Pew Global Attitudes Project 2015). It is true that statistics recorded by the police in Scotland in 2013/14 show a 4 per cent increase in racist incidents (4,807) compared to 2012/13 (4,628) (Scottish Government 2013a). But much of this increase is due to higher numbers of incidents involving white British victims and complainers (1,423 in 2013/14 compared to 1,139 in 2012/13). These figures must also be contextualised within an overall trend of decreasing numbers of racist incidents recorded by the police between 2006/7 and 2013/14 (Scottish Government 2015c).[3] Yet, unreported hate crimes (McBride 2016) and a climate of fear of new Islamist terrorist attacks (Swindon 2016c) might disrupt this trend, while Pakistanis (20 per cent – that is, 1,107) and Bangladeshis (1 per cent – that is, 41), two predominantly Muslim ethnic groups,[4] still constitute 21 per cent (1,148) of victims and complainers of racist incidents (5,626). They also contribute towards 35 per cent of the total population of Asian origin (Bangladeshi, Chinese, Indian, Pakistani and other Asian) who are victimised and complain about racism across the country.

Urban areas tend to record higher numbers of racist incidents. In fact, Glasgow, Edinburgh and Aberdeen are the three cities recording the highest proportion of racist incidents, respectively 20.7, 19.2 and 11.9 racist incidents for every 10,000 people in their local authority areas against a mean of nine racist incidents per 10,000 people in Scotland. Dundee is in line with the mean of nine racist incidents for every 10,000 people (Scottish Government 2015c). Religiously aggravated offences (Scottish Government 2015b and 2016) for conduct derogatory towards Islam under Section 74 of the Criminal Justice (Scotland) Act 2003 oscillated between fifteen and one hundred and thirty-four in the years between 2010 and 2016. Although the last iteration of the Scottish Government (2016a) survey recorded an increase in reported offences, under-reporting still constitutes an issue (Meer 2015b). Similarly, the problematic nature of disentangling religion from race and ethnicity makes it hard to provide an accurate picture of anti-Muslim sentiments.

While not reaching such negative peaks as in England, where Muslim communities face more serious problems of socio-economic deprivation, prejudice against Muslims in Scotland follows on from the wider post-9/11 questioning of Muslim loyalties to Great Britain, a progressive European shift to the radical right[5] and an understanding of Muslim presence in Europe as a cultural, social, economic and security threat (Savage 2004). This perceived threat includes a more than threefold numerical perception of Muslim presence across several European countries compared to the actual numbers and a perception that Islam is not compatible with the West (*Economist* 2015a). At the institutional level, Great Britain has followed a security approach that is particularly focused on net-widening preventative measures (Bonino 2012, 2013 and 2016b), often to the detriment of social cohesion. This is especially problematic when well-meaning policies end up being 'disproportionately experienced by people in the Muslim community' (House of Commons 2005: 46) and translate into 'day-to-day harassment of Muslims through stop and search [and] high-profile police raids [that have] had a corrosive effect on the relations between Muslim communities and the police' (Pantazis and Pemberton 2009: 662).

In a wider context in which some authors claim that ethnic minority populations are the victim of both under-protection and over-control (Loader and Mulcahy 2003), British Muslims have also faced public hostility in different forms and shapes. Some politicians and journalists believe that Muslims have problems in both feeling and being British and constitute a cultural and political threat to the country (Uberoi et al. 2011). Moreover, there is a distorted perception that Muslims are anti-modern and that Islam is unfavourable to democracy and human rights. This is connected to the idea that Britishness is a product of Western cultural sensitivities and is 'presented as a take-it-or-leave-it affiliation with little room for contestation or revision' (Meer 2010: 194).

Although the phenomenon dates as far back as the English Renaissance, when it was part of a 'process of creating a "demonized Other"' (Hellyer 2007a: 237), the term 'Islamophobia' itself was officially coined in the late 1980s, appeared in print in an American periodical in 1991 and entered the British political and social landscape via the Runnymede Trust report in 1997 (Commission on British Muslims and Islamophobia 1997). In short,

Islamophobia[6] 'is recognisably similar to "xenophobia" and "Europhobia," and is a useful shorthand way of referring to dread or hatred of Islam – and, therefore, to fear or dislike of all or most Muslims' (Commission on British Muslims and Islamophobia 1997: 1). Social exclusion, discrimination, prejudice and violence are the main interconnected and mutually reinforcing elements defining Islamophobia. Far from being uncontested, the notion of Islamophobia has attracted criticism from ordinary Muslim people, who prefer the term 'racism' (Hopkins et al. 2015), but also from experts who claim that the concept wrongly conflates discrimination against Muslims with criticism of Islam (Malik 2005; Joppke 2009).

Research has shown that Islamophobia, at least in the sense of discrimination against Muslims *qua* Muslims, leads to the social exclusion of Muslim communities (Commission on British Muslims and Islamophobia 2004). Although on a scale ranging from 'very high' to 'low' Great Britain scores 'low' on governmental restrictions on religion, it scores 'high' on social hostilities towards religion,[7] while most European countries score either 'moderate' or 'low' (Henne 2015). Far from being a purely post-9/11 problem, pre-9/11 studies on prejudice demonstrate that Great Britain and other European countries already suffered from discrimination against their Muslim and immigrant populations (Strabac and Listhaug 2008).

Among British ethnic groups, Pakistanis and Bangladeshis are the groups that are most likely to fall victim to crime, including racially aggravated crime (Spalek 2005). Non-Muslims in Great Britain tend to display discriminatory attitudes based on both narrow and negative views of Islam and Muslim institutions, such as mosques, and concerns over immigration,[8] multiculturalism and the distribution of resources and welfare services (Hussain and Bagguley 2012) that were further energised during the EU referendum campaign. Fear and mistrust among British Muslims are inflamed by counterterrorism practices and broader issues of discriminatory portrayals in the media, daily interactions with ordinary citizens, disapproval of foreign policy and the feeling of being part of a suspect community (McDonald 2011).

On a more positive note, polls reveal that two thirds of non-Muslim Britons have a generally favourable view of British Muslims (Field 2007). However, such a socially diffuse positive attitude could be undermined by the harassment and violence that a minority of non-Muslims carry out against

Muslims (Lambert and Githens-Mazer 2011). Despite being quite content with their life in Great Britain, a majority of Muslims 'express anger at attacks on Islam and feel vulnerable in the face of worsening Islamophobia' (Field 2011: 170). Historically, the problem of 'discrimination against [. . .] and exclusion of Muslims from mainstream political and social affairs' (Spalek 2002: 20) had operated within a legal framework that only recently protected Muslims against religious discrimination with the enactment of the Equality Act 2010. Since they were not legally protected until that date due to a loophole in the legislation, Muslims could face religious discrimination that would remain unpunished (Allen 2005). The media, which sometimes publish offensive content (Winkler 2006) and display unconscious biases (Baker et al. 2013), have played an important role in reinvigorating anti-Muslim attitudes (Allen 2005), criminalising Muslim communities and spreading moral panics (Frost 2008), based on strengthened societal boundaries and collective conscience (Goode and Ben-Yehuda 1994).

In the job market, data from the Fourth National Survey of Ethnic Minorities show that Muslims experience an employment penalty based on religion more than other characteristics, such as ethnicity or language (Lindley 2002). By analysing data on the probability of being in employment across fourteen ethno-religious groups in the United Kingdom, Khattab and Modood (2015) found that Muslim people and black groups suffer from a labour market penalty, which, however, varies in nature and extent. Racial prejudice and ethnic discrimination are alive and well. A sting operation conducted between 2008 and 2009 unearthed widespread racial discrimination by hundreds of British employers against people with names of Asian and African origin (Syal 2009). Moreover, a later study maintains that '25 per cent of the ethnic minority unemployment rate for both men and women could be explained by prejudice and racial discrimination' (All Party Parliamentary Group on Race and Community 2012: 4).

Other research further shows 'strong empirical evidence for the existence of religious penalties [affecting Muslims] operating alongside colour racism' (Khattab and Johnston 2013: 1370) and exacerbating ethno-religious penalties in the labour market during the recession that began in 2008 (Khattab et al. 2015). Moreover, Pakistanis and Bangladeshis face a double disadvantage in terms of both educational performance (Smith 2005) and employment

(Khattab et al. 2011). Pakistani and Bangladeshi women suffer from a 'triple paralysis' in the job market, as being immigrant, Muslim and female (Dyke and James 2009) negatively impacts on their employment prospects. This condition also affects skilled individuals who end up not being able to make full use of their abilities in Western countries, thus producing a 'brain waste' that is detrimental not only to Muslim communities but also to mainstream society (Mogahed 2007). Pakistanis are more likely to go to university than white people; however, they are less likely to receive university offers (Noden et al. 2014) and they perform worse than South Asian peers and most other groups in the General Certificate of Secondary Education (Dwyer et al. 2011).

The gap between educational attainment and human potential utilisation was paralleled by the numerical under-representation of ethnic minorities in British politics (Anwar 2001) in the late 1990s, although by 2010 'some British Muslims [had] been actively involved in politics for several decades' (Kabir 2010: 32). At the time, these people included a few mayors and mayoresses in London boroughs (for example, Brent in 1981; Hackney in 1995 and 2001; and Sutton in 2000); four Muslim Labour members elected in the 2005 general elections; two Conservative Muslims at the European Parliament; and several Muslims in the House of Lords. By August 2016, Muslims were represented at all levels of British politics and included thirteen Members of the British Parliament;[9] seventeen Members of the House of Lords;[10] two Members of the Scottish Parliament;[11] one Member of the National Assembly for Wales;[12] and four Members of the European Parliament.[13] The more sustained political engagement of British Muslims is not only evidenced by a record thirteen elected Muslim MPs in 2015, a notable increase from eight Muslim MPs in 2010, and the election of Sadiq Khan as Mayor of London in 2016, becoming the first ever Muslim mayor of a European capital city. It also includes enhanced activity and effectiveness within governance, policymaking and in the areas of equality and recognition of religious difference, security and cohesion (O'Toole et al. 2013).

Episodes of abuse and discrimination against Muslims have increased since 9/11 (Saeed 2015) and, as a consequence, daily encounters between Muslims and non-Muslims have suffered. Visible markers of Muslimness increase the likelihood of suffering from discrimination, harassment, marginalisation and employment difficulties. When coupled with the maintenance or adoption of foreign ethnic and/or Muslim norms and mannerisms, markers of Muslimness play an important role in both reinforcing exclusionary processes (Botterill et al. 2016) and placing Muslims within a discriminated against category. Furthermore, low-quality interactions between Muslims and non-Muslims promote non-positive behavioural intentions towards the former (Hutchison and Rosenthal 2011). In a study conducted by Hopkins et al. (2007), it appears that most Muslims would welcome increased contact with non-Muslim communities; however, it is necessary that people interacting with them do not misrecognise their identities or disrespect them under the influence of socially widespread prejudices and stereotypes.

Perceptions and Experiences of Discrimination in Everyday Scottish Life

A consistent pattern observed throughout fieldwork with Muslims in Edinburgh relates to the ways in which their distinctive body markers and visible 'signs of Muslimness' (for example, skin colour, beard, traditional clothes and hijab)[14] may position them within an a priori stigmatised group. Other studies have found that 'young [Scottish] Muslim men who have a beard and wear Islamic dress are likely to experience discrimination and marginalisation compared with those who do not' (Hopkins 2009: 307). The public display of negatively perceived cultural diversity could class Muslims as 'discreted' individuals through mere visual contact (for example, seeing a 'coloured' man who wears a long beard or a woman who wears a hijab) and without requiring communication to establish such diversity (Goffman 1990b [1963]). In this sense, the essentialisation of Muslimness may preclude the use of front stage techniques of self-presentation (Goffman 1990a [1959]) that would otherwise help Muslims to positively negotiate their multiple identities across different sociocultural spaces, ease interactions with non-Muslims and define their own social positioning on a more equal level.

The way in which signs, or visible markers, of Muslimness can cast Muslims outside the realm of power-balanced relationships and accepted cultural boundaries due to the symbolic power of race and religion to signal social differences is also identified by Hopkins (2004a and 2004b) in his study of Pakistanis in Glasgow and Edinburgh in the early 2000s and broadly follows other British (Spalek 2002; Allen 2014 and 2015) and European

(Choudhury et al. 2006) studies on the subject. Kyriakides et al.'s (2009) research in Glasgow further confirms that, when people only display 'foreign Muslim signs', extensively including foreign accents and non-mainstream mannerisms, these are perceived to be culturally problematic. However, the authors argue that when people utilise hybridised codes of cultural belonging, which rely upon both Scottish cultural norms, such as command of English and a Scottish accent (Virdee et al. 2006), and Muslim cultural norms, they can make claims of national belonging and be more easily included in society. Muslim hyper-visibility is both a trigger for ethno-religious discrimination and a catalyst for positive interest in, and support of, Muslimness. Ghedi, a Somali man, encapsulates the reality of being a member of a visible minority, particularly being a Muslim in a post-9/11 world, and the shift from a racial to an ethno-religious understanding of his identity:

> Being a Muslim in Edinburgh has been difficult compared to back home. Over there, the majority of people are Muslim so it 'forces' you to be a Muslim. Here, Muslims are a minority and there is a minority issue. For example, people define Muslims by how you dress. If you are a Muslim man and you wear a *shalvar kameez*, it says that you are a Muslim even before you talk. If you wear a turban, again it is the same thing. If you have a beard, that is again the same thing. At the beginning, Muslims were treated as a racial group. people would say to you, 'Paki,' as happened to me a number of times. Then, 9/11 changed things. If you have a beard and wear a *kameez*, they call you 'Bin Laden'. (Ghedi, Somali man in his mid-fifties)

A recent survey conducted among over 500 black and minority ethnic (BME) people in Scotland confirms that religion (44 per cent) and ethnicity (82 per cent) are perceived to drive discriminatory attitudes (Meer 2015b). Of the same cohort, 31 per cent of respondents reported having experienced discrimination in Scotland between 2010 and 2015, particularly while using transport services and in the areas of employment and education. Surveys conducted in England and Wales also demonstrate that Muslims are among the most victimised groups in racially motivated hate crimes (Corcoran et al. 2015). Leaving aside loci of security and interactions with the police and security officers for now, the workplace and the job market also appear to be areas of concern in other larger studies of Scottish Muslims (see Kidd and

Jamieson 2011), since visibly presenting oneself as a Muslim is perceived as a potential hindrance in both reaching certain positions and securing a job. A few respondents in Edinburgh mentioned the absence – if not the impossibility for society to even conceive – of Muslims in positions of power due to the very essence of them being visibly Muslim. In other words, they believed that institutional discrimination could potentially hamper Muslims' opportunities to access services and reach positions of authority and leadership. Arif stresses this issue. He alleges that discrimination in Scotland is deeply institutionalised and seriously affects the life goals of highly educated and motivated individuals of ethnic minority origin. Problems accessing services are also recorded in other research, where Muslims believe they have experienced 'greater barriers to [national] health service use in terms of the (negative) attitudes of receptionists and service opening hours compared with non-Muslims' (Love et al. 2011: 3). Similarly, Raza thinks that being a Muslim is a major impediment to reaching certain positions of institutional authority and leadership:

> *Stefano*: Do you think that some authorities or agencies are more supportive of Muslims?
>
> *Raza*: I think that authorities that have Muslims within them are more supportive, within Parliament and whatnot. However, first I feel that it is difficult for Muslims to get into that line, that level of authority, first and foremost. So that is an obstacle in itself.
>
> *Stefano*: In your opinion, what are the major impediments for Muslims to getting into positions of authority?
>
> *Raza*: First, because they are Muslim, it is unfortunate to say it. [. . .] I feel that it is slightly more difficult to get a job, to get that respect initially, so you have to work a lot harder. (Raza, Scottish Pakistani man in his early twenties)

This line of thought is supported by a Muslim who works at the headquarters of the National Health Service in Edinburgh. He reports that there have been no Muslim directors or chief executives since his employment there. Some evidence to support these arguments is contained in a report on Scottish local councils, which found that the workforce does not reflect the size of the ethnic minority community (Hussain and Ishaq 2008). The Scottish Government also claimed that the country has no head or deputy head teacher from an ethnic minority background (BBC News 2015). Raza is one of the very few respondents who maintain that exclusion, in this case from a position of authority, does not necessarily signify discrimination. Muslim exclusion from positions of leadership could derive from many other factors ranging from mere statistical reasons (non-Muslims largely outnumber Muslims in society) to meritocratic reasons.

Some other interviewees reported difficulties in negotiating their need to pray, for example being requested not to perform prayers during work hours, or feeling ashamed to pray whenever non-Muslims are around in case they react in a negative fashion. Sarmad reported issues with a colleague who would interrupt and verbally abuse him during prayer breaks in the workplace. Nasha recounted a personal experience as a volunteer at a Christian caring organisation, which she had decided to leave after being explicitly requested not to perform prayers at work. The nature of Muslimness interplays with social understandings of Islam as a religion, a culture and an ideology that some non-Muslims find hard to conceptually and practically integrate within the Scottish sociocultural system. In her own negative experience, Nasha was not able to negotiate her right to pray during lunch break, because prayers were allegedly considered to be offensive by the Christian organisation. Eventually, she had to resign. In the bleakest scenario, through the normative regulation of ethnic and religious values that are different from the dominant values of a cultural constituency, 'certain cultural practices of the minority cultural groups become [social and cultural] crimes, subject to sanctions and penalties imposed by the dominant group or elite' (Lemert 1972: 33).

Nasha's experience demonstrates the potential for Muslim-related practices to be subject to discrimination from a majority that defines the boundaries of Muslim engagement with society. Other respondents argued that visible Muslim identities drive stigmatisation and exclusion. Alena mentioned occasions on which she had felt that the discrepancy between her virtual image and her real image could be a key impediment to job hunting. In other words, she claimed that she had routinely managed to make job contacts over the phone thanks to her Western-sounding name but had failed face-to-face interviews due to her hijab and her requests to perform prayers on Fridays:

Looking for jobs was a big hit for me. I could not help thinking that the hijab was the way you do not get jobs and I do not like to think that way but felt like that I was forced to think about it that way. I was also trying to tell myself that there is something about me that is not right for this job and not the hijab and all the rest but I also thought about the hijab. I was fine on paper and I used to get lots of interviews for jobs. But then I would go for the interview and would never get the job. I think that, because my name is Alena, they think I am okay but when they meet me everything changes. (Alena, Palestinian woman in her late twenties)

Several other interviewees shared similar concerns in line with the findings of a study conducted by Kidd and Jamieson (2011) in the Central Belt that registered 'fears about the possibility of facing [. . .] discrimination when looking for work' (Kidd and Jamieson 2011: 52). Rebecca, a Scottish female convert to Islam who wears the burqa, also laments a mismatch between the expected identity that she communicates during phone interactions and the visual identity that people ascertain during face-to-face interactions:

I remember when I was phoning the council and trying to sort out some things for my kids. I explained the situation and they told me, 'Yes, no problem,' to my request. Then I turned up at the building and they ignored me. I do not say it in a bad way but I was standing in the queue and I was giving eye contact. You can see my eyes so I was giving eye contact. The receptionist was trying not to look at me. It is as if she was thinking, 'Oh my God, that woman is covered up and I do not know how to deal with her, she is not going to be able to speak English and so on.' I went to the front of the desk and said, 'Hello, I am trying to sort out this school thing.' The receptionist was a bit uneasy. People deal with me on a face-to-face basis differently than when I am on the phone. (Rebecca, Scottish woman in her early forties)

The fact that visibly displaying religious symbols affects interactions with Scottish people is not simply a perception but finds support in the Scottish Social Attitudes Survey 2015 (Scottish Government 2016d). Of the surveyed respondents, 18 per cent maintained that a Muslim woman being interviewed for a job involving contact with customers should be asked by the prospective employer to remove her hijab at work. A recent report by the Women and Equalities Committee (2016) further shows that stereotypical views of Muslim women act as a barrier to finding work. A few interviewees shared other, similar experiences. Arif recounted his own experience as a temporary worker in a legal aid office where he believed that he had been constantly assigned the hardest admin tasks, while his colleagues had been quickly promoted and had been given better duties. Akhtar pinpoints this very issue by arguing that Muslims could receive differential treatment simply because of their religious and ethnic identities:

> I think that sometimes, even if you have the best qualifications out there, they say that you do not get a job because you are not what they are look-ing for or they tell you a simple excuse that can be applicable to anyone. However, because of the way things are, I would not be chosen because I am Pakistani, because I am Muslim. It is not necessarily right to do it but I do not blame it either. This is because of the ways the media perceive Islam, the way in which things have been done. (Akhtar, Scottish Pakistani man in his early twenties)

Akhtar's words resonate with wider community perceptions of an a priori prejudice towards Muslims and Islam, which is often blamed on the media and radical right political parties. There is certainly a diffuse sense of media negativity around Muslims that some Scottish people accept uncritically. Encounters between Muslims and non-Muslims reveal the underlying sense of discomfort that some Scottish people have developed towards Muslims in a post-9/11 world. On a more positive note, Muslims feel fairly safe when dealing with non-Muslim friends and acquaintances because these people are able to avoid either stereotyping Muslim communities or making them pay a penalty for the wrongdoing of a tiny minority of Islamist terrorists.

Large-scale studies indicate that only 20 per cent of Scottish people hold negative views of Muslims (Homes et al. 2010) and that those who dis-criminate against Muslims are typically low-skilled male workers, pensioners, elders and Conservatives (Hussain and Miller 2006; see also Ormston et al. 2011). However, the display of a visibly Muslim identity, particularly in a post-9/11 world, affects the interaction between Muslims and non-Muslims. Hussain and Miller's (2006) study of Pakistanis in Scotland reveals that the majority of their respondents (61 per cent) believed ordinary people to be the most prejudiced Scots. Only a minority (23 per cent) of their respondents mentioned politicians and officials. Akhtar sheds further light on the perceived hostility suffered from Scottish people:

> Obviously due to recent circumstances it is more and more difficult for me to express myself as a person, not so much of a Pakistani background, but of a Muslim background. It has become more and more difficult. For example, my sister wears the hijab. I know that these are little things that people might perceive as silly but, like, when she gets on the bus people look at her. I know how it was before and I know how it is now and if you ask anybody they will tell you the same thing – I found myself being treated differently. These are little things but they do get to you. They really get to you. The way people see you, the way they act towards you and so on. Little, minor things but they just get to you sometimes. (Akhtar, Scottish Pakistani man in his early twenties)

At the extreme end of the scale of negative perceptions are respondents such as Babar, who recognises that British people are less prejudiced towards Muslims compared to continental Europeans, yet he believes that the religious persecutions and the dictatorships that marked European history prove that 'it is inherently in the European psyche that people are racist'. Clearly, different Scottish Muslims perceive themselves to be subject to prejudice and discrimination at different scales of intensity. But it is important not to fall into the trap of uncritically supporting a victimhood tendency that blames Europe and whiteness for all of the problems that contemporary Muslims face. While a hegemonic European white culture has partly fed close-minded social attitudes, different nation states have experienced different Muslim settlements. Their responses to the emergence of a Muslim consciousness have been shaped by an intricate set of historical, geopolitical and economic factors.

Certain expressions of cultural prejudice, such as staring at members of other ethnic groups on the bus, are often problematic to assess and evaluate objectively, and can relate to forms of behaviour other than pure racism (see also Kidd and Jamieson 2011). But discriminatory attitudes, such as being called a 'terrorist' or a 'Paki' and other forms of verbal abuse, are unequivocally suffered by several, predominantly male, visibly Muslim people in Edinburgh and across Scotland (see Kidd and Jamieson 2011). Verbal abuse tends to take place on the street, which is the location recording the highest number of general racist incidents between 2004/5 and 2013/14 (Scottish Government 2015c). This finding is in line with Kidd and Jamieson's (2011) study, which reports Scottish Muslims' experiences of hostility and unfriendliness both on the streets and in local neighbourhoods. But Kidd and Jamieson also notice more positive relationships between Muslims and non-Muslims, particularly in colleges and schools. This element should not be underestimated. It is well known that the formation of national identities passes through the educational system and that 'in Scotland it is one of the three national institutions which were preserved in the Union of 1707 and continued to preserve a sense of Scottish "national" identity while not colliding with British state identity' (Weber n.d.: 8).

Scottish Muslims often claim that, besides the media and the post-9/11 climate, the low exposure to ethno-religious diversity of Scottish people living in some parts of the country (see Kidd and Jamieson 2011) is to blame for discriminatory attitudes. Troublingly, some Muslims are routinely victims of serious abuse:

> I got eggs thrown at my house. Here in Edinburgh you get called 'Paki' routinely on the street, but mainly at night, not in the day. This year a Pakistani colleague of mine, on the very day that he arrived in Edinburgh, in three or four hours of arriving, was assaulted on Nicolson Street during daytime. That was within three or four hours. Probably that could happen anywhere, it could happen in England, it could happen in America, probably even more, but I think that everybody here does have an experience. (Arif, Canadian Bangladeshi man in his early thirties)

Other similarly serious incidents involved a female respondent having her hijab pulled off on the street and a mosque being vandalised in the aftermath of 9/11. A study conducted between 2013 and 2015 and involving 100 Muslims across Scotland (Hopkins et al. 2015) further recorded several incidents of verbal and physical abuse suffered by Scottish Muslims. In a notorious incident, a man entered Taj Madina Mosque in Dundee and destroyed several framed prayers (BBC News 2016e). Edinburgh Central Mosque was also recently vandalised

(BBC News 2016h). On the positive side, many Muslims who took part in both the author's own primary research and in Hussain and Miller's (2006) study perceive discrimination to be less serious than in England.

Yet, ethno-religious discrimination, even when it results only in a few minor incidents, appears to take an emotional and psychological toll on Muslims. Muslims are often apt to consider the complexities of their fragile position in society, take into account the generally positive experiences that they have had and avoid letting a few negative experiences shape their overall perceptions of life in Scotland. But some Muslims have been badly affected by perceived and real discrimination. People such as Arif are resigned to the idea that discriminatory incidents are routine experiences in Scotland. But while ordinary everyday experiences are not homogeneous across the Scottish Muslim population, Muslims' perceptions of discrimination at airports converge. As crucial loci of security, where any post-9/11 worry about an impending Islamist terrorist attack shows itself, airports are the most contested social spaces among the Scottish Muslim community.

Policing and Securitising Muslims after 2001

Within a global context in which, after 9/11, some Muslims have been stigmatised (Bonino 2012 and 2013; Kundnani 2014) and have been treated as a 'suspect community' (Pantazis and Simon Pemberton 2009), stops and searches at airports and on the street have targeted British Muslims through the use of Schedule 7[15] and the now-repealed Section 44[16] of the Terrorism Act 2000 and other counterterrorism measures. Academic research demonstrates that 'the combination of local-level (individual and community) and macro-level accounts of the use of [now-repealed] s44 powers has resulted in Asian men feeling as though the perception of them as inherently suspicious has become normalized' (Parmar 2011: 379).

In a study conducted by Human Rights Watch (2010) it appears that 450,000 stops and searches under Section 44 of the Terrorism Act 2000 were conducted in Great Britain between April 2007 and April 2009. Allegedly, 'no one was successfully prosecuted for a terrorism offence as a result, and according to Great Britain's independent reviewer of terrorism legislation, little if any useful intelligence about terrorist plots was obtained' (Human Rights Watch 2010: 1). Relying on sources such as the Metropolitan Police

Authority, interviews with Lord Carlile (the former Independent Reviewer of Terrorism) and its own research, the quality of which may vary, Human Rights Watch strongly criticises stops and searches under Section 44 of the Terrorism Act 2000. It alleges that, during the period under examination, powers were used improperly, in a discriminatory manner, without authorisation, inconsistently and unlawfully. More generally, it argues that stop and search activities damaged community relations, problematised trust in the police, especially in London, and undermined confidence within Muslim communities. Moreover, it maintains that it is difficult to establish exactly how many Muslims are stopped, and their likelihood of being stopped compared to people of other religions, because religion, unlike ethnicity, is not recorded during stops and searches.

The Scottish context is rather different. A pre-9/11 study (Scottish Executive 2002) found that 3.6 per cent, 7.4 per cent and 2.9 per cent of ethnic minorities were among those stopped and searched on the street by, respectively, Lothian and Borders Police, Strathclyde Police and Tayside Police, against a minority ethnic population of 4.1 per cent in Edinburgh, 5.5 per cent in Glasgow and 3.7 per cent in Dundee in 2001 (Scottish Executive 2004). These numbers and the response from the Scottish Executive (2003) show that pre-9/11 street stops and searches were not a very high-profile issue and had not dramatically impacted on minority ethnic people other than in Glasgow. In this sense, although disproportionality – which is defined as 'the extent to which searches of people from black and minority ethnic groups exceed that which would be expected given their share of the population' (Scottish Executive 2002: ii) – is highly problematic to measure, there is no strong evidence to support claims of police targeting of BME groups through stop and search activities in the pre-9/11 Scottish context. However, the report recognises anecdotal evidence that young people across several different groups (BME and white) 'appear alienated from the police, do not trust them, and feel that they are being harassed' (Scottish Executive 2002: iii).

In the years since 2001, there is still no evidence that stops and searches on Scottish streets disproportionately target people from BME backgrounds (Murray 2015). Unlike in England, where stops and searches often focus on race and ethnicity (Equality and Human Rights Commission 2010), in Scotland they are instead directed towards young people 'over and beyond the probability of offending' (Murray 2014: 19; see also Murray and Harkin 2016). In 2013/14, 4.1 per cent of recorded stops and searches were conducted on people from BME backgrounds (Police Scotland 2014). This figure is very close to the proportion of the Scottish BME population in the 2011 Census (4 per cent). Equally, Strathclyde Police (2011) recorded an increasing number of overall stop and search activities between 2004 and 2011, but these did not disproportionately impact on Glaswegian BME groups. In 2011, stops and searches conducted on BME groups accounted for 2.5 per cent of all searches against a BME population that was about 8.1 per cent of the total population at that time (Glasgow City Council 2012). The same report records that, after the Glasgow bombings, only seventeen stops and searches were conducted under Section 44 of the Terrorism Act 2000.

The impact of anti-terror legislation at airports is difficult to quantify due to the fact that data on stops and searches, as conducted under Schedule 7 of the Terrorism Act 2000, were not disclosed by three main Scottish police forces (Lothian and Borders Police, Strathclyde Police and Tayside Police)[17] in response to Freedom of Information requests submitted by the author in 2012. Although the airport context is rather patchy, Scottish Muslims have a perception of being targeted and discriminated against by security activities, which have silenced the negotiation of their identities and rights in interactions with police and security officers.[18]

A public Stop and Search Consultation Meeting organised by Edinburgh and Lothian Regional Equality Council (ELREC), in partnership with Lothian and Borders Police and Edinburgh City Council, in central Edinburgh in early December 2011[19] shed some light on airport stops and searches in Scotland. The meeting was generally aimed at giving a voice to members of affected ethnic minority communities, not necessarily only Muslims, in order to understand the situation in Edinburgh and beyond, and potentially develop good practices that better address the problematic over-policing of certain strata of the population in the post-9/11 social, political and legislative climate. It was chaired by a member of ELREC and included, as panel members, authorities from Lothian and Borders Police, the Association of Chief Police Officers and the Scottish Government. In the audience, there were around thirty or forty people, mostly members of ethnic minorities, some of whom openly described themselves as Muslim.

All of the panel members recognised that the practicalities of policing ethnic minorities had become problematic in the wake of 9/11. Schedule 7 had disproportionately impacted on certain communities in town and the South Asian community had been particularly stereotyped. But panellists also suggested that airports are key spaces for counterterrorism activities, especially in an age in which the threat posed by international terrorism continues to be severe (MI5 2016). Edinburgh Airport might therefore appear to be over-policed because it is the busiest airport in Scotland and one of the busiest airports in Great Britain. All members of the panel seemed to understand the issues that have affected South Asians and other ethnic minorities in Edinburgh. At least verbally, they showed an open attitude to developing fairer and more effective airport security practices.

A few Muslim men took the floor and expressed their anger, grievance and disillusionment. These men recounted their individual and collective experiences of being part of an alleged 'suspect community', which had been subject to frequent airport stops and searches and had suffered from highly intrusive actions at the hands of police and security officers. Allegations included private data from laptops and mobile phones having been transferred into the police security system without any apparent justification. These men voiced their distrust of the police and of the government, possibly confirming the link between frequency of contact with law enforcement agencies and dissatisfaction with policing activities (Scottish Executive 2002).

Muslims also lamented a lack of communication between the police and institutional community channels, such as mosques and other religious or social organisations. Yet, here it is important to remember that Police Scotland (formerly Lothian and Borders Police), in partnership with Edinburgh Council and the Edinburgh Chamber of Commerce, has, since 2009, organised an annual series of events called 'Edinburgh Community Resilience Week'. This week-long series of events includes workshops,[20] a 'National Security Conference' and other events[21] for business people, private security officers and the general public. These events aim to both raise awareness of counterterrorism strategies and illustrate the role that these different stakeholders can play in order to prevent, and prepare for, a potential terrorist attack. Some Muslims who were interviewed during research maintained that the police, and politicians too, had actively made their presence visible at mosques through courtesy visits, reassurance and/or protection. The police also engaged in important bridge-building exercises after the London bombings in 2005, taking 'necessary action in order to stem the [related] rising tide of racism' (Maan 2014: 93).

The Stop and Search Consultation Meeting suggested that Edinburgh Airport and other Scottish airports are fragile and contested social spaces. They are spaces where police and security officers often maintain order and control by, consciously or unconsciously, relying on power-imbalanced strategies that can negatively impact on ethnic minorities. It is true that international terrorism predominantly springs from certain Muslim-majority countries and, therefore, that security authorities could be targeting the geographical roots and destinations where certain flights originate and end, such as Pakistan,'rather than Muslims *qua* Muslims. Airport security staff's way of thinking illuminates counterterrorism actions: several airport security staff members believe that Muslims' negative experiences are unfortunate but should be understood as part of both the current, fragile geopolitical context and the nature of airports (Blackwood 2015).

The Stop and Search Consultation Meeting demonstrates that decreasing levels of confidence and trust in both police officers, who are often conflated with airport security personnel, and, more broadly, the government[22] can hinder the full inclusion of Muslims within the fabric of Scottish society, politics and institutions. The negative impact that stops and searches have had on the confidence of Muslims in entering spaces of security, interacting with security officers and having their own identities, liberties and rights respected and recognised is also a running theme for Scottish Muslims.

The Emotions of Discriminated Against Diversity at Scottish Airports

Stories of negative experiences at Scottish airports abound among the predominantly male Muslims interviewed and surveyed across different studies: primary research conducted by the author in Edinburgh; wider Scottish research conducted by Kidd and Jamieson (2011); and media reports (*Herald Scotland* 2011; Naysmith 2015). Many Muslims have either themselves experienced or know relatives or friends who have been subjected to perceived undue targeting or harsh treatment when leaving from or arriving at Scottish airports. In 2011, Humza Yousaf and Aamer Anwar publicly lamented that

South Asian men had been regularly stopped at airports (*Herald Scotland* 2011). This has become a typical narrative among Scottish Muslims. Muslims often consider ethno-religious profiling to be a main driver for airport checks or stops and searches and question the operational randomness of security activities. They believe that Muslims *qua* Muslims are targeted due to the fears associated with their cultural and religious difference:

> I have never been stopped at the train station but I have been stopped and searched at the airport. It is always a 'random' [sarcastic] search. [. . .] Random search – how come I am always the one randomly stopped? (Babar, Scottish Pakistani man in his mid-twenties)

> Stop and search at airports is a widespread issue. People are getting stopped. We get stopped. We see it ourselves. Not once but twice, three times. We see it a number of times and then we realise that it has become part of our life. The concern is the actual questioning and the perception that it puts on other passengers on the same flight. People think that you are being stopped for a reason. (Nasir, Scottish Pakistani man in his early thirties)

Within the social space that is constructed around the perceived stigmatisation of visible diversity, Muslims could end up being placed in a position of unequal standing before police and security officers. These actors operate as the human tools of the securitisation of Muslims and represent what Wacquant (2009) argues is the law-and-order wing of the state, which employs penal means to deal with social 'problems'. Other research conducted across Scotland confirms that Muslims believe that the 'frequency and nature of airport stops signal that [. . . they] are targeted as a group and regarded as a dangerous "other"' (Blackwood 2015: 258).

The securitisation of Muslims has produced several effects. In line with the findings of Blackwood et al.'s (2012b) study, these effects converge in a mixture of disempowerment, anger, humiliation, alienation and distrust towards security authorities. As Blackwood et al. demonstrate, 'Muslim airport stories' are often spread, shared and socially represented within Muslim communities. Such stories present negative encounters with police and airport security staff and perceptions that Muslims occupy a position of relative powerlessness, where: (1) Muslim identities are misrepresented and misunderstood; (2) for those people who uphold them, Scottish or British national identities are partially denied, since Muslims are treated as social aliens; and (3) 'respectable identities', which are based on high social status within the Muslim community, are not recognised by wider society. The authors further suggest that this threefold identity denial impacts on both Muslims' actions and perceptions of their position in society.

This process of identity misrecognition, which is the absence of others' recognition of a person's understanding of who he or she is (Taylor 1994) and which is promoted by the hyper-visibility of Muslim identities (Hopkins and Blackwood 2011), can hamper the way in which people are able to play out their own ways of being British, Scottish or Muslim during social interactions with police and airport security staff. The most significant negative consequence of misrecognition is the mirroring back of 'a confining or demeaning or contemptible picture' (Taylor 1994: 25) to those whose identity is denied. As Blackwood (2015: 257) postulates, 'this is particularly [. . . consequential] for minority group members (or those in low power positions) who are especially attuned to and affected by what they think other groups think about them'.

Chanda, a Bangladeshi woman, offers one of the most powerful accounts of being subject to the securitisation of visible Muslimness and describes her emotional state when walking through airports as follows:

> I feel as if I want to vanish. If I am at Edinburgh Airport, I feel so bad. Why me? I feel hundreds of thousands of pairs of eyes looking at me. This is very damaging sometimes. It is very scary, very upsetting. I feel very empty, very isolated, I feel like crying. It is such a bad feeling. (Chanda, Bangladeshi woman in her mid-forties)

Chanda's feelings are not unique among Scottish Muslims and add up to a perception that airports are detrimental social spaces for understanding one's positioning within society. This perception illustrates the emotional barriers that can hamper the negotiation of identities and rights on an equal basis with security officers. Significantly, it explains why some Muslims in Glasgow, Edinburgh and Dundee decide to utilise stratagems to minimise encounters with airport authorities, including avoiding others' gaze and changing one's posture (Blackwood et al. 2015). Hamid, a middle-aged Pakistani man, claims that police officers allegedly abused their position of power to try to extract information that he did not possess during an airport interview. A British passport-holder, Hamid further claims to have been harassed and threatened with deportation to Pakistan. He paints a very bleak picture of airports:

> Stop and search is a big issue at airports. It is really a big issue at airports. I would use the word 'harassment' because on a plane that has 200 people only those who have a beard or are Asians get stopped. I am using these words here deliberately: I use the word 'harassment' and I also use the word 'victimisation' because certain people are targeted. (Hamid, Pakistani man in his mid-fifties)

Institutional mistrust as a consequence of both the post-9/11 political and military tensions with Muslim countries, such as Afghanistan and Iraq, and the domestic policing of Muslim people runs high in Scotland. It particularly affects male members of the Muslim community who have had more frequent contact with the police and security authorities. There is a danger that post-9/11 security practices could depict law enforcement agencies as being dismissive of Muslims' belonging to the country. Overt abuse of power can only reinforce Muslims' perceptions that the security system is hostile. The frustration, anger and humiliation of travelling to or from Scottish airports have prompted some to look for different travelling arrangements:

> I know of people that got fed up with travelling by air as a result of that. I think that initially it was far from random. (Ali, British Pakistani man in his mid-forties)

> I have had so many bad experiences – and friends of mine too – at airports here in Scotland, both in Edinburgh and in Glasgow, that I do not even want to fly into Scottish airports anymore. I am serious. I will go to Manchester. I will go to wherever. London[23] is probably the easiest because there are so many different people coming in and they have to push them through. (Arif, Canadian Bangladeshi man in his early thirties)

The fact that a number of Muslim people 'got fed up with travelling by air' is confirmed by Blackwood's (2015) research that found that avoiding particular airports, travelling less frequently and playing down Muslim identities are common strategies used to avoid unwelcome attention. This situation reached its highest point with the boycott of Glasgow International Airport in 2006 (BBC News 2006) and in 2011 (Campsie and Leask 2011). Certainly, tensions between Muslims and the police have never exploded in episodes of violence as in England (Malik 2011). But it is remarkable that some Muslims have decided to boycott a key Scottish airport as a result of what they perceive to be widespread discrimination and hostility.

Conclusion

In an age of hostility and distrust towards Islam, discrimination against Muslims on the street, in the workplace and at loci of security is not surprising. The emergence of scapegoats, onto which society can pour its fears and insecurities, is not a novel event. Jews in Nazi Germany (Nachmani 2016), communists in the United States after the Second World War and gays in the 1980s played a role that, at least symbolically, resonates with the discrimination faced by numerous peaceful and law-abiding Muslims in the past fifteen years. A new way to 'unite a faltering civic society by invoking a common threat [. . .] and deflect attention away from the genuine causes of insecurity' (Vaughan 2002: 205), exaggerated cultural worries about Muslims represent a historical continuum. Visibly displaying a Muslim identity affects social interactions with some Scots. An a priori negative categorisation of Muslims has restricted them to an ethno-religious diversity that is considered lesser by wider society. Power-imbalanced relations with police and airport security officers have affected the social confidence and the sense of belonging of some community members. As Blackwood's (2015) research unequivocally demonstrates, people's perceptions that authorities treat them disrespectfully leads to a loss of trust and confidence, as well as passive non-compliance and active defiance.

But while it is true that Muslims have suffered prejudice, hostility and discrimination, the case put forward by Hopkins (2004a: 91) that racism 'is an everyday experience for many of Scotland's black and minority ethnic population' needs to be reconsidered. Trends of decreases in prejudice (Scottish Government 2016d) and recorded racism, which nonetheless still *do* exist and impact predominantly on Muslims, and the specific locales where discrimination happens must both be carefully considered. It is also important to contextualise prejudice and racism within those porous Scottish sociocultural boundaries that have the potential to shape a fully integrative

Scottishness and to appreciate that Muslim hyper-visibility is not only a trigger for ethno-religious discrimination but also a catalyst for attracting the curiosity of non-Muslims towards Islam. Such forces have allowed Muslims and non-Muslims to come together and challenge both global stereotyping and local discrimination through acts of resilience, engagement and mutual interest.

Notes

1. Even today, Pakistanis have the highest proportion of self-employed people of all minority ethnic groups. Half of Pakistanis work in the 'distribution, hotels and restaurants' industry. Pakistanis are also the most likely minority ethnic group to be 'managers, directors and senior officials' (20 per cent) and to work in 'sales and customer service occupations' (22 per cent) (National Records of Scotland 2013).
2. Another contractor later took up this job and finished building the mosque. The new mosque opened for use in 2005 (Maan 2014).
3. The decrease in recorded racist incidents follows a wider trend of decreasing crime rates in Scotland, which at the time of writing are at their lowest levels since 1974 (Scottish Government 2015a and 2016c).
4. Religion is not recorded in these statistics, thus making it difficult to quantify the exact extent of discrimination against Muslims.
5. Prejudice towards Muslims has characterised, brought together and mobilised a variety of right-wing groups, from populist to extremist ones (Hafez 2014).
6. For a critique of the Runnymede Trust's definition of Islamophobia and for an alternative definition of the term, see the work of Allen (2010).
7. The other European countries which score 'high' on social hostilities towards religion are Bulgaria, France, Germany, Greece, Italy, Romania and Sweden (Henne 2015).
8. According to the 2014 British Social Attitudes report, a large majority in Great Britain would like to see a reduction in immigration levels, although opinions about the impact of immigration on Great Britain's culture and economy vary considerably (Ford and Heath 2014).
9. Affiliation: nine Labour, three Conservative and one SNP.
10. Affiliation: six crossbench, five Conservative, three Labour and three Liberal Democrats.
11. Affiliation: one Labour and one SNP.
12. Affiliation: Conservative.

13. Affiliation: three Conservative and one Labour.

14. While many of the respondents who took part in primary research conducted in Edinburgh displayed at least one 'sign of Muslimness', it is true that not all Muslims in the general population do so. This is the case for those Muslims who have white or light-brown skin or carry no distinguishable visible markers of their faith. Also, some 'signs of Muslimness' might not identify one's faith, but ethnicity or culture, and could therefore be wrongly assigned to people (for example, Sikhs, Hindus, and so on) who are not Muslim (see also Hopkins et al. 2015).

15. This power allows authorities to carry out stops and searches at airports without needing reasonable suspicion.

16. This power allowed authorities to stop and search people in any location without needing any reasonable suspicion. It was repealed by the Terrorism Act 2000 (Remedial) Order 2011 so that the police could only stop and search people if reasonable suspicion of potential involvement in a terrorist act was proved under Section 43. Eventually, the Protection of Freedoms Act 2012 scrapped Section 44 and replaced it with Section 47a, which requires a senior police officer to authorise a stop and search upon reasonable suspicion that an act of terrorism will take place and that conducting a stop and search will prevent it.

17. Since 1 April 2013, these three police forces, the other five former regional police forces of Scotland (Central Scotland Police, Dumfries and Galloway Constabulary, Fife Constabulary, Grampian Police and Northern Constabulary) and the Scottish Crime and Drug Enforcement Agency have become part of a single, national police force called Police Scotland.

18. Given that security is managed in partial cooperation between airport security personnel, the police and counterterrorism units, it is often hard to understand who exactly conducts stop and search activities. Furthermore, 'people may not readily distinguish between authorities, and even where they do so, psychologically negative experiences have been shown to have stronger effects than positive experiences' (Blackwood 2015: 258).

19. The first such meeting was organised in 2008 and similar events have also been organised in Glasgow.

20. For example: 'Project Griffin', 'Project Argus' and 'Workshop to Raise Awareness of Prevent (WRAP)'. The latter workshop has been criticised by Blackwood et al. (2012a) for encouraging people with a duty of care, particularly those within the public sector, to report signs of vulnerability that they have recognised, especially in young Muslim males, to the authorities. According to the authors, this process might promote the targeting of Muslims and minority groups since pro-

fessionals and authorities, no matter how well intentioned, could be perceived as discriminatory by those that come to their attention. More broadly, they argue that this process could both isolate Muslims from the wider non-Muslim community and negatively impact on the former's confidence in, and cooperation with, authorities.

21. For example, a simulated terrorist attack during which members of the public are invited to take the role of policemen in the decision-making and operational process of dealing with an imminent terrorist attack.

22. On this note, it needs to be pointed out that British Muslims appear to be more likely than Christians to trust the government. Maxwell (2010) explains this finding by arguing that positive evaluations of British society are more prevalent among migrant communities – and many Muslims are indeed migrants.

23. Interestingly, Arif's perception that airports other than Scottish ones, such as those in London, are easier to travel to clashes with the reality that the city of London (although not necessarily its airports too) bore the highest stop and search rate of 60 per 1000 people of all ethnic backgrounds in 2007/8, as evidenced by a report published by the Equality and Human Rights Commission (2010).

6

DISCRIMINATED AGAINST YET INTEGRATED: MUSLIM RESILIENCE AND SCOTTISH ENGAGEMENT WITH DIVERSITY

At the other end of a period of more than a decade of discrimination and prejudice towards Muslims *qua* Muslims resides a less dark and more optimistic side of the story. It is a story that weaves together Muslim and non-Muslim populations in a common path of mutual discovery and understanding. Following the tragic events of 9/11 and the global sociopolitical response to the ever-present threat of terrorism, Scotland has been at the forefront of fostering safe social and cultural spaces where its Muslim community can thrive. Muslims and non-Muslims have come together to challenge global stereotyping and local discrimination through acts of resilience, engagement and mutual interest. Open days at mosques, outreach events organised by universities and the voluntary sector, political partnerships with Muslim causes and support from national and local institutions have all helped allay intercommunity tensions. The Scottish superstructure has proved to be a congenial hub for these efforts: racist organisations have never gained a foothold and sectarian, more than racial, issues have shaped the countours of religious discrimination in Scotland. The peculiar features of Scottishness and the country's inclusionary ethos and cultural history of perceived tolerance have further supported integration and promoted a relatively harmonious relationship between Muslims and the indigenous Scottish community. The much more widely researched Glasgow might well overshadow other locales in academic studies; however, it is Edinburgh, the capital city of Scotland, which emerges as a model of local pluralism where Muslims can openly express their visible diversity. Set within a Scottish context of relative acceptance of minorities, the lack of urban segregation, economic prosperity, political power, international character and multicultural nature of Edinburgh are unique features that contrast with major British conurbations hosting large Muslim communities, where issues of socio-economic disadvantage, ethnic concentration, experiences of discrimination and racial conflicts have intensified cultural tensions between Muslim and non-Muslim populations.

A Tolerant Scotland

When the negative personal experiences and collective stories previously presented are left aside for a moment, there soon emerges a body of Muslim voices that speak highly of the many Scottish virtues of tolerance and openness. Many Muslims praise the Scottish capital for offering a uniquely positive social space where families can comfortably settle. The vibrant and cultured nature of Edinburgh, 'a metropolitan meeting place for different ethnic traditions' (Qureshi and Moores 1999: 327) and home to the world's largest arts festival, the Edinburgh Fringe Festival, and other sociocultural events, has undoubtedly helped desensitise the population to ethno-religious diversity. Similarly, open days at mosques, the Islamic Festival during the Edinburgh Fringe Festival, the popular Mosque Kitchen attached to Edinburgh Central Mosque and events organised by universities and local interfaith organisations across Scotland continue to offer constant opportunities for Muslim and non-Muslim communities to gather together and mix.

These opportunities positively contribute to a limited two-way integration, which studies demonstrate to be susceptible to both friendly and positive inter-ethnic contact and people's positive views of, and attitudes towards, different ethnicities (Bekhuis et al. 2013). But while Edinburgh certainly does not represent the whole of Scotland, especially given that the experiences of the larger Glaswegian Muslim population are more diverse (see Hopkins 2004a and 2004b), an increasing amount of research supports the view that Scottish tolerance and egalitarianism is as much a result of popular imagination as it is deeply rooted in society, culture and politics. In other words,

The Scottish myth is not dependent on 'facts', because it represents a set of social, self-evident values, a social ethos, a celebration of sacred beliefs about what it is to be Scottish. It helped to underpin a social and cultural order, which placed a premium on collective, cooperative and egalitarian commitments. It is an ideological device for marking off the Scots from the English, which seems to grow in importance the more the two societies grow similar, and it played a key role in accounting for political divergence between the two countries in the second half of the twentieth century. (McCrone 2001: 102–3)

Chapter 4 hinted at how a notion of nationalism based on a Scottish oppressed identity has been played out in contrast with the idea of England as an oppressive force. This notion highlights the ever-present tension between being Scottish and being English, a feature that is very much part and parcel of the life experiences and the sense of identity of many Scottish Muslims. Moreover, this notion reinforces perceptions that Scotland is more tolerant and less Islamophobic than England, which find support in the data and the research presented so far. Very importantly, racist and neo-fascist organisations, such as the National Front and Oswald Mosley's British Union of Fascists, never built much support in Scotland (Dunlop 1993; Sutherland 2012). The Scottish lack of interest in the BNP was evident in March 2004. A week after five members of a local Pakistani gang had kidnapped and murdered 15-year-old Kriss Donald in Glasgow, the BNP organised a march in town to stir up racial hatred. However, the then BNP leader Nick Griffin and his associates 'came in the dark and left in the dark, and most people never knew anything about it' (Sarwar 2016: 8).

In more recent times, the historical absence of a strong fascist tradition has also weakened the appeal of modern racist groups, such as the Scottish Defence League (SDL), in a context where, 'when [neo-] fascist parties based in England have attempted to organise in Scotland since 1945, they have tended to agitate upon the "Irish question"' (Miles and Muirhead 1986: 127). Miles and Dunlop (1987) take this argument forward and note that, while sectarian issues in Scotland predated the arrival of Irish immigrants and were linked with the persecution of Catholics after the Reformation, throughout the nineteenth century Irish immigrants suffered from physical abuse and had their properties damaged. The twentieth century brought further political and ideological divisions via the institutionalisation of a segregated, denominational education system, the daily rivalry between the football clubs in Glasgow (Catholic and Republican Celtic versus Protestant and Unionist Rangers) and the political activism of militant Protestantism, particularly during the 1920s and 1930s. These elements, Miles and Dunlop posit, kept alive the fire of sectarianism and, in turn, blocked the fascist advance in Scotland: the attempts of fascists, for example the Scottish Fascist Democratic Party, to plant their roots in the country were very short-lived. In this way, 'militant Protestantism [, institutionalised by the Scottish Protestant League and by the Protestant Action,] became an effective substitute in the context of a distinct political process in Scotland' (Miles and Dunlop 1987: 128).

The arrival and settlement of South Asian, and by inference Muslim, communities took place in a society already fragmented along cultural lines, although in more recent times the sectarian-related religious discrimination against, and the social disadvantage of, Catholics have been fading (Bruce et al. 2005) and have affected some areas – notably, West Central Scotland – more than others (Goodall et al. 2015). Nowadays, more or less intense sectarian divisions between Celtic and Rangers football clubs act as a prophylactic against the creation of mass support for the SDL, which fails to draw members from the typical targets for recruitment of the Defence Leagues – that is, football casuals (Sutherland 2012).

Another key element reverberating through the idea of Scottish tolerance is the perception that people are more friendly and accommodating towards strangers than English people. It is a notion that some have connected to an alleged Scottish tradition of empathy whereby 'in India during 200 years of the [British] Raj, the Scots were usually far more forbearing and far more considerate towards their Indian subjects' (Maan 1992: 205). In somewhat melodramatic terms, but certainly conveying the deeply poignant personal experiences of a key figure in Scottish Muslim history, Maan further argues that such a 'characteristic of the Scots could be due to the mixed make-up of Scottish society or to their sympathies being with the other underdogs, considering that they themselves have been underdogs to the English for a long time' (Maan 1992: 205). Part reality and part myth, such perceptions go hand in hand with a Scottish tradition that has historically considered race relations as an English problem, even though 'what distinguishes Scotland from England is the absence of a racialization of the political process in the period since 1945 rather than an absence of racism *per se*' (Miles and Dunlop 1987: 119, emphasis in the original).

Miles and Dunlop (1986 and 1987) suggest that such an experience of racialisation has been framed in opposition to English politics. That is, while England tends to perceive the causes of economic crises to be located within its national boundaries and, therefore, uses New Commonwealth migrants as scapegoats, Scotland blames its economic problems to its unbalanced political relations with England. From this point of view, the Scottish historical experience is laden with 'a memory of a loss of nationhood, of being the object of a different form of "colonial" domination by England, and this has been the dominant element which has shaped the political agenda in the post-1945 period' (Miles and Dunlop 1987: 133). The rise in the support for the SNP in the 1960s, the authors suggest, was promoted by a realisation that British political parties had failed to reverse the Scottish economic decline and trumpeted the independence manifesto by appealing to the alleged economic self-sufficiency offered by North Sea oil. The dramatic increase in Scottish self-identification among Scots compared to British self-identification since the 1970s (McCrone 2001) is evidence of a proud sense of belonging to Scotland that finds resonance in the increasing public support for the SNP in both the Scottish Parliament elections and the general elections. Such strong national sentiments go hand in hand with a Scottish political identity that marks the process of being or becoming Scottish – that is, even migrants who were not born in Scotland can commit to Scotland and 'invoke the ability to be a "political" Scot' (Kiely et al. 2005: 170).

Affiliation to Scotland also hinders support for the English Defence League (EDL). By wrapping itself around the flag of Englishness, the EDL fails to appeal to Scottish people who are left with the smaller, rather insignificant SDL as the main racist group of choice in the country. Powerful political statements against the SDL and the sectarian issues previously highlighted have prevented it from building as strong a support base as the EDL has in England (Sutherland 2012). Notably, Scottish political parties, Sutherland argues, have opposed Defence Leagues and have supported anti-racist organisations, whereas in England the EDL's ideologies have thrived within a more

fertile political ground. Further credence towards both a relaxed Scottish attitude towards visible ethnic minorities and the evergreen cultural opposition
to England is offered by studies that highlight 'the theory that Anglophobia
itself [both] displaces Islamophobia by providing another target and [. . .]
helps to reduce within-Scotland phobias by providing Scots with a common,
external, and very significant "Other"' (Hussain and Miller 2006: 83).

Linking back to the settlement of South Asians in Scotland described in
Chapter 1, the first-hand experiences of community pioneer Bashir Maan suggest that a certain degree of complacency about racial prejudice and discrimination among first generations 'contributed towards the "no problem here"
concept' (Maan 1992: 205). But even if problems with the majority population
might have been self-concealed and might have remained unaddressed, Maan
claims that Scottish ethnic minorities themselves have helped foster positive
relationships with the non-Muslim majority: they so far have not created major
social difficulties and have tended to act as responsible citizens.

This theme became particularly relevant in the wake of 30 July 2007,
when Bilal Abdullah, an Iraqi-born Briton, and Kafeel Ahmed, an Indian-
born British resident, drove a Jeep Cherokee loaded with propane gas canis-
ters into Glasgow Airport. The attack killed Ahmed and injured five members
of the public. In most circumstances, this incident would have caused a political knee-jerk reaction against Muslims. After all, this was the first terrorist
attack to happen in Scotland after the Lockerbie bombing on 21 December
1988. Notably, it took place in a national climate shaken by the ongoing
security threats posed by Islamist terrorism. Only two years before, on 7 July
2005, a series of coordinated suicide bombings perpetrated by four Muslim
men, three British-born Pakistanis and a Jamaican-born Briton, struck at the
heart of the London transportation system, killing over fifty people and injur-
ing about 700. The day before the attack on Glasgow Airport, on 29 June
2007, two cars loaded with gas cylinders, petrol and nails were removed and
rendered ineffective just before they could kill and maim people in central
London. Connected to this foiled terrorist plot were the two men who would
attack Glasgow the following day (Crown Prosecution Service 2008).

But instead of denouncing the evils of terrorism, former Scottish First
Minister Alex Salmond offered the world a unique example of political astuteness by pledging his solidarity with the Muslim community through a public

statement delivered from Glasgow Central Mosque.[1] What is also remarkable in this story is the reaction, or lack thereof, of the Scottish Muslim community a few years on. During interviews and informal conversations with Muslims between 2011 and 2013, very few people mentioned the Glasgow bombing. Indeed, some argued that the fact that the perpetrators were not 'some of us' – that is, they were not Scottish-born or resident Muslims – quickly washed off any sense of collective responsibility. Increased intolerance against Muslims obviously followed the incidents (Homes et al. 2010), but the communities soon resumed their normal lives and four years afterwards almost no respondent mentioned the bombings unless explicitly asked to discuss them.

It is during such intense moments that Scottish society has united in public displays of the 'One Scotland' manifesto. On 11 September 2011, religious leaders and interfaith officers in Edinburgh organised a 'walk for peace' to commemorate the 3,000 people who had died during the terrorist attacks against the United States ten years before. Around 200 Christians, Jews, Muslims, Baha'is, Hindus, Sikhs, Pagans, Unitarians, Buddhists, Brahma Kumaris and agnostics gathered at Hindu Mandir on St Andrews Street and walked through the city, stopping at various places of worship for gifts of peace candles, prayers and blessings from the host faith communities: Anwar e-Madina Mosque on Annandale Street; the Baha'i Centre on Albany Street; St Mary's Metropolitan Cathedral (Catholic) on Leith Street; and St John's Church (Scottish Episcopalian) on Princes Street (Edinburgh Interfaith Association 2011).

Promoting peace and inter-religious dialogue through mutual cultural understanding is high on the agenda in Scotland. The activities of interfaith organisations and more formal institutions, such as the Alwaleed bin Talal Centre for the Study of Islam in the Contemporary World[2] within the University of Edinburgh, are a reminder that Scotland has actively mobilised to reach out to its diverse faith communities. A telling example of how Muslim and non-Muslim communities have embraced each other and have attempted to project a positive, normalised sense of Muslimness is the 'peace mural' painted by Muslim graffiti artist Mohammed Ali on the outer wall of the Anwar e-Madina Mosque in Edinburgh in 2011. It is thanks to the joint financial and organisational effort of Edinburgh City Council, the Scottish Government and the Alwaleed Centre at the University of Edinburgh that

Ali's mural now adorns one of the main Edinburgh mosques. In it is contained a strong message of reconciliation and peace. The mural features the silhouette of Edinburgh Castle, the word 'saalam' (peace) in Arabic and the following message in English:

> If there is righteousness in the heart there will be beauty in the character. If
> there is beauty in the character there will be harmony in the home. If there
> is harmony in the home there will be order in the nation. If there is order
> in the nation there will be peace in the world. So let it be . . . Spread peace
> among yourselves.

An online video (Ali 2012) released shortly after the mural was completed brings together Muslim and non-Muslim voices to both counter negative portrayals of Islam and promote its largely peaceful nature – a largely peaceful nature that today is impressed on the very physical and spiritual structure of a place of worship in Edinburgh. The good relations between Muslim and non-Muslim communities reached another high point in 2013, when Reverend Isaac Poobalan handed over part of St John's Episcopal Church hall in Aberdeen to the local Muslim community, as the local Syed Shah Mustafa Jame Masjid was too small to fit its increasing number of worshippers. This is believed to be the first church in Great Britain to share its premises with Muslim worshippers (Lawson 2013). Over twenty years after Muslims performed their evening prayer next to the altar of St Giles' Cathedral in Edinburgh, this event marks another key moment in the religious and cultural accommodation of Islam in Scotland.[3]

The country still falls short of institutional diversity within the education system compared to England (Weedon et al. 2013). However, in the past few years there have been plans to endow Glasgow with the first Muslim school in Scotland (Cowing 2013; Denholm 2015), a decision that could endanger tolerance towards Muslims, especially among the conservative and secular sections of the non-Muslim Scottish community. But Scotland's welcoming nature is far from being purely a myth and the fact that the general public in Scotland is less opposed to immigration than anywhere else in Great Britain except in London (McCollum et al. 2014; see also Migration Observatory 2014) is a case in point. Scotland's openness is very real and this has become even more evident in the wake of 9/11.

Scotland and Islam in a Relationship of Mutual Discovery

Hand in hand with discrimination, stigmatisation and exclusion, the terrorist attacks on the United States and fifteen years of sociopolitical attention on Muslims throughout the Western world have promoted a renewed and increased interest in Islam across Scotland. The post-9/11 climate has not only revived and strengthened the relationship between Muslims and their faith but has also encouraged non-Muslims to better understand Islamic principles, beliefs and practices. Alena maintains that many non-Muslims living in Scotland do not simply buy into the negative portrayals offered by the media but take a more independent stance towards Islam and Muslim communities:

> If you look at 9/11 from the bright side, more and more people are asking about Islam, finding out more about Islam. Islam is the fastest-growing religion, so there must be a reason for that. In a way 9/11 was a sad incident but something good is coming out of that, although this does not mean that I want more 9/11s to happen! (Alena, Palestinian woman in her late twenties)

The post-9/11 interest in Islam has not stopped at the level of superficially increased understanding but has marked for some people the beginning of a personal journey of self-discovery and identity redefinition, eventually leading to conversion.[4] There are no specific numbers for Scotland, although anecdotal evidence suggests that conversions are on the rise, especially among young women (Azam and Godwin 2015). The total number of converts to Islam in Great Britain was around 100,000 in 2010 and numbers continue to increase (Brice 2011), notwithstanding contradictory experiences of 'acceptance and rejection, inclusion and exclusion, integration and isolation' (Suleiman 2013: 9; see also Suleiman 2016). According to research conducted by Brice, books, the Internet and Muslim acquaintances are the major catalysts and direct actors promoting conversion. For all the contentiousness that surrounds the public display of signs of Muslimness, particularly the hijab, and the ways in which they attract prejudicial attitudes from some non-Muslims, several Scots demonstrate positive attitudes, interest and curiosity. Adila recounts her experience of visibly projecting a Muslim identity when she started to wear the hijab at work and the positive response from her colleagues:

> Six months into my volunteering job, I started wearing the hijab. People did not question me. They looked at me once and thought, 'Oh, she is wearing the hijab,' but did not ask why I started wearing it or that kind of thing. It was quite nice because during those days Ramadan was happening and they would ask me information about it. They would not ask me questions when I used not to wear the hijab. I thought that it was very good. I could tell them about my religion. (Adila, Kenyan Pakistani woman in her mid-forties)

The relationship between Muslim and non-Muslim communities in Scotland is certainly more nuanced than the highly negative one described in Chapter 5. It forms part of a very complex picture, in which the bright colours of societal interest in exploring and understanding Islam tone down the dark colours of prejudice and discrimination. It is a picture made even brighter by the power of visible symbols of Muslimness to counterbalance negative reactions and to negotiate cultural and religious diversity in the Scottish social and cultural arenas. While some Muslims certainly endure stigmatisation and discrimination, many people from different ethnic and socio-economic backgrounds, both in interviews with the author and in other research (Colourful Heritage 2016), reported positive encounters with non-Muslims at various levels of social engagement. It is a powerful body of voices that consider negative incidents to be a combination of low educational achievement, poor social skills and alcohol abuse rather than a peculiarly Scottish attitude:

> Generally speaking, I think that non-Muslims are very positive. I have lived here for ten years and have come across just three or four times in which someone said something to me because I am a Muslim woman. That is all. Those comments came most of the time from someone who was drunk or uneducated. (Nyanath, Sudanese woman in her mid-thirties)

> I have a good relationship with non-Muslims. I used to have my own shop, a takeaway. I worked in catering so I had contact with a lot of non-Muslims. We get along fine. Most of my customers are non-Muslims and are very nice. (Anis, Tunisian man in his late fifties)

I think that the attitude of non-Muslims towards Muslims is very good. I work [in a hotel] with Spanish people. There are also Scottish people and English people there. There is no difference. Wherever you go – hospitals or police stations – non-Muslims behave very well towards us. They try to help us. (Imran, Pakistani man in his mid-thirties)

There is a general consensus that the Scottish majority is accepting and tolerant of people of Islamic faith, particularly so in Edinburgh. Other qualitative research, involving over fifty Scottish Muslims in Dundee, Glasgow and Edinburgh, confirmed existing negative experiences at airports but highlighted the positive relations with the wider Scottish community (Blackwood 2015). Some Muslims are certainly wary about visibly and publicly identifying themselves as Muslim. But some other Muslims feel that it is their duty to reach out to Scottish society and engage widely with the public to dispel perceived misconceptions around Islam. These are not merely vague activities of interfaith dialogue. Instead, they are effective ways to foster intercommunity contact, given that 'negative or positive views [towards Islam and Muslims] correlate strongly with the amount of knowledge of Islam and of direct contact with Muslims' (Field 2007: 465).

The nature of the relationship and the level of engagement between Muslim and non-Muslim communities are very important. They can build bridges and break sociocultural barriers through quality contact and, eventually, shape positive attitudes towards Muslims (Hutchison and Rosenthal 2011). It is well established that quality contact with people of Islamic faith has the potential to inspire 'more positive attitudes towards Muslims, the perception of Muslims as distinct individuals rather than a homogeneous entity, greater intentions to behave positively towards Muslims, and less anxiety about coming into contact with Muslims' (Hutchison and Rosenthal 2011: 55).

Many young Muslims have resiliently challenged post-9/11 stereotypes and have not let global and national negative narratives affect their feelings of belonging to society. These Muslims have been proactive in both promoting intercommunity engagement and facilitating a process that seeks to normalise the image of Muslims living in Scotland. Akhtar used to be involved in both personal activities and community projects to challenge social suspicion towards, and misunderstanding of, Islam and Muslims:

Sometimes when you are speaking to non-Muslims they get really self-conscious. This gets to me even if I understand that they do not want to offend. But, because of the fact that they have been so over-conscious, I feel that I do not want to be treated differently. I want to be treated normally. That is it. [. . .] It makes me more determined to show that some of the ways people perceive Muslims nowadays are not true. It makes me more determined to be myself the way I am. I am not going to change for anyone or anything like that. (Akhtar, Scottish Pakistani man in his early twenties)

The annual Islamic Festival within the Edinburgh Fringe Festival in August is a telling example of the ways in which Muslim people and institutions, especially mosques, have attempted to reach out to wider society. The Islamic Festival consists of an exhibition (Islamic Exhibition) showcasing excerpts from the Qur'an, Islamic art, banners and other visual tools to illustrate Islamic beliefs, principles and attitudes to religion, society and life. Numerous related events, such as lectures and workshops on Islamic-related topics, ranging from Arabic calligraphy to women in Islam and shari'a law, make it a very popular event in Scotland. The Islam Festival Edinburgh documentary (Islam Festival 2010) is a testament to the positive reception of the festival among non-Muslim people, who often speak in laudatory terms of the exhibition as a valuable effort to address the many stereotypes surrounding Islam. Besides the exhibition, a number of other intercommunity activities regularly take place during the year across the major Scottish cities, such as Islam Awareness Week and various Mela festivals. The latter are annual South Asian festivals that are best described as 'an example of how minority cultures can become part of the mainstream [. . .] *without* surrendering the ongoing, parallel evolution of their own separate cultures and identities' (Penrose 2013: 19, emphasis in the original).

Interfaith seminars, peace talks and social gatherings also take place at churches, mosques, universities and other institutions. Far from being a secluded group purely subject to tyrannical patriarchal norms, Scottish Muslim women have been very active in this arena too. Notably, Amina Muslim Women's Resource Centre launched the successful 'I Speak for Myself' campaign in 2012 in an attempt to reduce stereotypes and mistaken perceptions of Muslim women. While it is hard to measure the effectiveness of these activities in enhancing tolerance and respect towards Muslims, ongoing processes of intercommunity dialogue and interaction are at least attempting to normalise the meanings of being Muslim in Scottish society. Yet, it would be naïve to consider all of these activities as disinterested acts of reconciliation with Scottish society. For all the good intentions behind Muslim engagement with wider society, proselytism (*da'wa*) often plays an important role in driving much outreach effort.

A major public engagement event, running under the title of 'Hope Conference' and held in Edinburgh during Islam Awareness Week in 2013 and 2015, hosted about 1,000 attendees who joined in force from across Scotland. The event featured Islamic scholars and Muslim public speakers promoting the so-called 'true teachings of Islam and everlasting uplifting notions and concepts of Hope' (Hope Conference 2015). Live conversions to Islam in front of the large audience were met with rounds of applause, while a smooth-spoken presenter tried to lure more people onto the same path. Speakers excitedly praised the alleged truest nature of Islam, while criticisms levelled by the non-Muslim audience towards religiously sanctioned violence against children at mosques and women (see, for example, Suleiman 2012) were quickly dismissed. All in all, the event was an opportunity to proselytise on a large scale and, in the absence of more moderate and contradictory perspectives, the various speakers resembled loud American televangelists rather than modest, learned religious scholars.

Less explicitly one-sided events are organised throughout the year by community organisations, mosques and interfaith groups. In this sense, Aberdonian Muslims have given a splendid example of community engagement by offering free meals to homeless people in the city (BBC News 2016f). While young people tend to be more active than the older section of the community, often because they have more time to spend volunteering and fewer family or business commitments, mosques historically attended by first-generation Muslims have gradually started embracing a more open attitude:

[Talking about intercommunity events:] I do know in terms of 'Mosque A' and some other mosques I go to as well – a new mosque, 'Mosque C'. They do some stuff there. The imam at 'Mosque C' goes to schools and meets teachers. Again, that mosque is very proactive. Some of the old-school mosques are not as engaged but they are getting there. These are little things and small steps to become more open. A project I am involved in locally is called 'Charity Week'. Again with that, this year too, I have a big, massive push in terms of getting other people involved. I had a meeting with the guys from the Church of Scotland to try and get people from other faiths. I emailed a lot of the ministers, some of the other faiths' people, trying to get them involved in this project. [. . .] We have different events. 'Charity Week' starts on 24 October. We have got a cricket event, we have got a ladies' night, we have got a general fundraising event for the community and then we have got a dinner and auction on Sunday and a lot of other things going on. (Akhtar, Scottish Pakistani man in his early twenties)

Besides bringing the Scottish Muslim and non-Muslim communities closer to one another, 9/11 has also allowed people of high social status to gain even more visibility. This is the case for Ali, who has enjoyed many opportunities for public speaking and writing since 2001:

The other way of thinking is that, post-9/11, what happened is that there were all sorts of opportunities to speak and write, all sort of things. I took up various of those opportunities, whenever possible. For example, I have been able to speak at international conferences, meetings and interfaith dialogues and to write pieces. (Ali, British Pakistani man in his mid-forties)

Ali's public visibility may not necessarily be a benefit shared by the majority of Muslims but it is true that those who have enjoyed the same rewards have done so within local Scottish contexts that openly embrace the positive aspects of Islam and actively foster dialogue between different ethnic and religious communities. Far from being drawn to Muslims and Islam out of mere curiosity, a section of the Scottish non-Muslim population has also been supportive of global and local Muslim causes, such as peace marches, anti-racism protests or pro-Palestine campaigns. While this support can potentially hide all sorts of political interests and ideological agendas, it nevertheless demonstrates the existence of social partnerships between Muslims and people of different faiths and no faiths across Scotland.

Scottish Social Support for Global and Local Muslim Affairs

The series of global events that marked the history of the early twenty-first century have undoubtedly drawn Scottish society closer to the fate of Muslims in foreign countries. The Western military involvement in Afghanistan (2001–14) and Iraq (2003–11), the ongoing Israeli–Palestinian conflict and the Arab Spring (2010–12) have acted as catalysts to several actors in Scotland. The Scottish Government has historically positioned itself closer to traditional Muslim views than Westminster has. Opposition to the war in Iraq and the more recent condemnation of the Israeli bombing of Gaza in 2014 (Rahim 2015) are two fitting examples. Local political and activist groups have played a key role in endorsing Muslim causes too. Not only concerned with the well-being of Muslims living abroad, political groups are often joined by other religious groups, unaffiliated individuals and institutions in supporting local Muslim communities, particularly at anti-racist demonstrations. Scottish activists often stand with Muslims during counter-marches against the SDL. They also tend to outnumber the SDL's demonstrators (see, for example, Tell MAMA 2016):

> Most of the time when you see protests of the EDL or the SDL, you see non-Muslims who are representing Muslims, supporting Muslims or staying on the side of Muslims. At the same time, you have Muslims who fight for justice. We have so many protests against the foreign policies of Israel and America. During pro-Palestine protests, most of the time you see more non-Muslims than Muslims there. (Yasir, young Pakistani man in his mid-forties)

A large presence of non-Muslim Scots congregating to counter the SDL's demonstrations is part of a wider strategic plan, which the spokesperson of a prominent Scottish anti-racism group elucidated during an anti-Islamophobia event at Islam Awareness Week in 2013. A key strategy to respond to the SDL's street activities is to gather large numbers of non-Muslim counter-demonstrators. Given that non-Muslims are not the direct targets of discrimination, they can mobilise more powerful narratives in opposition to the SDL's message than Muslims would be able to. The same event brought together many prominent British Muslim and pro-Muslim speakers from the anti-racist, anti-war and Islamist scene. These speakers discussed and lamented the perceived negative media portrayals of Islam and responded to the protests that the SDL had organised in the previous few weeks. A similar protest was underway on that same day outside the venue, Augustine United Church in Edinburgh. But, as the event progressed, the boundaries between the local and the global started blurring and, while the event was taking place *in* Scotland, one was left wondering whether such an event was at all *about* Scotland. Undoubtedly, counterterrorism measures, such as stops and searches at airports, and anti-Muslim activities carried out by racist groups have salience in the life of the Scottish Muslim community. But, equally, the degree of seriousness posed by such threats to Scottish Muslims should be properly assessed.

Without dismissing discrimination and prejudice, it is crucially important to consider these issues from a relative, rather than an absolute, point of view. Arguing that racism 'is an everyday experience for many of Scotland's black and minority ethnic population' (Hopkins 2004a: 91) resonates well within ultra-liberal academic circles. Yet, the Scottish landscape presents unique nuances that need to be recognised. Discrimination and prejudice must be reconsidered in light of both decreasing numbers of recorded racist incidents (a trend which might be disrupted by both the divisive post-'Brexit' referendum climate and renewed fears of Islamist terrorism) and the specific locales where they happen. From a relative point of view, both the literature and the data presented so far unequivocally point to one single conclusion: Scotland suffers from discrimination and prejudice but at lower levels than England does and, presumably, at much lower levels than several continental European countries do.

Anti-Islamophobia or anti-SDL campaigns and the Israeli–Palestinian conflict continue to capture the interest of both Scottish anti-racism and anti-war activist groups and unaffiliated non-Muslims (see BBC News 2012a and 2013; Nicholson 2012). The controversial disruptions of events, sponsored by the University of Edinburgh, featuring prominent Israeli figures such as Ismail Khaldi, a Bedouin diplomat in the Israeli Ministry of Foreign Affairs, in February 2011 and Daniel Taub, the former Israeli Ambassador to the United Kingdom, in October 2012 (Student Rights 2012) are two significant examples. However, non-Muslims do not blindly support local Scottish Muslim communities. Following the 'Scotland for Marriage' campaign, which drew support from a few Christian groups,[5] the MCS stepped up pressure against politicians and the government to halt proposals to pass same-sex marriage legislation in 2013[6] (Duffy and Azzam 2013). In this instance, Muslim campaigners managed to draw little support from the wider Scottish population.

Same-sex marriage is a very sensitive subject for Muslims, who constitute the most conservative religious group in Great Britain and record much lower levels of approval for same-sex marriages compared to other religious groups: 33 per cent as compared with 70 per cent (Lewis and Kashyap 2013). It is even more of a distinctively Muslim, rather than Scottish, issue given that over two thirds (68 per cent) of Scottish people believe that same-sex couples should be able to marry, including almost 60 per cent of Christians of the various denominations combined (ScotCen Social Research 2014). Action against same-sex marriage was one major undertaking that brought Muslims together in the pursuance of shared religious, moral and ideological causes without much support from wider society. Instead, non-Muslims selectively support Muslim causes, with a preference for those conforming to their own individual and collective political and social stances.

The benevolence towards, and support of, Muslims from local authorities and the police are very visible during committee meetings, intercommunity events and other social occasions at 'Mosque B'. Members of the Scottish Government and MSPs can often be seen participating in various events, while local councillors pay occasional visits to the mosque to enquire about persistent community grievances. After 9/11, 7/7 and the murder of British Army soldier Lee Rigby in Woolwich (London) perpetrated by two British-born Nigerian converts to Islam in May 2013, the police were on the front line to minimise the impact of any much-feared backlash against Muslim people and properties. Police efforts ranged from visiting mosques to provide reassurance to giving security advice to community leaders. Soon after the Woolwich murder, Police Scotland, through the Edinburgh Contest[7] Group, circulated an email to local minority ethnic groups warning of potential community tensions and hate crimes, particularly directed towards Muslims, encouraging community members to report such crimes and promising that the police 'have a grip on this' and that 'members of the BME community are safe to go about their lives as normal'.[8]

Similarly, after the Paris terrorist attack in November 2015, Deputy Chief Constable Iain Livingstone circulated an email to communities reassuring them that Scotland faced no known and imminent threat of terrorism and encouraging people 'to work together in ensuring that no person or group in Scotland feels marginalised or isolated'.[9] The email also reassured communities that Police Scotland would respond swiftly to any incident of hate crime. The day after the Brussels terrorist attack in March 2016, Police Scotland made a public commitment to reach out to Scottish Muslim and Jewish communities, fearing a backlash against them (Leask 2016c). In the same month, Asad Shah, a member of the minority Ahmadiyya Muslim community in Glasgow, was murdered by a Sunni Muslim man from Bradford hours after wishing his customers a happy Easter on social media (BBC News 2016a). Ultra-orthodox Muslims accuse the Ahmadiyya community of heresy because they believe their founder, Mirza Ghulam Ahmad, to be a Prophet and persecute them in some Muslim-majority countries, including Pakistan (BBC News 2010). The incident in Glasgow was a religiously prejudiced murder, motivated by Shah's adherence to Ahmadiyya beliefs (BBC News 2016c).

The MCS issued a statement of concern for the murder and affirmed the right of the Ahmadiyya community to uphold its beliefs (*Herald Scotland* 2016c). Hundreds of Scottish people, including First Minister Nicola Sturgeon, MSP Humza Yousaf and Glasgow City Council leader Frank McAveety, attended a silent vigil in remembrance (Armour 2016). Police were also on the front line and offered a strong message of solidarity to the community. Ruaraidh Nicolson, Police Scotland's Assistant Chief Constable, and Mak Chishty, the National Police Chiefs' Council lead for race, religion and belief, sent a letter to people living in the south side of the city reassuring that police would put in place additional patrols, would work 'very closely with all communities' and would deal with 'any sectarian conflict, hatred or extremism [. . .] swiftly and strongly' (*Herald Scotland* 2016b).[10] Observation of several anti-SDL and pro-Palestine demonstrations and interviews with local people between 2011 and 2013 made it very clear that Scottish police officers are active in protecting the Muslim community, both physically and psychologically.

Stressing the positive role played by Police Scotland is even more important as a way to counterbalance the negative experiences of stops and searches at airports. These positive relationships find evidence beyond media reports (Rahim 2015). Even academic research, which has critically assessed the negative interactions between Muslims and security officers at airports, has conceded that Muslim–police relationships at the local level are positive (Blackwood 2015). Partnerships between the police and the Scottish Muslim community take various forms. In more recent times, and in light of the global and national threat posed by Islamist terrorism, the MCS and Police Scotland have arranged joint workshops for religious personnel and mosque representatives to debate extremism and radicalisation (*Herald Scotland* 2015a). Importantly, Police Scotland have also supported the 'United Against Extremism' campaign, which was launched by the Scottish Ahmadiyya Muslim community with other faith and community groups in April 2016 (BBC News 2016d). A few months later, Edinburgh Central Mosque launched a programme of teaching and study called 'Against Extremism'. Police Scotland have recently planned to increase the number of people from BME backgrounds who join the force. The formal introduction of the hijab as an optional part of their uniform for Muslim female officers is one step in that direction (BBC News 2016g). When coupled with a strongly empathetic attitude displayed by the Scottish public, the benevolent disposition of the police becomes a crucial factor in shaping feelings of collective safety and belonging to the country:

> The day of 9/11 the police came to my mum, to the shop, and said, 'We are worried that there might be a backlash against Muslims. So any problem, contact this number.' They gave a special number for us to contact, which was nice to know. And then regular customers, and even people who used to come for years and had never said anything to us, came to us and said, 'We know what happened and we know that this has nothing to do with you, because we know you personally and you are nothing like that. And if there is any trouble you can call me, you can contact me.' And my mum started crying. She did not expect that. She was overwhelmed with support.
> (Babar, Scottish Pakistani man in his mid-twenties)

Scholars, policymakers and the public should certainly not become too complacent about the tolerant Scottish environment in which Muslims live. Scotland's tradition of racism towards migrant labour (Miles and Muirhead 1986) and as generated and reproduced through its involvement in the British Empire should not be forgotten. But today's reality is much rosier. Perceptions of Scotland as a welcoming country go hand in hand with Muslims' affiliation with Scottishness. Increased levels of Scottishness, which have been recorded since the 1970s at the expense of, and played out against, Britishness (McCrone 2001; Bond and Rosie 2002), marry well both with the ethnically flexible nature of Scottishness (Kyriakides et al. 2009) and with Scotland's 'aspirational pluralism' (Meer 2015a). The romantic and often political idea of a Scottish egalitarian and inclusive society (McCrone and Bechhofer 2010) is evidenced by the interest in Islam and in the support for Muslim causes that many people have demonstrated. Not only a cause of ethno-religious discrimination, the visibility of Muslimness in everyday Scottish life has also taken the forms of genuine interest in, and tolerance towards, Islam, particularly in Edinburgh. The Scottish capital has in itself the potential to blossom as a local model of pluralism by mobilising its porous sociocultural boundaries in the shaping of a fully integrative Scottishness that can valorise and include Muslim diversity.

The 'Promised Land'? Edinburgh as a Model of Local Pluralism and Integration

Edinburgh perfectly encapsulates the inclusionary ethos and the cultural history of perceived Scottish tolerance. Set within a Scottish context of relative acceptance of minorities, the lack of urban segregation, economic prosperity, political power, international character and multicultural nature of Edinburgh make it a truly successful model of local pluralism where Muslims can openly express their visible diversity. Such unique features are all the more evident when contrasted with the less favourable conditions offered by major conurbations hosting large Muslim communities in both Scotland, such as Glasgow, and England, such as Bradford, Birmingham, Manchester and some parts of London. Muslims across the socio-economic and gender spectra maintain that the geography and the scale of Edinburgh, as well as the range of sociocultural activities that it provides, entice people to settle there for life:

> I think that Edinburgh is a nice place to live, because it is not huge and it is not too small. There is a good Muslim community but it is not huge. We

have mosques and activities, so from a Muslim perspective I think that it is a nice, cosy place to live in general. I also think that Edinburgh is a nice place to raise children, while in big cities it is just a nightmare. (Alena, Palestinian woman in her late twenties)

The cosmopolitan and culturally active nature of Edinburgh, as well as its small Muslim community and the absence of urban segregation, are all the more important in light of the fact that 'the larger the non-White component to an urban area's population, and the larger the South Asian share of that component, the greater the degree of clustering into neighbourhoods whose populations contain only a minority of Whites' (Johnston et al. 2016: 12). A small, diverse and dispersed ethnic minority community can facilitate positive interactions and relationships with the indigenous population. It is well known that racial violence and exclusion from 'those important spheres of social life that constitute the basic elements of citizenship in a democratic welfare State' – namely, 'the spheres of employment, housing, sports and social cultural entertainment, and political institutional life of the wider society' (Wardak 2000: 242) – can alienate and push minorities to the social and geographical boundaries of a city.

Self-segregation can occur and take disparate forms, such as (1) the appearance of small communities of shopkeepers; (2) ethnic concentration within certain neighbourhoods; (3) the emergence of independent sports clubs and bhangras (Punjabi disco clubs); and (4) political actions aimed at seeking minority rights (Wardak 2000). In his study conducted in the 1990s, Wardak found that some Scottish Pakistanis living in the Leith area of Edinburgh responded to mainstream exclusion by insulating themselves within social, cultural, economic and political micro-worlds. These were predominantly first-generation migrants who needed to find cultural and linguistic support via a community of similarity. Today, younger generations are dispersing more and more across the Scottish capital.

With the exception of the continued clustering around the Leith area of a small section of the Pakistani population, there is no predominant South Asian or Muslim neighbourhood in Edinburgh or in Scotland more generally, apart from Glasgow. Unlike major British conurbations hosting large, predominantly Pakistani, Muslim communities where ethnic concentration, economic deprivation, serious discrimination and racial tensions have created a social rift between Muslim and non-Muslim populations, the geographical dispersal of the Muslim community in Edinburgh puts contact theory to the test and the results are very optimistic. Edinburgh Muslims and non-Muslims are socially and geographically forced to be in contact with each other. Overall, they harmoniously share neighbourhoods, social networks and public services through individual, community and institutional efforts. This situation allows an ethnically diverse community bound by a renewed Islamic impetus to integrate and thrive within Scotland's porous sociocultural boundaries:

> I have not spent time in England but I am really glad that I am Scottish. I really am! I do think that here we are better off than anywhere else in the United Kingdom. Basically, I think that Edinburgh has the right balance between the amount of Muslims and the amount of non-Muslims. Whereas, in other places where there are far too many Pakistanis you have troubles. For example, in Bradford and places like that, they have got issues. (Rabab, Scottish Pakistani woman in her late twenties)

> I really love Edinburgh. That is why I decided to stay on. One thing about Edinburgh is that it is multicultural, so you do not really feel all that different from other people. Even though the Muslim community is small, there are people from all over the world. (Zoe, Singaporean woman in her mid-thirties)

> Edinburgh is a university town. There are so many changes of students and of course the Festival. And I know it might seem just a bunch of students having fun for a month but this is key for Edinburgh people to deal with foreigners. Edinburgh is such an international city. The Muslim community is very scattered in Edinburgh. There are halal shops here and mosques there. There is no predominantly Muslim area here. (Rebecca, Scottish woman in her early forties)

Often taking forward the evergreen political and cultural 'Scotland versus England' rhetoric, some local Muslims define their positive experiences of life in the capital in opposition to either personal experiences in, or stories about, England. Zakir's life experiences in Huddersfield, where he lived for around twenty years, and Edinburgh, where he lives now, have been very different.

His enthusiasm for the Scottish social environment, for example at school, is often contrasted with gloomy stories about life in England:

> *Stefano*: Have you noticed any difference between Scottish people and English people?
> *Zakir*: I think that Scottish people are more tolerant. They hate the English more than the Asians! When I was younger it was common to be called Paki [in England]. In high school, in Huddersfield, we had three levels – 'a', 'b' and 'c'. Asians were pushed into 'c'. I was put into 'c' as well. By chance, one of the teachers said that I should not be in that class. At the end of the year I came first in four exams so automatically in the second year I was pushed into 'a'. Otherwise, all Asians were automatically put into 'c'. That was discrimination. [. . .] Edinburgh is more tolerant, also of Asians. The school experience here has been much better than in England. And the religious element is more tolerated here. (Zakir, British Pakistani man in his mid-forties)

A man very well connected with Muslim communities across Scotland, Zakir is able to provide a very insightful overview of the historical reasons that have made the Scottish capital so attractive for Muslims, especially due to the unique economic opportunities that have allowed minorities to enter self-employment and thrive:

> We originally moved from Huddersfield to Edinburgh over twenty years ago because there was an economic depression there. Here [in Edinburgh] there were more opportunities. My father is a weaver and had been working there since the 1960s. The factory where he was working closed down and there was a lot of unemployment, which continues nowadays. I saw it when I was back in Huddersfield last year. There is poverty, backwardness and a rural mentality. When they come here, they find that there is money and business. Most of them go into the business trade. At the time, we got a newsagent's shop so we started our own business. We knew some people who had originally come from Huddersfield and we set up our own business. People who came here from Huddersfield were those who had a bit of money. They looked for business and then started it. First they would live in rented accommodation, and then they would buy their own houses. They all came here to Edinburgh because they had a bit of money, unlike the

first generation of migrants. Most [Asian] people in Edinburgh went into self-employment instead of working in factories. (Zakir, British Pakistani man in his mid-forties)

The fact that the internal migration of Zakir's parents and friends was mediated by their knowledge of British culture is certainly a convincing explanation behind the smooth settlement of a section of the Muslim community who moved from England to Scotland. Equally important is the socio-economic make-up of the Pakistanis who have settled in Scotland. As already noted, they tend to originate from the well-off Faisalabad area in the Punjab. The variety of ethnic groups making up the Muslim community that lives in Scotland is also a factor that prevents the formation of ethnic clusters and promotes the shaping of a much more ethnically transversal community bound by both religion and nation. Several Muslims further praise Edinburgh's desegregated environment, where diversity can find expression in a context of tolerated pluralism. Muslims with experience of life in other European countries can often provide very valuable insights. Bilel, a Tunisian man who lived for many years in Italy and France before settling in Scotland, praises the country and Edinburgh for their welcoming and accommodating nature:

> The good thing in Edinburgh is that they facilitate places for us to worship in the mosque, at airports, at hospitals, I think even at universities. So there is respect for religion, not just Islam but also Christianity and other beliefs. Some time ago Edinburgh University removed Bibles from one of its rooms in respect for other religions. (Bilel, Tunisian man in his mid-fifties)

Some migrants to Scotland from Muslim-majority countries share this way of thinking, particularly when they realise that the freedoms available in Scotland are liberating and empowering. Nasha faced serious challenges when returning to Pakistan for a monthly holiday. Being unable to attend the mosque or to pray in public or semi-public spaces in her town of origin, as she normally could do in Edinburgh, made Nasha more aware of her sense of belonging to Edinburgh:

> Interestingly, I went back to Pakistan after eight years this summer and I felt very strange there. I felt it was really hard to accommodate to different things. That is when I realised that Edinburgh is my home. I was very young

when I came here [early teens] so I would say that I grew up here and my ideas have matured here. You know when you have a sense of the environment and the people and you start realising things in the world. I started understanding the world – that is what happened in Edinburgh. (Nasha, Pakistani woman in her mid-twenties)

While respondents might well be looking at Edinburgh through rose-tinted glasses, the Scottish capital has received positive appraisals far and wide. The most important political, financial and cultural city in Scotland, and home to both the Scottish Parliament and the Scottish Government, Edinburgh has consistently won awards as 'best UK city'[11] (BBC News 2009a; *Guardian* 2012; *Edinburgh News* 2016) over the years for its harmonious atmosphere and reputation, as well as its culture, its safety and the friendliness of the locals. The previously mentioned annual Islamic Festival, part of the Edinburgh Fringe Festival; events arranged by the university and interfaith organisations; and the efforts of various voluntary groups make the city a uniquely favourable place for ethnic and religious minorities.

Across Scotland, a section of the non-Muslim population that sides with Muslims in their efforts to advance Muslim political causes, challenge discrimination and clear up misconceptions around Islam has not gone unnoticed. Similarly, the tight-knit and well-integrated nature of the Scottish Muslim community has facilitated good relationships with the wider society. Good community relationships have prevented the spread of the extremist Islamist ideologies of groups such as Hizb ut-Tahrir and Al-Muhajiroun, which instead found fertile ground south of the border and, particularly, in London. According to prominent community members, the narratives of isolation and division propagated by these groups failed to find supporters when they attempted to enter the Scottish landscape, via Glasgow, in the 1990s. The visits to Scotland of leading Islamist Omar Bakri Muhammad in that period were carried out on the quiet (*Herald Scotland* 2015a). Similarly, more recent public opposition to Islamist terrorism from Scottish Muslim organisations and individuals (BBC News 2007; O'Leary 2014; Weldon 2014; *Herald Scotland* 2015b) testifies to the fact that the relatively well-off, small, educated and dispersed Scottish Muslim community places a strong emphasis on unity and tolerance.

This situation should certainly not overshadow the ongoing risk of radicalisation among Scottish Muslims, the evergreen threat posed by lone wolves (Marshall 2016) and the recent notable cases of individuals who joined violent jihad: Glaswegian Aqsa Mahmood fled to Syria and turned into a recruiter for the Islamic State in 2013 (Fantz and Shubert 2015), while Aberdonian Abdul Rakib Amin joined the Islamic State in 2014 and was killed in a drone strike conducted by the Royal Air Force in Raqqa, Syria, one year later (Maddox 2015). Allegations (BBC News 2016b) that Sabir Ali and Haziz Abdul Hamid, two senior figures at, respectively, Glasgow Central Mosque and Idara Taleem ul Quran Mosque in Edinburgh have occupied senior positions in the UK branch of Sipah-e-Sahaba Pakistan (SSP), a Home Office-banned militant anti-Shi'a organisation aimed at turning Pakistan, also via violent means, into a Sunni state ruled by shari'a law (Home Office 2016), raise some concerns about the ultra-orthodox section of the Pakistani community living in Scotland.[12] Revelations that the imam of Glasgow Central Mosque, Maulana Habib ur Rehman, defined Mumtaz Qadri's[13] murder of former Governor of Punjab in Pakistan, Salman Taseer, for alleged blasphemy 'the collective responsibility of the ummat [sic]' confirm these concerns (Leask 2016d and 2016e). This incident also spotlights the cultural fractures that divide members of Glasgow Central Mosque. On the one hand, conservative Scottish Pakistanis cling on traditional views of Islam and want to solve community problems internally. On the other hand, there are liberal Scottish Pakistanis, such as Aamer Anwar, who champions mosque reform and received death threats (Brooks 2016) and abuse (*Herald Scotland* 2016a) for condemning violent extremism and calling for unity within the Muslim community. An outpouring of political support for Anwar followed the death threats (Goodwin 2016).

But while the threat of violent extremism in Scotland exists, it is likely to be lower than in major European countries, thanks also to the limited availability of weapons in the country (Marshall 2016), the peculiar socio-political Scottish environment, the sentiments of affiliation to Scotland that many local Muslims express (Bonino 2015b) and the positive role played by Edinburgh in making Muslims feel welcome. The fostering of belonging to the country is nowhere more evident than in the experiences of (re)discovered religiosity among Muslim women.

Muslim Women (Re)Discover their Religiosity in Scotland

There is no doubt that Scotland still presents fragmentations and contradictions in the ways in which different religions and beliefs intersect and relate to each other in the public sphere (Allison and Siddiqui 2014). Nonetheless, particularly for Muslim women, Scotland and Edinburgh have actively supported a process of strengthening of religious identity. This is especially true of Muslim women who migrated from a Muslim-majority country to Scotland. While for some of these women a heightened religious identity represents nothing more than a mechanism of cultural transition, some other Muslims narrate journeys of self-discovery in which their affiliation to Islam has become more self-conscious and actively internalised, not just in adaptation to, but also through, the Scottish context. Nyanath, a Sudanese woman who had lived in Sudan and the United Arab Emirates before relocating to Edinburgh, 'found' Islam in Scotland:

> At the beginning, I was not confident about being a Muslim here. Because when you come from a Muslim country you do not appreciate what you believe in and you do not understand why you believe in it. [. . .] But then I came here and this gave me a chance to think over my beliefs. When I saw that there are many nice people who are really good-hearted people, I started thinking, 'What is the difference between me and them? Why do I need to be a Muslim? Why do I need to believe in Islam? Why do I need to believe in a God if I cannot see him?' So I started to think and reflect and this made me more religious. [. . .] This is more about understanding Islam. Understanding the almighty God. Understanding people. [. . .] This happened once I moved to Edinburgh and I am now able to be a Muslim around people who are not Muslim. (Nyanath, Sudanese woman in her mid-thirties)

Similarly, Chanda believes that she is part of a self-conscious minority within a supportive Scottish environment – an environment that not only affords her rediscovered Muslimness space for expression but that also actively promotes its expression:

> When you are in an environment and you think that your existence is talked about, you feel that your existence has an added value for society.

In Bangladesh we do not overly practise Islam. Eighty-six per cent of the population is Muslim but Islam is taken for granted. We do not have strong obligations to practise in Bangladesh. Also, in terms of Islamic symbols, such as scarves, these are not very much in practice in my home country. There are a lot of mosques in Bangladesh but it is not like in Middle Eastern countries where shops would close as soon as they hear the call for prayer. It is up to you whether you want to pray or not. Here in Edinburgh I really enjoy my spiritual life. I totally enjoy it. This is without question. It does not mean that I have become more Islamic or more spiritual. It is that, whatever I am doing, I feel that the environment is supporting me. I think that this is due to human nature. When your identity is talked about, then you want to come out and show that you have very good things to offer. (Chanda, Bangladeshi woman in her mid-forties)

A number of Muslims, mostly women, suggest that Edinburgh could have the potential to nurture their religious experiences. Pushed by externalities to think deeply about their own identity, and internally stimulated to discover their religion and spiritual self at a much deeper level, these Muslim women look for certainty and stability in Scotland despite the global distrust of Islam. Equally importantly, the freedoms that the majority of male and female Muslims experience in Scotland are conducive to a more participatory Muslimness, through cultural and religious negotiations, within a Scottish environment in which, for example, women attend mosques more often than they would do in some Muslim-majority countries:[14]

I was at Edinburgh University and I was in George Square and the mosque was nearby, so it just made sense that I went there. Of course, my family goes there. But as a woman it was different. Back home women did not really go to the mosque as much. This is not a religious issue. It is a cultural issue that men go to the mosque and women just pray at home. So I started to pray at home here too, but then I saw a lot of people going to the mosque – both men and women – so I said, 'Why should I not go too?' (Alena, Palestinian woman in her late twenties)

Scottish Muslim women have also taken a public role in reducing stereotypes and black-and-white perceptions about Muslim women. The organisation

Beyond the Veil and Amina Muslim Women's Resource Centre are two collective attempts to promote a better understanding of what it means to live as a Muslim woman in Scotland. Similarly, less formal groups have proliferated throughout the country and have pushed Muslim women to participate in Scottish sociocultural life:

> We set up a Muslim Women's Group about six years ago, it was just because we felt that Muslim women did not really have social activities to go to. Everything was mixed. You know, if you worked you would work and then go to a party. You would go to a pub. And we did not really want to go to a pub. If there was a party in somebody's house, people would be drinking and we did not really want to do that. So we will have our own gatherings. But what we will have is a gathering not just for Muslims. We will invite those people to our parties instead of them inviting us to theirs. It has been really good. It has developed. We have about 300 members. It is really good. We do lots of activities, we run the mothers and toddlers group and we invite non-Muslims to it as well. It just shows people that the mosque is not a scary place where you get beaten up or whatever. It is just like any other church or any other synagogue or whatever. (Adila, Kenyan Pakistani woman in her mid-forties)

But life for Muslim women in Scotland is not always so positive and certainly presents intra-community nuances and complexities that need to be untangled. The onus that is placed on women to publicly perform a 'respectable femininity' (Siraj 2012) at the intersection between religious visibility and cultural conformity highlights the importance of female self-representation and the maintenance of honour[15] by adhering to expected moral behaviours both within and outside the domestic arena (Qureshi and Moores 1999). Conformity to a strongly visible Muslim identity is often promoted through the hijab as a way of 'increasing one's [at least performed] accountability as a Muslim' (Hopkins and Greenwood 2013: 446). When used as a tool of physical concealment from men (*purdah*), the hijab can also further a woman's status (Siraj 2011), actively resist Western sexualisation and enable adherence to cultural codes of conduct based on honour and shame[16] (Werbner 2012). The experience of an active member of the Muslim student society who was strongly criticised for wearing Western clothes without a hijab (see Chapter 2) demonstrates that, while united to some extent through Islam, the Muslim community still presents fragmentations and contradictions that are yet to be resolved. This is especially true when considering that Muslim women often disagree on the nature and the purpose of wearing a hijab.

In her study of Glaswegian Muslims, Siraj (2011) found that more than half of participants who wore the hijab had been regular attendees of *dars*, which is a religious study curriculum widely used in South Asian Islamic schools and which recommends the use of the veil. For some of Siraj's participants, the hijab was not a gender segregationist tool. Instead, it represented a source of empowerment and a way to access public spaces more smoothly. Yet, other respondents noted the sociocultural expectations and pressures placed on women to wear the hijab, to the extent that Siraj (2011: 724) argues that

> The practice of wearing the hijab is not always a personally motivated deci-
> sion, but is open to subtle expectations and parental influence. Early sociali-
> sation of gendered space fostered by a set of moral teaching creates spatial
> identities and an acute awareness that men and women conduct themselves
> differently depending upon the space they occupy. Yet, when one enters the
> space of the other (male), it is women who preserve the boundaries.

According to Siraj's findings, those who do not wear the hijab might do so because they are worried that the veil places women in a submissive and secondary position. These women believe that they can still show modesty by dressing appropriately, for example by not wearing clothes that reveal sexual body parts. Aside from sociocultural connotations, the hijab displays religiosity and obedience to the Islamic faith[17] and this is particularly true for those Muslim women who found in Scotland a home for their rediscovered Muslimness. These social, cultural and religious elements signal the multiple layers underpinning the symbolic meanings of the hijab and the fact that, among Muslim women, who are a very heterogeneous and cosmopolitan group (Bhimji 2012), 'doing femininity' is a very intricate process that brings up interrelated questions of theology, ethics and morality that are difficult to address in a satisfactory fashion. The very complexity of this issue signals an even more important point – namely, that Scotland offers a sociocultural environment generally positive towards, and supportive of, its Muslim population. Nonetheless, it is yet to fully heal Muslim intra-community tensions and theological, ethnic and cultural contradictions.

Conclusion

The transition from ethno-cultural-centrism towards a stronger commitment to Islam has interwoven with proudly national and local Scottish experiences of being Muslim. Coupled with both a political system that has at least aspired to, if not necessarily fully achieved, pluralism, and a sociocultural environment that has cut off racist organisations and Islamophobic sentiments at their roots, the inclusive, open and tolerant nature of Scotland and the friendliness of its population have made life for Muslims a largely enjoyable experience. A key theme that emerges from various pieces of research conducted in Scotland is that perceptions, as much as realities, of the country as a distinctive 'land of tolerance' – often in opposition to a less tolerant and welcoming England – have entered the public imagination and have shaped Muslims' positive feelings of social belonging. The relationship between Muslim and non-Muslim communities has been mutually strengthened in a process of a limited two-way integration, in which both sides have challenged the post-9/11 backlash and have discovered one another.

Muslims have resisted the global stigma attached to their community by proactively opening the doors of their homes and mosques to wider Scottish society, both figuratively and literally. At the same time, a section of the non-Muslim population has reached out to Muslims, driven by a mix of curiosity, solidarity and political sympathies. Formal and less formal organisations have been pivotal in both promoting interfaith and intercommunity dialogue and dispelling myths about what it means to be a Muslim in twenty-first-century Scotland. The role played by Police Scotland and by the Scottish Government has been crucially important too. The 'One Scotland' political manifesto has been proved to be more than simple rhetoric and has helped to create safe spaces for, and show support to, Muslims. Edinburgh's international character, economic and political power, geographically integrated minority groups, tolerant social attitudes and engagement with diversity hold the keys to the shaping of a post-ethnic and transcultural Scottish society. The Scottish future will be a model of local pluralism based upon a community of diversity bound by a set of shared civic values.

Notes

1. Similarly, the current Scottish First Minister Nicola Sturgeon visited Glasgow Central Mosque to give her public tribute to the victims of the Paris attacks in mid-November 2015 (*Scotsman* 2015).

2. Five other Centres exist in as many universities in the United Kingdom (University of Cambridge), United States (Georgetown University and Harvard University), Lebanon (American University of Beirut) and Egypt (American University of Cairo). All such Centres were funded through an endowment from Saudi Arabia's Prince Alwaleed bin Talal and are devoted to the promotion of better mutual understanding between the world of Islam and the Western world.

3. In March 2016, the Church of Scotland and the Islamic Finance Council (IFC) launched a joint plan to create ethical financial services to respond to what Omar Shaikh, a member of the IFC Advisory Board, defines 'morally questionable, somewhat toxic and inherently exclusive' banking and financial products (Bain 2016).

4. Muslim converts are technically considered 'reverts' (and not 'converts'). This follows the Islamic idea that everyone is born Muslim. Therefore, Muslims believe that embracing Islam at a later stage in life is simply a return to one's original, natural religion. Religion in Islam is considered to be a gift from Allah to humankind and not an individual choice.

5. These include the Catholic Bishops' Conference of Scotland, the Christian Institute and the Evangelical Alliance.

6. The legislation eventually came into effect in late 2014.

7. Contest, more often spelled CONTEST, is the acronym for 'COuNter-TErrorism STrategy' – that is, the set of measures to combat terrorism in the United Kingdom.

8. Email from Police Scotland (May 2013).

9. Email from Police Scotland (November 2015).

10. One month later, Sir Bernard Hogan-Howe, the head of the Metropolitan Police Service, visited the Ahmadiyya-affiliated Baitful Futuh Mosque (the largest British mosque) in London to reassure the community (Townsend 2016).

11. Recently, Edinburgh was named the fourth most beautiful city in the world by the *Rough Guides* (*Scotsman* 2016).

12. Leaders of Glasgow Central Mosque, the MCS, the Ahmadiyya Muslim Community Glasgow and New Mercy Asian Church subsequently voiced condemnation of violent extremism (Swindon 2016b).

13. Qadri was sentenced to death for the murder of Taseer in 2011 and executed at Central Jail Rawalpindi, Pakistan, in 2016. While in jail, Qadri incited a prison guard to shoot Mohammad Asghar, a Scottish Pakistani man from Edinburgh, who has been on a death row for blasphemy since early 2014 (Buncombe and Aziz 2014). Asghar's case has been particularly controversial: the 72-year-old man was convicted and sentenced to death for writing that he was the Prophet Muhammad. However, his family has presented evidence that he suffers from paranoid schizophrenia and his lawyer, Aamer Anwar, has argued that there is no justification for the death penalty for blasphemy in Islam (Braiden 2016).

14. The more negative side of this story is that Muslim women have inadequate access to British mosques due both to Islamic sources that make attendance at Friday prayers compulsory for men and optional for women and to entrenched exclusionary practices (Suleiman 2012).

15. Zakir masterfully described the issue here by stating that in South Asian culture 'a man can always have his honour, but when a woman goes out [to a club, on a date and so on] her honour is gone'.

16. Other research found that the hijab both improves body image and decreases the internalisation of media-driven beauty standards (Swami et al. 2013).

17. Whether wearing the hijab is an Islamic prescription or not remains a highly contested issue. More liberal thinkers posit that the Qur'an does not explicitly mention that a woman should cover her hair, but her ornaments and bosom only, and also locate the use of the hijab within specific socio-historical contexts, for example within pre-Islamic Arabic upper-class customs (Siraj 2011).

EPILOGUE: TOWARDS A SCOTTISH COMMUNITARIANISM, WHERE DIVERSITY AND HUMAN UNIVERSALS MEET

Theories and practices of integration are much-needed tools to locate Scottish Muslim experiences within wider European and British contexts and to demonstrate that Scotland has sown the seeds for conciliation between Western society and Islam. Previous discussions on Edinburgh's cosmopolitanism, economic and political power, geographically integrated minorities, tolerant social attitudes and engagement with diversity traced the path of a post-ethnic, transcultural and inclusive idea of society that rests at the heart of the Scottish project. Beyond Edinburgh, and across the country, social bridges are shaped by a civic notion of Scottishness, which many Muslims have keenly embraced and which is grounded on an intercultural humanism driving a communitarian society. This book has described the joys and pains of Muslims' everyday life in Scotland. The final balance speaks of relatively positive experiences of sharing a non-Muslim country with the largely white Scottish majority community. Ten key factors, which have been uncovered throughout this book, play a key role in the successful integration of Muslims in Scotland and will be summarised in the second half of this Epilogue. Taken together, these factors give birth to a 'Scottish dream' of relative tolerance and inclusivity – a relative tolerance and inclusivity that sets Scotland in stark contrast to England and to many European countries.

Integration in Theory and Practice

The idea of integration remains at the heart of early social theorists' concern to understand social relations and labour division in modern societies (Meer 2014a). While this book is not a treatise on theories of integration, it is useful to remind readers of the key concepts that have shaped the field. Tönnies (1974 [1887]) skilfully posited that social relations in modern societies had migrated away from a traditional form of community called *Gemeinschaft*. *Gemeinschaft* was characterised by the strong personal relationships typical of a family, by a unity of will (that is, the idea that the interests of the community come before self-interest), by a moderate division of labour and by fairly simple social institutions. Tönnies's idea of a traditional form of community goes hand in hand with Durkheim's (1984 [1893]) concept of mechanical solidarity, which features cohesive, homogeneous, typically traditional and simple kinship-based societies. On the other hand, Tönnies proposed that modern society, which he termed *Gesellschaft*, is based upon looser and more superficial and transitional, yet wider, social networks, associations and mechanical aggregations, which pursue self-interest within a structured system underpinned by strong labour division and class conflicts. Modern society marries well with Durkheim's idea of organic solidarity, which expresses itself in advanced societies characterised by the interdependence of their members through division of labour, socio-economic organisation and social bonds.

Notions and practices of integration remain ambivalent. In Great Britain, a model of integration 'has never been clearly defined' (Saggar and Sommerville 2012: 1). Wider European policies rolled out to advance the integration of Muslims within European societies normally gravitate around four main proposals: state neutrality, legal pluralism, group-based autonomy for national or regional minorities, and special rights for minority groups (Angenendt 2007). In Statham's (2016) study of Great Britain, the Netherlands, France and Germany, ordinary non-Muslim people and Muslims report different views of what Muslim group rights should be. Unsurprisingly, Muslims are more in favour of extending Muslim group rights than the non-Muslim majority is. In Great Britain and in the Netherlands, 'significantly extending Muslim group rights does not seem to bring majorities and Muslims to a consensus' (Statham 2016: 233). This is almost paradoxical in a country, Great Britain, where a supportive range of policies and public debates are not matched by a similarly positive public attitude to the extension of Muslim group rights (Statham 2016). Statham's explanation is very intriguing, albeit speculative. According to the scholar, the absence of strong anti-Islamic political actors coalesces majority public frustration at both Islam and perceived Muslim privilege, which some people believe to be promoted by a politically correct Establishment. Research conducted among British Somalis (Scuzzarello 2015) adds an important nuance to discussions on integration policies. It demonstrates that British Somalis construct their membership in the polity over and beyond the integration concepts that are propounded by policymakers and politicians.

Recent theorisations of integration often refer to post-migration relations and to the ways in which societies deal with cultural difference in contexts coloured by a plurality of races and ethnicities (Meer 2014a). Eriksen (2006: 14) posits that diversity is 'largely aesthetic, politically and morally neutral expressions of cultural difference' and, therefore, tends to be more easily accepted in the public sphere. On the contrary, difference is often considered in negative terms as

> Morally objectionable or at least questionable notions and practices in a minority group or category, that is to say notions and practices which are held to (i) create conflicts through direct contact with majorities who hold other notions, (ii) weaken social solidarity in the country and thereby the legitimacy of the political and welfare systems, and (iii) lead to unacceptable violations of human rights within the minority groups. (Eriksen 2006: 14–15)

Difference is popularly associated with immigrants and their descendants and considered to cause social problems (Eriksen 2006). Somewhat in line with the arguments espoused by Sartori (2000), Eriksen logically concludes that the demarcation between acceptable and unacceptable cultural differences risks hiding broader and deeper political and class conflicts. Since who and what people are is discerned by understanding who and what they are not (Cesareo 2000), difference underpins individual identities (Jenkins 2008). It is therefore unsurprising that difference plays such a key role in social relations. It is from this position that some intellectuals advocate for 'the right to have one's "difference" (minority ethnicity, etc.) recognised and supported in both the public and the private spheres' (Modood 2003: 105). Social acceptance and recognition of difference lie at the heart of heated contemporary debates on the place of religion in the public sphere. Tensions over Islamic symbols are encapsulated by public discussions on the burqa in Great Britain (Meer et al. 2015). In France, the role of the burqa led to long-standing social issues (Choudhury 2007) and legal arguments, eventually culminating in its official ban from public life in 2010. The British tradition of giving asylum to radical Islamist preachers has also tapped into concerns over the integration of highly political forms of Islam, which were brought onto the streets of London and other major cities in the 1980s and 1990s. During those years, fundamentalist preachers, such as Omar Bakri Muhammad, Abu Hamza al-Masri and Abu Qatada al-Filistini, arrived in the country 'fresh from the politically repressive societies of the Muslim world' (Hellyer 2007b: 3) and soon encouraged 'followers to adopt extreme political narratives and pursue activities designed to support the global fundamentalist struggle' (Herrington 2015: 15; see also Pantucci 2015).

Going even further back in time, British policies of opening the door to mass immigration after the Second World War have been accused of being responsible for Muslim communities' isolation from mainstream society (Leiken 2005). Leiken's criticism of overly stretched British liberalism is, in Brighton's (2007) work, better described as the failure of multiculturalism to tackle socio-economic marginalisation and grant political equality to minorities. The Brixton Riots of 1981 and the Rushdie Affair of 1988–9 are clear examples of the troubled relationships between ethnic and religious minorities and wider society. Community cohesion and the integration of diversity in Great Britain rest on the fragile terrain of fragmented Muslim communities. The country lacks the ethno-cultural mix of Northern Ireland, which is composed of 'longstanding and now approximately equally-sized communities' (Herbert 2012: 357). Lacking such distinctiveness and being 'a product of rapid immigration creating a multicultural, multi-religious society within a couple of generations' (Herbert 2012: 357), Great Britain has not yet managed to reconcile its ethno-cultural fragmentations.

In Brighton's (2007: 10) own words, racial segregation has shaped 'a multi-ethnic [Great] Britain composed of "communities" without a "meta-community" to tie them together'. These arguments became particularly pertinent in the wake of 9/11 and, especially, 7/7, when British society and the government started focusing on integration in order to re-conceptualise the meanings of citizenship and group identity formation (Modood and Salt 2011). Emerging policies and evolving ideas around citizenship, social cohesion and social capital led to criticism of previous understandings of integration, multiculturalism and equality. An attack on multiculturalism as 'the culprit of [Great] Britain's security woes' (Meer and Modood 2009: 481) was born out of both the increased security focus on Muslim communities in the early twenty-first century and the belief that Muslims have problems accommodating to the values of liberal democracy. To counterbalance this view, scholars such as Meer (2014d) maintain that historical colonial dynamics play a key role in today's postcolonial environments and that European civilisation has traditionally encountered difficulties in accepting difference as part of common life.

While blaming either European societies or Islamic values risks significantly overlooking the sociocultural nuances of the debate, at the core of European polities rests an imperfect project of 'cultural conversation'. Converging Islamic and Western values (Coles 2009) have not been fully recognised by different European countries. Continuing obstacles to implementing a neutral state, or a moderate secular state (Modood 2010), which should allow the accommodation of different religions (Madeley 2003), demonstrate the limits of the current cultural conversations between different ethnic, faith and non-faith groups in Europe. In Great Britain, the ongoing debates over shari'a law courts (Zee 2016) and forced marriage (Bonino 2016a) are a warning that some conservative Muslims are yet to fully adapt to existing legal frameworks and social norms.

The religious expectations from some Muslim leaders that legal duality and shari'a be applied in private law (Klausen 2005) or in the resolution of any dispute, collides with traditional understandings of the cultural, legal and political boundaries of Western societies. At the same time, different Western integration policies have often proved to be contradictory, if not paradoxical. Demonstrating the limits of British integration policies, Joppke (2009: 467, emphasis in the original) argues that

> Considering that, in the dreaded 'Jacobin state' across the Channel, which did much less on the 'respect and recognition' front and instead prescribed

one-size-fits-all *citoyenneté* on its Muslim minority, the non-Muslim majority *and* the Muslim minority held equally benign views of one another,
one might take this as a failure of British multiculturalism and a success of
French Republicanism.

How diversity and difference play out, or should play out, in society generally
depends on what position one takes on integration: the one-way assimilationist stance or the two-way adaptive stance. The receiving sociocultural context also matters. This issue is particularly magnified in discourses around the
sociocultural values, norms and positions that Muslims should adopt within
host European countries. Cultural and ethnic separateness and the creation of
parallel societies,[1] such as the French *banlieues* and 'Londonistan', are often
used as evidence of a perceived integration problem within Muslim communities (Tibi 2010). This position sits within the idea that cultural and ethnic
conflicts between Muslims and Europeans have been drawn along the lines
of a lack of mutual acceptance and recognition, as well as tensions over the
validity of differing values.

In this respect, Tibi (2007 and 2010) has called Muslims to adjust to
Europe's foundational values, such as secularism, cultural modernity, religious
pluralism, individual human rights and tolerance. Heated debates (Phillips
2006) over the increasing numbers of Muslims living in Europe (Taspinar
2003; Savage 2004), often fuelled by high birth rates and migration, have
gone as far as to posit the ongoing emergence of 'a flourishing young Islamic
civilization'[2] (Sendagorta 2005: 70) and the so-called 'Islamisation' of Europe
(Fallaci 2004; Caldwell 2009). While these claims have been contested as exaggerated European worries (Meer 2012), such discourses highlight the problematic nature of integration in practice. This is particularly true when Muslim
religious, ethnic and cultural diversity and national values are considered to be
mutually exclusive components of society, despite the sociocultural benefits of
upholding both an ethnic identity and a national identity (Kymlicka 2012).
Global surveys demonstrate that the relationships between Europeans and
Muslims are very complex and heterogeneous (Pew Global Attitudes Project
2006 and 2011). The refugee crisis and the emergence of the Islamic State have
resulted in increasingly unfavourable views about Muslims among Europeans
(Pew Global Attitudes Project 2016). However, people living in Spain (52 per

cent), Germany (69 per cent), the United Kingdom (72 per cent) and France (76 per cent) hold more positive views of Muslims than people in Poland (30 per cent) and Italy (31 per cent) (Pew Global Attitudes Project 2015).

The idea of an Islamic bond of faith that could provide unconditional solidarity and support calls into question the identity of Muslims as a global community and the values in which Western and Islamic societies are grounded. It is true that Muslim political identities based on religion alone collide with European secularism (Hellyer 2007b). However, it is equally true that, as Tibi (2010: 128) posits, 'an individual can simultaneously be a Muslim by faith and a European by civic values'. In this sense, Scuzzarello (2015: 1230) claims that

> The British 'civic' citizenship model has created an institutional structure within which minority groups can participate fully. The British model of race relations, focusing on equality, is paralleled by a culturally pluralist conception of citizenship which seeks to retain diversity among minorities living in [Great] Britain by allowing its residents to follow a variety of cultural patterns. Religion is relegated to a matter of private individual conscience within public institutions.

This argument could not be any stronger than in Scotland, where a civically oriented nationalism and a strong political narrative of ethnic inclusion have drawn into their net a large chunk of the Muslim community. Scotland demonstrates that John Esposito's preoccupation, which is achieving 'mutual understanding that leads to a healthy sense of pluralism and tolerance' (Kalin 2001: 158), has been allayed through a mixture of political astuteness, cultural acceptance and social openness.

Scotland at the Crossroads of Diversity and Human Universals

The proposition for an integrationist and pluralist society – a community of communities (Parekh 2000b; Farrar 2012) – is grounded on a shared set of liberal values, sense of citizenship and belonging and recognition of minorities (Meer and Modood 2009). Such a society retains a strong communitarian ethos in the form of

> A social philosophy that maintains that society should articulate what is good – that such articulations are both needed and legitimate. [. . .]

> Communitarians examine the ways shared conceptions of the good (values) are formed, transmitted, justified, and enforced. Hence their interest in communities (and moral dialogues within them), historically transmitted values and mores, and the societal units that transmit and enforce values such as the family, schools, and voluntary associations (social clubs, churches, and so forth), which are all parts of communities. (Etzioni 2003: 224)

But the sort of communitarianism that Scottish Muslims have enacted is far from a historically driven and culturally imposed one. Instead, it is a jointly and democratically shaped communitarianism through which individuals share mutual social responsibilities within and towards their wider community (Taylor 1994). It is bound by social capital, which are those social bridges and bonds that can bring together different people (Putnam 2000) under an overarching sense of being Scottish, albeit one that is played out in multiple and fragmented ways. The communitarian ethos is already inscribed within Islam, given that 'Muslims may be seen to give to the common good when conflict of interest arises between the individual and the community' (Suleiman 2012: 15). However, for committed Muslims, community interests do not precede individual rights: Islam will always remain 'a religion, a moral code, and a way of life which, like all religions, must take the individual as its primary focus' (Suleiman 2012: 15). In this respect, the communitarianism proposed here takes into account the competing interests that religion, nation and society play in the shaping of the Scottish Muslim community. While Islam continues to be the primary identification of many Scottish Muslims, belonging to the country and active participation in the affairs of the polity allow civic notions of being Scottish to enter a fruitful dialogue and engagement with religion. This process follows the proposal that Goodhart spells out for Great Britain in terms of

> A 'citizen nation' – crossing class and ethnic boundaries – in which as many people as possible move beyond being 'mere' citizens who obey the law and pay their taxes to 'virtuous' citizens [. . .] who join in the social and political life of the country, in however small a way. (Goodhart 2013: 315)

This idea has taken a distinctive form and has gained traction in Scotland, with its 'firsts' in politics, Bashir Maan and Mohammad Sarwar, and a Muslim community that is increasingly active in the public life of the country. Open and proud identification with Scotland only strengthens Muslims' expressed commitment to the country. Muslim narratives of belonging to Scotland are favourably located within notions of an inclusive Scottish nationalism that can fend off the assault of a less palatable politics emanating from south of the border (McConaghy 2015). In this respect, McConaghy (2015: 9) wisely reminds readers that

> Scotland, having more progressive attitudes on a range of economic and social issues than the rest of the United Kingdom, allows Scottish national-ism to highlight the potential for an independent Scotland to escape the conservatism that is imposed on them as a result of their membership of the United Kingdom.

The quest for a 'good society', one that Etzioni (2002) defines as striking the right balance between, on the one hand, autonomy and liberty and, on the other hand, social bonds and social order, takes place within social environ-ments that are sensitive to the variegated yet often common needs of their different cultural constituencies. Whenever these sets of elements are in a mutually high and antagonistically low relationship, authentic communi-ties based on the true needs of their members flourish (Etzioni 1996). A good society therefore emerges within a context that 'allows communities to maintain some limitations on new membership while at the same time greatly restrict[s] the criteria that communities may use in forming such exclusivity' (Etzioni 2003: 85). In Etzioni's (2003) worldview, exclusion in a good soci-ety must not be driven by race, ethnic origin, religion, sexual orientation or other similar criteria. On the contrary, a good society remains glued together through admittedly vaguely defined bonds of affinity. Brown's human uni-versals (1991) help define these values – values that find a fertile ground in the Scottish civic landscape. According to Brown (2004: 47),

> Human universals – of which hundreds have been identified – consist of those features of culture, society, language, behavior, and mind that, so far as the record has been examined, are found among all peoples known to ethnography and history.

In his exploration of the nature versus nurture debate and in a convincing use of key psychobiological and evolutionary tools to explain human nature,

Brown describes human universals as the transcultural and trans-historical elements at the core of world societies. The common traits that Brown (1991 and 2004) identifies as cutting through different cultures (daily routines, myths, legends and so on), societies (division of labour, kinship systems, family, social groups and so on), languages (grammar, phonemes and so on), behaviours (gestures, facial expressions and so on) and mental states (empathy, emotions and so on) demonstrate that communities have at their disposal a common 'space' and 'language' for dialogue. Widely popularised in Steven Pinker's (2002) masterpiece *The Blank Slate: The Modern Denial of Human Nature*, Brown's human universals constitute the basis of an intercultural humanism that drives much thinking behind the civic notion of Scottishness.

Throughout this book, Scottishness has emerged as a fluid and inclusive sociocultural category that brings together a variegated pool of people, who share a sense of belonging, however defined, to Scotland. The Scottish capital city, Edinburgh, with its cosmopolitan nature, economic and political power, geographically dispersed and integrated minorities, tolerant social attitudes and engagement with diversity exemplifies a post-ethnic, transcultural society. Held together by the recognition of human universals and naturally located within Scotland's tradition of social justice and equality, 'good community' in Edinburgh and in Scotland emerges also thanks to Muslims' contribution to the fostering of social bridges and the shaping of a democratically agreed set of civic values.

The sociopolitical mobilisation of young Scottish Muslims is an element that well illustrates the landscape against which a Scottish sense of being Muslim has been played out in the country. Admittedly, this mobilisation does not represent a uniquely Scottish or Muslim phenomenon. Sander and Putnam (2010: 11) demonstrate that youth interest in politics has surged in the years since 9/11, to the extent that, in the United States, 'the share of college freshmen who said that they had "discussed politics" [. . .] has more than doubled and is now [, in 2010,] at an all-time high of 36 percent'. In her in-depth study of English Muslims, Kabir (2010) contends that biculturalism can help Muslims integrate within wider society by retaining ethnic cultures and languages while adding the cultures and languages of the host society. From a social cohesion perspective, this position is impeccable, although it overlooks the fact that many Muslims in Great Britain are born and bred in the country and do not require much directed learning activity. British-born Muslims speak English as their mother language. Many of these Muslims eat fish and chips like any other native British person does. But in Scotland this situation presents further nuances, insofar as the appeal of Scottish nationalism has drawn into its net a large quota of (predominantly Scottish-born) Muslims. The fusion between Scottish identity and Islam, rather than ethnic culture and language, within younger generations opens up possibilities for mutual dialogue between nation and religion in the shaping of a moderate Islam that can be accommodated within the porous cultural structures of Scotland.

But the dividing lines between the older generations and the younger generations have partly fractured the Scottish Muslim community, demonstrating the significance of ongoing generational changes. In January 2016, public revelations that Glasgow Central Mosque had breached legal duties (Leask 2016a) and could be exploited by money launderers (Leask 2016g) spotlighted issues of governance and institutional development, as well as the tensions between the orthodox and the reformist sections of the Scottish Pakistani community. Amid claims (Leask 2016a) that the management of the mosque funnelled £50,000 to the European headquarters of the Tablighi Jamaat, an orthodox revivalist Sunni movement, in Dewsbury in 2011, the younger liberal generations have collided with the 'founding fathers', who have controlled the mosque since it was built in 1984. Younger generations who feel that they are silenced by older community leaders (BBC Radio 4) want to pass on a new message to the community: the mosque is a place open to all Muslims, irrespective of ethnic and national origin.

This is the cry of a new local *umma*, which feels Muslim but belongs to Scotland. Yet, members of the older, socially conservative Pakistani-born generation of Muslims have resisted institutional reform and cultural change (Leask 2016b), save for the appointment of a Somali man as the first ever non-Pakistani committee member in May 2016 (Leask 2016m). In a scathing attack published in the *Herald Scotland* a few months earlier, Aamer Anwar (2016) denounced the older Pakistani generation's quasi-feudal system of managing mosques and their demeaning approach to women. Noticing the irony of 'standing in photo calls with First Minister Nicola Sturgeon' but finding it 'so difficult to call on Muslim women to join them, even for a photo' (Anwar 2016), Anwar lamented the absence of women among the committee members and the trustees of Glasgow Central Mosque. Similarly, Humza Yousaf called the exclusion of women from the mosque committee 'a disgrace' (Leask 2016f).

Still considered too much of a sexual temptation for male Muslims to bear at a sacred place, women are not allowed to pray in the same room with men, while white converts to Islam suffer from deep-rooted prejudice at the hands of what Anwar (2016) describes as '"Citizen Khan wannabes" [. . . who] are in essence frightened old men, who fear losing their status'. But this situation is not uniquely Scottish, given the fact that 'over 40 per cent of Deobandi mosques in the UK do not admit women' (Bowen 2014: 30). Liberal Scottish Pakistanis, who had briefly managed to take control of Glasgow Central Mosque, were forced to resign in February 2016. Mosque president Maqbool Rasul, general secretary Nabeel Shaikh, joint general secretary Jamil Moghul and office-holders Chaudhary Shahid, Imran Bashir, Munawar Akbar and Rashid Khaliq left their positions, alleging that they and their families had received threats from orthodox members of the community (Coyle 2016; Leask 2016h and 2016k). The latter dismissed the accusations (Leask 2016j and 2016k), maintained that Islam is unchangeable and argued that rules for mosques are inscribed in the religion (Leask 2016i). Once the associates of the orthodox elders retook control of the mosque, they sent a clear message to the reformists, by suspending the weekly lunches for visitors and worshippers that had been instituted as a symbol of openness (Leask 2016l). The cultural turf war between the older and orthodox and the younger and liberal Scottish Pakistanis exemplifies the slow and troubled process of generational change.

The murder of Asad Shah and the security concerns expressed by his family demonstrate that Scottish Muslims are divided along sectarian lines too. Imam Daud Ahmad of Bait Ur Rahman Mosque in Glasgow, the only place of worship for the around 500 members of the Scottish Ahmadiyya community, posits that divisions trouble different Islamic denominations (Swindon 2016a). Anti-Ahmadiyya conferences and leaflets at Glasgow Central Mosque are cases in point (Porter 2016). While intra-community tensions are likely to persist for the foreseeable future, the increased diversity within the Muslim community – a community that is expanding and is not bound by ethnic ties alone – reflects the changing nature of being Muslim in the Scottish context. In a country that is still largely populated by white Scottish people (84 per cent of the total population), and by whites more generally (96 per cent of the total population) (National Records of Scotland 2013), the concept of diversity finds particular relevance *within* the Muslim community, rather than *outside* it. As Aberdeen, Dundee and Edinburgh demonstrate, Muslim communities are a variegated mix of ethnicities, languages and cultures. Islam is the 'universal' that glues these different Muslim constituencies together, as much as Scottishness is the 'universal' that glues Muslim and non-Muslim communities together through common civic values and a sense of national belonging. In this real-world case study of Brown's human universals, many Scottish Muslims and non-Muslims have found common ground in their shared sense of being human, however differently it is played out in a variety of contexts. The basis for the 'Scottish dream' rests on the unique experiences of Muslim life in the country, as well as in Scotland's peculiar social, political and cultural environment.

The Scottish Dream

The migration, settlement and development of Muslim communities in Scotland examined in this book have highlighted several elements suggesting a trend of generally positive life experiences in the country. These final pages will summarise the ten key factors that bring together the author's primary research and other studies explored throughout this book that can help explain the good relationships between Scotland and its Muslim population. These ten factors, and the book overall, should not be interpreted as promoting the myth of Scotland as a paradise on Earth or overlooking the socialisation difficulties, the ethno-religious discrimination and the institutional problems faced by Scottish Muslims. Instead, it should be considered as the starting point for understanding what makes Scotland a certainly imperfect yet a relatively successful model for the integration of Muslim communities in a European country.

1. A small, dispersed community

The Muslim community in Scotland is small both in absolute numbers and relative to the total Muslim population in Great Britain. With fewer than 77,000 members in 2011 – although the figure today could reasonably be over 100,000 – and accounting for a very small proportion of the total Scottish population, the presence of Muslims in Scotland is not bound to fuel as much public resistance as in England or in major continental European countries. Integration within the wider urban space is enforced by virtue of necessity. The reality is that ethnic segregation is not very widespread, with the exception of East Pollokshields and Govanhill in Glasgow, where ethnic clustering persists but levels are falling and remain lower than in major cities in England and Wales. With generally positive experiences of life in Scotland, Muslims may well confirm the validity of contact theory. Moreover, a small Muslim population makes it easier for local authorities to address social grievances and for police and the security service to monitor risky individuals. Social grievances constitute the key ingredient in community tensions, resentment among Muslims and insecurity within the non-Muslim population. The Scottish environment and the small Muslim population conveniently ensure that these grievances do not grow out of proportion.

2. A predominantly self-employed community

The Scottish Pakistani tradition of self-employment (Bailey, Bowes and Sim 1995) has evolved from low-paying jobs as pedlars in the mid-1920s to today's more lucrative ownership of grocery shops, takeaways, restaurants and cash and carry warehouses. Boasting the highest proportion of self-employed people among all minority ethnic groups and employing half of its members in the distribution, hotels and restaurants industry, the Pakistani community has stayed away from job competition with the non-Muslim majority. Instead of taking jobs away from native Scottish people, Pakistanis have created job opportunities for both Muslims and non-Muslims. As the minority ethnic group most likely to feature managers, directors and senior officials among its members, Scottish Pakistanis have sown the seeds for economic success in the country and have presented a public image as a hard-working community. The relatively well-off status of the first Pakistani migrants originating from the Punjab has also helped the community to establish financially stable living conditions for subsequent generations. Through a mixture of continuing self-employment and entry into the professions, the future of today's community looks much brighter than the future of the Pakistani families who migrated from the Mirpur to major English cities.

3. Muslims have stayed away from major troubles

Not only have Pakistanis in Scotland promoted a positive business image to the public and preferred house ownership and private renting, thus avoiding competition for public services in the 1950s and 1960s, but they have also, and very importantly, stayed away from major troubles. The 1988–9 disturbances related to the Rushdie Affair and the 2001 and 2011 England riots were not mirrored by similar violent action in Scotland. It is true that the small Scottish Muslim community has a limited capacity to mobilise on the streets compared to its English counterpart. It is also true that South Asian gangs, who have populated Glasgow since the 1960s (Azam 2006) and have mostly fought against other South Asian gangs, have also clashed with the white majority. However, violent tensions between South Asians and white people, such as those in Pollokshields in 2003, have 'never reached the scale of the riots of Bradford, Burnley or Birmingham [. . . mostly] due to the good relations between the local Asian community leaders and the local white community' (Sarwar 2016: 8).

Notably, the English riots in 2001 and 2011 were also a result of context-specific relations between local ethnic minorities in the English cities involved and the white community, including the police. In Scotland, a lack of violent street protests and riots, possibly coupled with a relative lack of concern about discrimination on the part of the first generations of Muslim migrants, has had a widely positive effect on community relations. Alex Salmond's public statement from Glasgow Central Mosque following the Glasgow bombing of 2007 demonstrates that Scotland's political astuteness has managed to keep a lid on those feelings of anger that have troubled a section of the English Muslim community and that have been directed towards Westminster and English society.

4. Anglophobia and sectarianism can displace Islamophobia

It would be misleading to claim that Scotland is a paradise of cultural tolerance. Yet, it would be equally inaccurate to treat the subject of discrimination in Scotland without contextualising it within the country's sociocultural structures. This book has demonstrated that discrimination against Muslims, or ethnic minorities normally describing themselves as Muslim, *does* exist but exists to a *relatively* lower extent than it does in England. Structurally, there are two key elements that help explain the relatively lower levels of discrimination in Scotland: Anglophobia and sectarianism. Anglophobia has been well documented in Hussain and Miller's research and has gained traction with the independence impetus. While a quest for independence per se does not entail a deep-rooted dislike for, and prejudice against, English people, the political stances taken by the SNP have often been shaped in open opposition to Westminster's policies. The Scottish Government's fierce opposition to the Trident nuclear programme, anti-Israel stances, open-door policies for Syrian refugees, condemnation for the air strikes in Syria, defence of Russian president Vladimir Putin, constant criticism of the British government and strong pro-European Union approach exemplify the fault lines that divide Scottish and English politics and that, at the same time, unite Muslims and the Scots.

At the cultural level, Muslims resort to proud Scottish identities, which are often conceptualised in opposition to notions of English identity. Being Scottish 'because we are not English' may well have become a new badge of identity for a generation of Scottish people, whether Muslims or non-Muslims, who are disenfranchised by a political system that is perceived to be concentrated in the palaces of power in London. At the same time, the historical sectarian tensions between Catholics and Protestants have partly cushioned other religious minorities from more serious prejudice. Muslims have certainly suffered ethno-religious discrimination, particularly after 9/11. But the hostilities that Irish Catholics faced until recent times may have lessened the impact of anti-Muslim prejudice, in a country, Scotland, where the 'Other' and the religious scapegoat is historically identified as white and Catholic, rather than brown and Muslim.

5. Police stops and searches on the street do not target black and minority ethnic groups

Lower levels of discrimination against Muslims in Scotland compared to England are not simply a matter of perception. In certain aspects of everyday life, they are a documented fact. This book has presented statistics demonstrating that stops and searches on Scottish streets have not targeted BME groups to the same extent that they have in England and Wales. In this respect, policing activities south of the border have disproportionately entailed the securitisation of black and Asian ethnic minorities, thus fuelling discontent and feelings of being institutionally discriminated against. Conversely, police in Scotland have disproportionately stopped and searched young people rather than ethnic groups per se. As Murray's (2015: 63) research on stop and search demonstrates, 'in Scotland, there appears to be no robust evidence of discrimination in terms of race and ethnicity'. Within a fragile sociopolitical context, in which Muslim communities in England lament intrusive police action, Scotland has managed not to alienate its minorities. Controversial as they are, stops and searches in Scotland have at least managed to redirect criticism towards the extensive use of the non-statutory variety (Murray 2014), rather than the targeting of BME groups.

6. A lack of minority claims

The fact that Muslims in Scotland form part of a small, dispersed and relatively well-off community has facilitated social integration. This same community has ostensibly refrained from advancing serious minority claims. As Meer notes in his research, neither faith nor language claims have been strongly pursued in the quest for institutional recognition. Scotland has yet to open the doors to its first Muslim school, while Urdu, the language spoken by many Pakistani Muslims, is nowhere near achieving institutional recognition or the cultural importance that Gaelic possesses. A lack of serious minority claims, in a context that has not restricted Muslims' capacity to voice their aspirations for recognition, has played out to the advantage of sociocultural cohesion. Although Urdu and Islamic schools have not entered the institutional landscape, Muslim communities have still managed to make Scotland their home, express strong allegiance to the country and achieve positions of political power.

7. The 'no problem here' attitude

The relatively positive experiences of Muslims in Scotland hide a darker side: the so-called 'no problem here' attitude (Dunlop 1993) among first-generation Muslims. As the earlier South Asian migrants were primarily focused on improving their baseline financial conditions, it is likely that discrimination was relegated to the status of a 'lesser evil' compared to the 'greater evil' that a life of economic hardship in India (and, subsequently,

Pakistan) would have afforded them. The foundations of the Scottish myth of tolerance may well have been laid through a mixture of social inaction in the face of discrimination and a life of relative financial gratification compared to the experiences of countrymen both back home and in England. While younger Muslim generations have been very vocal about the prejudice that they suffer, particularly so after 9/11, and have mobilised politically for both global and local causes, it would be naïve to assume that their parents' and relatives' memories have not impacted on their views of Scotland. Much like a placebo, the 'no problem here' attitude has helped foster the notion of a country that positively caters for its Muslim community. Perceptions and realities do not always and necessarily match. Yet, the key to social cohesion lies in different ethno-cultural constituencies' feelings of belonging to the values, symbols and traditions of a nation. While maintaining their own religious principles, Scottish Muslims have managed to foster a Scottish sense of being Muslim.

8. 'One Scotland' and a shared national narrative

The 'One Scotland' manifesto has been the shrewdest political stratagem that the Scottish Government could put in place to take forward the narrative of a civically based nationalism. While the spectre of populism looms behind any type of nationalism, and the SNP has ostensibly embraced rabidly anti-English positions, the political stances taken by the SNP have undoubtedly gained unprecedented popular consent. The various factors summarised so far have helped to give momentum to this manifesto. The small Muslim community has not advanced serious minority claims and, instead, has taken up the rhetorical and political idea of an inclusive Scottish identity, which people of various ethnic and religious groups can claim so long as they act for the good of Scotland. Although identity operates in much more complex ways, and Scots may not necessarily accept Muslims' claims of Scottishness at all times, the country offers a relatively safe space for public recognition.

The Scottish Government has also done much to support a shared national narrative by voicing a politics of inclusiveness rather than ethnic exclusivity. Political statements in favour of immigration,[3] asylum-seekers and refugees and in opposition to the Iraq War have won the support of many Muslims (*Economist* 2009). It is beyond the scope of this book to discuss the credibility and impact of these political stances. Domestic and foreign policies need to consider wider national and geopolitical dynamics and interests rather than simply meeting the expectations of Muslim communities. But, certainly, there can be no better sociopolitical marketing tool to draw Muslims into the SNP's ideological ranks than opposition to controversial policies enacted by the much-disliked London elites.

9. A progressive politics and a civic nationalism

Scotland's progressive politics functions as a shield against widespread anti-Muslim sentiments. Its long-standing social democratic and centre-left stances historically opposed Margaret Thatcher's conservatism (Devine 2016) and are mirrored by the persisting tensions with the British government. Scottish politics promotes a utopian, proto-social egalitarianism that symbolically connects with a historical sense of oppression at the hands of the English and conveniently allows Muslim communities to join the Scots on the 'oppression caravan'. Anti-English feelings and the lack of an established fascist tradition have starved racist movements of the oxygen that they need to take root in the country. The fact that EDL members have to join the ranks of the SDL to generate enough demonstrators encapsulates the invisibility of racist groups in Scotland. The fact of counter-demonstrators outnumbering members of the Defence Leagues speaks to the heart of Scottish intolerance for street bigotry. Arguably, the key Scottish feature that stands out is a strongly civic nationalism – a concept of nation that moves beyond strict ethnic boundaries and construes belonging to the polity around an inclusive approach to citizenship and a commitment to equality. The SNP's manifesto for an independent Scotland was built around 'a commitment to a multi-cultural Scotland' in which people 'are accustomed to multiple identities, be they national, regional, ethnic, linguistic or religious' (Scottish Government 2013b: 271). Scotland's progressive politics and civic nationalism manifest themselves in what Meer (2015a) has dubbed 'aspirational pluralism' and finds evidence in more migrant-friendly attitudes compared to England. Scotland's progressive politics and civic nationalism share some notable trans-Atlantic similarities with Canada, particularly so under the leadership of the Liberal Party led by Justin Trudeau. Canada has managed to foster some of the highest levels of Muslim integration (Vidgor 2011) and acceptance (Neuman 2016) and shares with Scotland a multicultural political ethos. What McGrath (2012) defines 'the "small n" Canadian nationalism of the 1970s onward: welcoming, inclusive, peaceful' closely resembles today's Scottish nationalism, with its power to alienate English elites and win Muslim hearts. Furthermore, Canadian refusal to invade Iraq in 2003 and primarily non-militaristic approach to the ongoing war against the Islamic State (Labott 2016) resonate with Scottish political attitudes toward war. Lastly, the Scottish government's promise to remove nuclear weapons from the country, yet join NATO, should the 2014 independence referendum have succeeded, shows striking similarities with the Canadian experience of abandoning its nuclear arsenal in 1984 while remaining a full member of NATO (McGrath 2012).

10. The myth of Scottish tolerance and historical amnesia

The idea that Scotland is somehow more tolerant than England continues to persist among various members of the Muslim community. Scottish Muslims are often apt to remember that 'there must be something' about Scotland that allowed a small community to boast both the first Muslim MP (Mohammad Sarwar) and the first Muslim councillor (Bashir Maan) in Great Britain. The stories of these two Muslim pioneers are now written in the history books.

Bashir Maan moved up the ranks from his position as a travelling salesman to the directorship of a grocery store chain, and later to his election as, first, a Justice of the Peace in Scotland in 1968 and, second, a Muslim councillor in Great Britain in 1970. His trilogy of books document the lives and the memories of numerous Muslim pioneers in Scotland. In his autobiography, Mohammad Sarwar (2016) reminisces about his rise to fame and political power from the hardship of his childhood and teenage years in rural Pakistan. Sarwar migrated to Glasgow aged twenty-four, in 1976, and built a wholesale cash and carry business empire with a turnover exceeding £200 million a year. His election as MP for Glasgow Govan in 1997 catapulted him to the forefront of British politics and his oath of allegiance on the Qur'an, in the House of Commons, made history. His re-election in 2001 (Glasgow Govan) and in 2005 (Glasgow Central) reaffirmed Sarwar's prominence within the Labour Party. More recently, he served as Governor of

Punjab in Pakistan before resigning in January 2015 and joining the Pakistan Tehreek-e-Insaf (PTI), a centrist political party promoting social welfare, in February of the same year.

At a very delicate time in the history of Islamic–Western relations, the generally positive relations between Muslims and many non-Muslim Scots bolster the notion of Scottish tolerance. People's interest in discovering Islam demonstrates the relative openness of the Scottish population towards other cultures and faiths. By reducing the existing strain on, and valorising, Muslims' visible diversity, Scotland has attempted to mobilise its porous sociocultural boundaries in the shaping of a sense of Scottishness that is civically inclusive. However, the myth of Scottish tolerance lives in a world of legends and facts, symbols and statistics, perceptions and realities. As is often the case, the truth resides in the middle. The success stories of Bashir Maan and Mohammad Sarwar should not overshadow historical problems of ethnoreligious discrimination. Prejudice against migrant labour and Scotland's active involvement in the British Empire – a major theme in Scottish historiography in recent times – are just two key examples. It is crucially important that any credible study of Scottish society drops the veil from the deep-rooted historical amnesia that conveniently forgets the country's past of active prejudice towards non-native Scots.

Conclusion

Fifteen years have passed since 11 September 2001, and yet Muslims remain in the public eye across every Western society. Political and media debates have forcefully discussed the fragile relationship between the West and Islam amid the rise of the Islamic State in the Middle East and the ongoing domestic security risks posed by Islamist terrorism. Theories and practices of integration have, at various times since the Rushdie Affair, sentenced Muslim and non-Muslim communities to an inescapable future of cultural wars and social antagonism. Pessimists have declared Europe to be slowly morphing into an Islamic colony. Propagandists have blamed white Europeans and Americans for every illness affecting Muslim communities.

European Muslim and non-Muslim communities indisputably face cultural conflicts. The ultra-conservative attitudes of some Muslims, a fixed notion of Europe as white and Christian, geopolitical tensions, and the coterminous rise of extremist Islamist organisations, such as the now proscribed al-Muhajiroun and its mutations, and anti-Muslim far-right groups, such as the Patriotic Europeans Against the Islamisation of the West (PEGIDA), are only a few factors driving these conflicts. While Scotland has not been left untouched by the cultural storm, it stands in a very privileged position. The ethnically fixed idea of Britishness is sidelined by a civic concept of Scottish nationhood that solves the multiculturalist 'problem' by creating fuzzy, yet inclusive, Scottish and Muslim identities. New generations contain, restrain and dilute, yet maintain, ethnic differences and produce a vague, yet functional, notion of being both Scottish and Muslim. In the ecology of an evolving Muslim community, Muslimness and Scottishness enter a relationship of peaceful civil coexistence. A cross-bred Scottish Muslim community is in the making and will eventually change the face of Islam in Scotland. By resorting to the power of human universals to make people of different cultures, ethnicities and societies so similar in their difference, Scottish society has managed to carefully handle Muslim diversity at a very fragile time in the history of Western–Islamic relations. The future of Scotland rests on the pluralism of different cultural communities bound by a set of shared civic values. The future of Scotland is that of a post-ethnic, transcultural society where tensions between Muslims and non-Muslims will gradually diminish and the Scottish tradition of equality and social justice will ultimately triumph.

Notes

1. Recent research challenges the idea that Muslims live in complete isolation from wider society. For example, in Birmingham, which hosts over 230,000 Muslims (about 22 per cent of the total local population), patterns of religious segregation are, albeit still rather high, falling (Gale 2013).
2. This concept is largely based on Yassine's (1998) idea of civilisational alternation.
3. It should be noted that there is 'a potentially widening gap between Scottish political discourse and public opinion' on migration in Scottish society (Lloyd 2015: 155).

BIBLIOGRAPHY

Abbas, Tahir (2005), 'British South Asian Muslims: State and Multicultural Society', in Tahir Abbas (ed.), *Muslim Britain: Communities Under Pressure*, London: Zed Books, pp. 3–17.

Abbas, Tahir (2013), '"Last of the Dinosaurs": Citizen Khan as Institutionalisation of Pakistani Stereotypes in British Television Comedy', *South Asian Popular Culture*, 11 (1): 85–90.

Abruzzi, William (1993), *Dam That River! Ecology and Mormon Settlement in the Little Colorado River Basin*, Lanham, MD: University Press of America.

Adewunmi, Bim (2012), 'Citizen Khan: An Asian Sitcom Star is Born', *The Guardian*, 22 August, <http://www.theguardian.com/tv-and-radio/2012/aug/22/citizen-khan-sitcom-star-born> (last accessed 25 February 2016).

Ager, Alastair and Alison Strang (2008), 'Understanding Integration: A Conceptual Framework', *Journal of Refugee Studies*, 21 (2): 166–91.

Ali, Mohammed (2012), *Edinburgh Mural*, <http://www.aerosolarabic.com/portfolio/edinburgh-mural> (last accessed 10 January 2016).

Ali, Sundas (2015), *British Muslims in Numbers: A Demographic, Socio-economic and Health Profile of Muslims in Britain Drawing on the 2011 Census*, London: Muslim Council of Britain.

All Party Parliamentary Group on Race and Community (2012), *Ethnic Minority Female Unemployment: Black, Pakistani and Bangladeshi Heritage Women*, London: Runnymede Trust.

Allen, Chris (2005), 'From Race to Religion: The New Face of Discrimination', in

Tahir Abbas (ed.), *Muslim Britain: Communities Under Pressure*, London: Zed Books, pp. 49–65.

Allen, Chris (2010), *Islamophobia*, Aldershot: Ashgate.

Allen, Chris (2014), 'Exploring the Impact of Islamophobia on Visible Muslim Women Victims: a British Case Study', *Journal of Muslims in Europe*, 3 (2): 137–59.

Allen, Chris (2015), '"People Hate You Because of the Way you Dress": Understanding the Invisible Experiences of Veiled British Muslim Women Victims of Islamophobia', *International Review of Victimology*, 21 (3): 287–301.

Allison, Anthony and Mona Siddiqui (2014), *Faith and Belief: A Contemporary Mapping of Attitudes and Provisions in Scotland*, Edinburgh: University of Edinburgh.

Allport, Gordon (1954), *The Nature of Prejudice*, Cambridge, MA: Perseus Books.

Amin, Ash (2002), 'Ethnicity and the Multicultural City: Living with Diversity', *Environment and Planning A*, 34 (6): 959–80.

Anderson, Benedict (1996 [1983]), *Imagined Communities: Reflections on the Origin and Spread of Nationalism*, London: Verso.

Angenendt, Steffen (2007), 'Muslims, Integration, and Security in Europe', in Steffen Angenendt, Paul Barrett, Jonathan Laurence, Ceri Peach, Julianne Smith and Tim Winter (eds), *Muslim Integration: Challenging Conventional Wisdom in Europe and the United States*, Washington, DC: Center for Strategic and International Studies, pp. 45–52.

Ansari, Humayun (2004), *The Infidel Within: Muslims in Britain since 1800*, London: Hurst.

Ansari, Humayun (2009), *Remembering the Brave: The Muslim Contribution to Britain's Armed Forces*, London: Muslim Council of Britain.

Anwar, Muhammad (2001), 'The Participation of Ethnic Minorities in British Politics', *Journal of Ethnic and Migration Studies*, 27 (3): 533–49.

Anwar, Aamer (2016), 'The Battle for the Soul of Islam in Scotland', *Herald Scotland*, 31 January, <http://www.heraldscotland.com/news/14242621.The_battle_for_the_soul_of_Islam_in_Scotland> (last accessed 2 February 2016).

Archambault, Hannah (2007), 'A Community United? Going in Search of Community with Edinburgh Muslims', *Edinburgh Papers in South Asian Studies*, 23.

Archer, Louise (2001), '"Muslim Brothers, Black Lads, Traditional Asians": British Muslim Young Men's Constructions of Race, Religion and Masculinity', *Feminism and Psychology*, 11 (1): 79–105.

Archer, Toby (2009), 'Welcome to the Umma: The British State and its Muslim Citizens Since 9/11', *Cooperation and Conflict: Journal of the Nordic International Studies Association*, 44 (3): 329–47.

Armour, Robert (2016), 'Donations Flood in for Murdered Glasgow Shopkeeper', *Third Force News*, 29 March, <http://thirdforcenews.org.uk/tfn-news/donations-flood-in-for-murdered-glasgow-shopkeeper> (last accessed 29 March 2016).

Azam, Imran (2006), 'Asian Gang Life in Glasgow', *Asian Image*, 26 November, <http://www.asianimage.co.uk/news/1020787.Asian_gang_life_in_Glasgow> (last accessed 5 May 2016).

Azam, Imran and Karin Goodwin (2015), 'Finding Allah: Why More and More Scots are Converting to Islam', *Herald Scotland*, 4 October, <http://www.heraldscotland.com/news/13802175.Finding_Allah__why_more_and_more_Scots_are_converting_to_Islam> (last accessed 21 February 2016).

Bailey, Nick, Alison Bowes and Duncan Sim (1995), 'Pakistanis in Scotland: Census Data and Research Issues', *Scottish Geographical Magazine*, 111 (1): 36–45.

Bain, Simon (2016), 'Faiths Collaborate to Create Ethical Financial Option', *Herald Scotland*, 23 March, <http://www.heraldscotland.com/business/14376620.Faiths_collaborate_to_create_ethical_financial_option> (last accessed 29 March 2016).

Baker, Paul, Costas Gabrielatos and Tony McEnery (2013), *Discourse Analysis and Media Attitudes*, Cambridge: Cambridge University Press.

Bauman, Zygmunt (2007), *Liquid Times: Living in an Age of Uncertainty*, Cambridge: Polity Press.

BBC2 (1966), *Minorities in Britain*, <http://thespace.org/items/e00008jc?t=ywfx> (last accessed 20 March 2014).

BBC News (2006), 'Muslims "Boycott" Glasgow Airport', *BBC News*, 23 July, <http://news.bbc.co.uk/1/hi/scotland/glasgow_and_west/5208082.stm> (last accessed 23 August 2016).

BBC News (2007), 'Hundreds Attend Anti-Terror Rally', *BBC News*, 7 July, <http://news.bbc.co.uk/1/hi/scotland/glasgow_and_west/6279416.stm> (last accessed 23 February 2016).

BBC News (2009a), 'Edinburgh "Most Desirable" City', *BBC News*, 13 August, <http://news.bbc.co.uk/1/hi/scotland/edinburgh_and_east/8199815.stm> (last accessed 10 January 2016).

BBC News (2009b), 'Glasgow "Invented" Tikka Masala', *BBC News*, 21 July, <http://news.bbc.co.uk/1/hi/scotland/glasgow_and_west/8161812.stm> (last accessed 10 February 2016).

BBC News (2010), 'Who are the Ahmadi?', *BBC News*, 28 May, <http://news.bbc.co.uk/2/hi/south_asia/8711026.stm> (last accessed 29 March 2016).

BBC News (2012a), 'Gaza Crisis: Pro-Palestinian Rally Taking Place in Edinburgh', *BBC News*, 17 November, <http://www.bbc.co.uk/news/uk-scotland-edinburgh-east-fife-20376594> (last accessed 10 February 2016).

BBC News (2012b), 'Sitcom Citizen Khan Prompts 185 Complaints to the BBC', *BBC News*, 29 August, <http://www.bbc.co.uk/news/entertainment-arts-19395994> (last accessed 10 January 2016).

BBC News (2013), 'SDL and Anti-Fascists Stage Protests at Holyrood', *BBC News*, 1 June, <http://www.bbc.co.uk/news/uk-scotland-edinburgh-east-fife-22742462> (last accessed 12 February 2016).

BBC News (2015), 'Scottish Schools "Have No Black or Asian Heads"', *BBC News*, 14 June, <http://www.bbc.co.uk/news/uk-scotland-33122160> (last accessed 16 February 2016).

BBC News (2016a), 'Arrest After Glasgow Shopkeeper Asad Shah Dies in Attack', *BBC News*, 26 March, <http://www.bbc.com/news/uk-scotland-glasgow-west-35898543> (last accessed 29 March 2016).

BBC News (2016b), 'Police Probe Scottish Mosque Figures' Links to Banned Sectarian Group', *BBC News*, 31 March, <http://www.bbc.com/news/uk-scotland-35928089> (last accessed 31 March 2016).

BBC News (2016c), 'Asad Shah Death: Man Admits Killing Shopkeer Because he "Disrespected" Islam', *BBC News*, 6 April, <http://www.bbc.com/news/uk-scotland-glasgow-west-35976958> (last accessed 12 April 2016).

BBC News (2016d), 'Ahmadiyya Muslims Launch Peace Campaign in Glasgow', *BBC News*, 18 April, <http://www.bbc.co.uk/news/uk-scotland-glasgow-west-36072051> (last accessed 18 April 2016).

BBC News (2016e), 'Man Faces Trial Over Mosque Vandalism in Dundee', *BBC News*, 27 May, <http://www.bbc.com/news/uk-scotland-tayside-central-36398500> (last accessed 17 June 2016).

BBC News (2016f), 'Muslim Community Offers Free Food in Aberdeen', *BBC News*, 25 May, <http://www.bbc.com/news/uk-scotland-north-east-orkney-shetland-36369329> (last accessed 17 June 2016).

BBC News (2016g), 'Police Scotland Uniform to Include Muslim Hijab', *BBC News*, 23 August, <http://www.bbc.com/news/uk-scotland-37166422> (last accessed 24 August 2016).

BBC News (2016h), 'Police Investigate Hate Crime at Edinburgh Mosque', *BBC*

News, 18 September, <http://www.bbc.co.uk/news/uk-scotland-edinburgh-east-fife-37400357> (last accessed 23 September 2016).

BBC Radio 4 (2016), 'The Deobandis – Episode 2', *BBC Radio 4*, 12 April, <http://www.bbc.co.uk/programmes/b076cg3d> (last accessed 12 April 2016).

Becker, Howard (1966), *Outsiders: Studies in the Sociology of Deviance*, New York, NY: The Free Press.

Bekhuis, Hidde, Stijn Ruiter and Marcel Coenders (2013), 'Xenophobia among Youngsters: The Effect of Inter-ethnic Contact', *European Sociological Review*, 29 (2): 229–42.

Bhimji, Fazila (2012), *British Asian Muslim Women, Multiple Spatialities and Cosmopolitanism*, Basingstoke: Palgrave Macmillan.

Blackwood, Leda (2015), 'Policing Airport Spaces: The Muslim Experience of Scrutiny', *Policing: A Journal of Policy and Practice*, 9 (3): 255–64.

Blackwood, Leda, Nick Hopkins and Steve Reicher (2012a), 'Divided by a Common Language? Conceptualizing Identity, Discrimination, and Alienation', in Kay Jonas and Thomas Morton (eds), *Restoring Civil Societies: The Psychology of Intervention and Engagement Following Crisis*, Oxford: Wiley, pp. 222–36.

Blackwood, Leda, Nick Hopkins and Steve Reicher (2012b), 'I Know Who I Am, But Who Do They Think I Am? Muslim Perspectives on Encounters with Airport Authorities', *Journal of Ethnic and Racial Studies*, 36 (6): 1090–108.

Blackwood, Leda, Nick Hopkins and Steve Reicher (2015), '"Flying While Muslim": Citizenship and Misrecognition in the Airport', *Journal of Social and Political Psychology*, 3 (2): 148–70.

Bolognani, Marta (2007), 'The Myth of Return: Dismissal, Survival or Revival? A Bradford Example of Transnationalism as a Political Instrument', *Journal of Ethnic and Migration Studies*, 33 (1): 59–76.

Bolognani, Marta (2009), *Crime and Muslim Britain: Race, Culture and the Politics of Criminology Among British Pakistanis*, London: Tauris Academic Studies.

Bolognani, Marta (2012), 'Good Culture, Bad Culture . . . No Culture! The Implications of Culture in Urban Regeneration in Bradford, UK', *Critical Social Policy*, 32 (4): 618–35.

Bond, Ross (2006), 'Belonging and Becoming: National Identity and Exclusion', *Sociology*, 40 (4): 609–26.

Bond, Ross (2016), 'Multicultural Nationalism? National Identities among Minority Groups in Scotland's Census', *Journal of Ethnic and Migration Studies*, DOI: 10.1080/1369183X.2016.1232162.

Bond, Ross and Michael Rosie (2002), 'National Identities in Post-Devolution Scotland', *Scottish Affairs*, 40 (Winter): 34–53.

Bond, Ross, Katharine Charsley and Sue Grundy (2010), 'An Audible Minority: Migration, Settlement and Identity among English Graduates in Scotland', *Journal of Ethnic and Migration Studies*, 36 (3): 483–99.

Bonino, Stefano (2012), 'Policing Strategies against Islamic Terrorism in the UK after 9/11: The Socio-Political Realities for British Muslims', *Journal of Muslim Minority Affairs*, 32 (1): 5–31.

Bonino, Stefano (2013), '*Prevent*-ing Muslimness in Britain: The Normalisation of Exceptional Measures to Combat Terrorism', *Journal of Muslim Minority Affairs*, 33 (3): 385–400.

Bonino, Stefano (2015a), 'Scottish Muslims through a Decade of Change: Wounded by the Stigma, Healed by Islam, Rescued by Scotland', *Scottish Affairs*, 24 (1): 78–105.

Bonino, Stefano (2015b), 'Visible Muslimness: Between Discrimination and Integration', *Patterns of Prejudice*, 49 (4): 367–91.

Bonino, Stefano (2015c), 'Muslims Feel at Home in Scotland but Concerns Persist about Security Practices at Airports', *Holyrood*, <http://www.holyrood.com/articles/comment/muslims-feel-home-scotland-concerns-persist-about-security-practices-airports> (last accessed 3 February 2016).

Bonino, Stefano (2016a), 'Policing Forced Marriages Among Pakistanis in the UK', in Margaret Malloch and Paul Rigby (eds), *Human Trafficking: The Complexities of Exploitation*, Edinburgh: Edinburgh University Press, pp. 159–74.

Bonino, Stefano (2016b), 'The British State "Security Syndrome" and Muslim Diversity: Challenges for Liberal Democracy in the Age of Terror', *Contemporary Islam: Dynamics of Muslim Life*, 10 (2): 223–47.

Botterill, Kate, Peter Hopkins, Gurchathen Sanghera and Rowena Arshad (2016), 'Securing Disunion: Young People's Nationalism, Identities and (In)securities in the Campaign for an Independent Scotland', *Political Geography*, 55: 124–34.

Bowen, Innes (2014), *Medina in Birmingham, Najaf in Brent: Inside British Islam*, London: Hurst.

Bowes, Alison, Jacqui McCluskey and Duncan Sim (1990), 'Racism and Harassment of Asians in Glasgow', *Ethnic and Racial Studies*, 13 (1): 71–91.

Braiden, Gerry (2016), 'Family of Scot on Pakistani Death Row Claim He Would be Free if He Was White', *Herald Scotland*, 6 March, <http://www.heraldscotland.com/news/homenews/14324647.Family_of_Scot_on_Pakistan_death_row_claim_he_would_be_free_if_he_was_white> (last accessed 29 March 2016).

Brice, Kevin (2011), 'A Minority Within a Minority: A Report on Converts to Islam in the United Kingdom', *Faith Matters*. <http://faith-matters.org/images/stories/fm-reports/a-minority-within-a-minority-a-report-on-converts-to-islam-in-the-uk.pdf> (last accessed 23 February 2016).

Brighton, Shane (2007), 'British Muslims, Multiculturalism and UK Foreign Policy: "Integration" and "Cohesion" in and Beyond the State', *International Affairs*, 83 (1): 1–17.

British Library (n.d.), *World Wars: Asians in Britain*, <http://www.bl.uk/learning/histcitizen/asians/worldwars/theworldwars.html> (last accessed 20 February 2016).

Brooks, Libby (2015), 'Police Scotland Confirm Spike in Hate Crime after Paris Attacks', *The Guardian*, 20 November, <http://www.theguardian.com/world/2015/nov/20/police-scotland-hate-crime-paris-attacks-muslim-community> (last accessed 21 February 2016).

Brooks, Libby (2016), 'Human Rights Lawyer Gets Death Threats after Plea to Scottish Muslims', *The Guardian*, 3 April, <http://www.theguardian.com/uk-news/2016/apr/03/human-rights-lawyer-aamer-anwar-death-threats-scottish-muslims> (last accessed 12 April 2016).

Brown, Donald (1991), *Human Universals*, New York, NY: McGraw-Hill.

Brown, Donald (2004), 'Human Universals, Human Nature and Human Culture', *Daedalus*, 133 (4): 47–54.

Bruce, Steve (1988), 'Sectarianism in Scotland: A Contemporary Assessment and Explanation', in David McCrone and Alice Brown (eds), *The Scottish Government Yearbook 1988*, Edinburgh: University of Edinburgh, Unit for the Study of Government in Scotland, pp. 150–65.

Bruce, Steve (2011), *Secularization: In Defence of an Unfashionable Theory*, Oxford: Oxford University Press.

Bruce, Steve, Tony Glendinning, Iain Paterson and Michael Rosie (2005), 'Religious Discrimination in Scotland: Fact or Myth?', *Ethnic and Racial Studies*, 28 (1): 151–68.

Buncombe, Andrew and Umair Aziz (2014), 'Mohammad Asghar: Notorious Killer Incited Assassination Attempt on UK Pensioner in Pakistani Jail', *The Independent*, 28 October, <http://www.independent.co.uk/news/world/asia/mohammad-asghar-notorious-killer-incited-assassination-attempt-on-uk-pensioner-in-pakistani-jail-9824021.html> (last accessed 29 March 2016).

Caldwell, Christopher (2009), *Reflections on the Revolution in Europe: Immigration, Islam and the West*, London: Allen Lane.

Campsie, Alison and David Leask (2011), 'Muslims Boycott Airport', *Herald Scotland*, 30 July, <http://www.heraldscotland.com/news/home-news/muslims-boycott-airport.14371950> (last accessed 8 February 2016).

Caraballo-Resto, Juan (2010), 'Contentions in the Making: Discussing Secularism Among Scottish Muslims', in Gabriele Marranci (ed.), *Muslim Societies and the Challenge of Secularization: An Interdisciplinary Approach*, Dordrecht: Springer, pp. 151–64.

Carling, Alan (2012), 'Towards a Shared Future? Opportunity and Denial in Bradford's Experience of Ethnic and Religious Change', in Max Farrar, Simon Robinson, Yasmin Valli and Paul Wetherly (eds), *Islam in the West: Key Issues in Multiculturalism*, Basingstoke: Palgrave Macmillan, pp. 169–86.

Carroll, Lucy (1998), *Dossier 20: Arranged Marriages: Law, Custom and the Muslim Girl in the UK*, London: Women Living Under Muslim Laws.

Castles, Stephen, Maja Korac, Ellie Vasta and Steven Vertovec (2002), *Integration: Mapping the Field*, London: Home Office.

Cesareo, Vincenzo (2000), *Società Multietniche e Multiculturalismi* [Multiethnic Societies and Multiculturalisms], Milan: Vita e Pensiero.

Choudhury, Tufyal (2007), 'Anti-Muslim Discrimination: Remedies and Failings', *Global Dialogue*, 9 (3–4): 33–46.

Choudhury, Tufyal, Mohammed Aziz, Duaa Izzidien, Intissar Khreeji and Dilwar Hussain (2006), *Perceptions of Discrimination and Islamophobia: Voices from Members of Muslim Communities in the European Union*, Vienna: European Monitoring Centre on Racism and Xenophobia.

City of Edinburgh Council (2013), *Ethnicity and Related Themes: Ethnic Group, Country of Birth, National Identity, Age and Year of Arrival in the UK, Religion, Languages*, Edinburgh: City of Edinburgh Council.

Clegg, Cecilia and Michael Rosie (2005), *Faith Communities and Local Government in Glasgow*, Edinburgh: Scottish Executive.

Cohen, Albert (1955), *Delinquent Boys: The Culture of the Gang*, Glencoe: The Free Press.

Coles, Maurice (2009), *Islam, Citizenship and Education: When Hope and History Rhyme*, Leicester: Islam and Citizenship Education Project.

Colourful Heritage (2016), *Colourful Heritage Project: Capturing the Memories, Stories and Adventures of the First Generation*, <http://www.colourfulheritage.com/watch-a-video.aspx> (last accessed 2 February 2016).

Commission on British Muslims and Islamophobia (1997), *Islamophobia: A Challenge for Us All*, London: Runnymede Trust.

Commission on British Muslims and Islamophobia (2004), *Islamophobia: Issues, Challenges and Action*, Stoke on Trent: Trentham Books.

Condor, Susan and Jackie Abell (2006), 'Romantic Scotland, Tragic England, Ambiguous Britain: Constructions of "the Empire" in Post-Devolution National Accounting', *Nations and Nationalism*, 12 (3): 453–72.

Cooley, Charles (1922), *Human Nature and the Social Order*, New York, NY: Scribner's.

Corcoran, Hannah, Deborah Lader and Kevin Smith (2015), *Hate Crime, England and Wales, 2014/15*, London: Home Office.

Cowing, Emma (2013), 'Islamic High School to Open in Glasgow', *Scotland on Sunday*, 1 April, <http://www.scotsman.com/scotland-on-sunday/scotland/islamic-high-school-to-open-in-glasgow-1-2868668> (last accessed 22 February 2016).

Coyle, Matt (2016), 'Police Probe Threats Against Former Central Mosque Leaders', *STV News*, 3 February, <http://stv.tv/news/west-central/1341461-police-probe-threats-against-former-glasgow-central-mosque-leaders> (last accessed 29 March 2016).

Croall, Hazel and Liz Frondigoun (2010), 'Race, Ethnicity, Crime and Justice in Scotland', in Hazel Croall, Gerry Mooney and Mary Munro (eds), *Criminal Justice in Scotland*, Abingdon: Willan Publishing, pp. 111–31.

Crown Prosecution Service (2008), *Doctor Bilal Abdullah Guilty of London and Glasgow Bomb Plot*, 16 December, <http://www.cps.gov.uk/news/latest_news/183_08> (last accessed 20 February 2016).

Cusick, Linda (1994), 'Scottish Inferiority', *Scottish Affairs*, 9 (Autumn): 143–50.

Dawkins, Richard (1976), *The Selfish Gene*, Oxford: Oxford University Press.

Deakins, David, Mohammed Ishaq and David Smallbone (2005), *Minority Ethnic Enterprise in Scotland: A National Scoping Study*, Edinburgh: Scottish Executive.

Denholm, Andrew (2015), 'Primary Bids to Become Scotland's First State-Funded Muslim School', *Herald Scotland*, 7 December, <http://www.heraldscotland.com/news/14127759.Primary_bids_to_become_Scotland_s_first_state_funded_Muslim_school> (last accessed 27 January 2016).

Devine, Tom (2012), *The Scottish Nation: A Modern History*, London: Penguin Books.

Devine, Tom (2016), *Independence or Union: Scotland's Past and Scotland's Present*, London: Allen Lane.

Duffy, Judith (2014), '"I May be Muslim but I Identify Myself as Scottish": The Indyref Battle for the Scottish Asian Vote', *Herald Scotland*, 16 February, <http://

www.heraldscotland.com/news/13145999._I_may_be_Muslim_but_I_iden-tify_myself_as_Scottish___the_indyref_battle_for_the_Scottish_Asian_vote> (last accessed 30 January 2016).

Duffy, Judith (2015), 'Tensions Rise in Scotland in Wake of Paris Attack', *Herald Scotland*, 22 November, <http://m.heraldscotland.com/news/14095367.Tensions_ rise_in_Scotland_in_wake_of_Paris_attack> (last accessed 8 February 2016).

Duffy, Judith and Imran Azzam (2013), 'Scotland's Muslim Leaders to Target Politicians over Same-Sex Marriage', *Herald Scotland*, 17 February, <http:// www.heraldscotland.com/news/home-news/scotlands-muslim-leaders-to-target-politicians-over-same-sex-marriage.20248632> (last accessed 17 February 2016).

Dunlop, Anne (1990), 'Lascars and Labourers: Reactions to the Indian Presence in the West of Scotland During the 1920s and 1930s', *Scottish Labour History Society Journal*, 25: 40–57.

Dunlop, Anne (1993), 'An United Front? Anti-Racist Political Mobilisation in Scotland', *Scottish Affairs*, 3 (Spring): 89–101.

Dunlop, Anne and Robert Miles (1990), 'Recovering the History of Asian Migration to Scotland', *Immigrants and Minorities*, 9 (2): 145–67.

Durkheim, Emile (1984 [1893]), *The Division of Labor in Society*, translated by Wilfred Halls, New York, NY: The Free Press.

Dwyer, Claire (1999a), 'Contradictions of Community: Questions of Identity for Young British Muslim Women', *Environment and Planning A*, 31 (1): 53–68.

Dwyer, Claire (1999b), 'Veiled Meanings: Young British Muslim Women and the Negotiation of Differences', *Gender, Place and Culture*, 6 (1): 5–26.

Dwyer, Claire, Bindi Shah and Gurchathen Sanghera (2008), '"From Cricket Lover to Terror Suspect" – Challenging Representations of Young British Muslim Men', *Gender, Place and Culture*, 15 (2): 117–36.

Dwyer, Claire, Tariq Modood, Gurchathen Sanghera, Bindi Shah and Suruchi Thapar-Björkert (2011), 'Educational Achievement and Career Aspiration for Young British Pakistanis', in Tariq Modood and John Salt (eds), *Global Migration, Ethnicity and Britishness*, Basingstoke: Palgrave Macmillan, pp. 177–204.

Dyke, Anna and Lucy James (2009), *Immigrant, Muslim, Female: Triple Paralysis?*, London: Quilliam Foundation.

Economist, The (2009), 'Islam in Tartan', *The Economist*, 7 May, <http://www.economist.com/node/13611699> (last accessed 29 March 2016).

Economist, The (2015a), 'Islam in the UK', *The Economist*, 7 January, <http://www.economist.com/blogs/graphicdetail/2015/01/daily-chart-2> (last accessed 9 January 2016).

Economist, The (2015b), 'The Thistle and the Crescent', *The Economist*, 15 August, <http://www.economist.com/news/britain/21661000-muslims-seem-happier-identify-scottish-english-thistle-and-crescent> (last accessed 16 February 2016).

Edinburgh Interfaith Association (2011), '9/11 Walk for Peace', *Interfaith Matters*, 9.

Edinburgh News (2016), 'Edinburgh Voted Best City in the UK for Third Year Running', *Edinburgh News*, 19 April, <http://www.edinburghnews.scotsman.com/our-region/edinburgh/edinburgh-voted-best-city-in-the-uk-for-third-year-running-1-4104729> (last accessed 13 June 2016).

Edinburgh Partnership (2014), *2011 Census Results for Edinburgh*, Edinburgh: City of Edinburgh Council, <http://www.edinburgh.gov.uk/downloads/download/699/the_2011_census_presentation_to_the_edinburgh_partnership> (last accessed 17 October 2015).

Edmunds, June (2010), '"Elite" Young Muslims in Britain: From Transnational to Global Politics', *Contemporary Islam: Dynamics of Muslim Life*, 4 (2): 215–38.

Elshayyal, Khadijah (2016), *Scottish Muslims in Numbers*, Edinburgh: University of Edinburgh, Alwaleed Centre for the Study of Islam in the Contemporary World.

Equality and Human Rights Commission (2010), *Stop and Think: A Critical Review of the Use of Stop and Search Powers in England and Wales*, <http://www.equality-humanrights.com/uploaded_files/raceinbritain/ehrc_stop_and_search_report.pdf> (last accessed 14 January 2016).

Eriksen, Thomas (2006), 'Diversity Versus Difference: Neo-Liberalism in the Minority Debate', in Richard Rottenburg, Burkhard Schnepel and Shingo Shimada (eds), *The Making and Unmaking of Difference*, Bielefeld: Transaction, pp. 13–36.

Etzioni, Amitai (1996), 'The Responsive Community: A Communitarian Perspective', *American Sociological Review*, 61 (1): 1–11.

Etzioni, Amitai (2002), 'The Good Society', *Seattle Journal of Social Justice*, 1 (1): 83–96.

Etzioni, Amitai (2003), 'Communitarianism', in Karen Christensen and David Levinson (eds), *Encyclopedia of Community: From the Village to the Virtual World*, London: Sage Publications, pp. 224–8.

Fallaci, Oriana (2004), *La Forza della Ragione* [The Force of Reason], Milan: Rizzoli.

Fantz, Ashley and Atika Shubert (2015), 'From Scottish Teen to ISIS Bride and Recruiter: The Aqsa Mahmood Story', *CNN*, 24 February, <http://edition.cnn.com/2015/02/23/world/scottish-teen-isis-recruiter> (last accessed 3 March 2016).

Farrar, Max (2012), 'Multiculturalism in the UK: A Contested Discourse' in Max Farrar, Simon Robinson, Yasmin Valli and Paul Wetherly (eds), *Islam in the West: Key Issues in Multiculturalism*, Basingstoke: Palgrave Macmillan, pp. 8–37.

Fenton, Steve and Robin Mann (2011), '"Our Own People": Ethnic Majority Orientations to Nation and Country', in Tariq Modood and John Salt (eds), *Global Migration, Ethnicity and Britishness*, Basingstoke: Palgrave Macmillan, pp. 225–47.

Field, Clive (2007), 'Islamophobia in Contemporary Britain: The Evidence of the Opinion Polls, 1988–2006', *Islam and Christian–Muslim Relations*, 18 (4): 447–77.

Field, Clive (2011), 'Young British Muslims Since 9/11: A Composite Attitudinal Profile', *Religion, State and Society*, 39 (2–3): 159–75.

Fletcher, Thomas and Karl Spracklen (2013), 'Cricket, Drinking and Exclusion of British Muslims?', *Ethnic and Racial Studies*, 37 (8): 1310–27.

Forced Marriage Unit (2016), *Forced Marriage Unit Statistics 2015*, London: Home Office and Foreign and Commonwealth Office.

Ford, Robert (2008), 'Is Racial Prejudice Declining in Britain?', *British Journal of Sociology*, 59 (4): 609–36.

Ford, Robert and Anthony Heath (2014), 'Immigration: A Nation Divided?', in Alison Park, Caroline Bryson and John Curtice (eds), *British Social Attitudes: The 31st Report*, London: NatCen Social Research, pp. 78–94.

Foucault, Michel (1998 [1978]), *The History of Sexuality: The Will to Knowledge*, translated by Robert Hurley, London: Penguin Books.

Frost, Diane (2008), 'Islamophobia: Examining Causal Links Between the Media and "Race Hate" from "Below"', *International Journal of Sociology and Social Policy*, 28 (11–12): 564–78.

Gale, Richard (2013), 'Religious Residential Segregation and Internal Migration: The British Muslim Case', *Environment and Planning A*, 45 (4): 872–91.

Gallup (2009), *The Gallup Coexist Index 2009: A Global Study of Interfaith Relations*, New York, NY and London: Gallup and the Coexist Foundation.

Gause, Georgii (1934), *The Struggle for Existence*, Baltimore, MD: Williams and Wilkins.

Gilbert, Julie (2016), 'Glasgow MSP Takes Oath in Urdu as Parliament Sworn in at Holyrood', *Glasgow Live*, 12 May, <http://www.glasgowlive.co.uk/news/glasgow-news/glasgow-msp-takes-oath-urdu-11324660> (last accessed 25 May 2016).

Gilliat-Ray, Sophie (2010), *Muslims in Britain: An Introduction*, Cambridge: Cambridge University Press.

Glasgow City Council (2012), *Population and Households by Ethnicity in Glasgow: Estimates of Changes 2001–2010 for Community Planning Partnership Areas and Neighbourhoods*, Glasgow: Glasgow City Council.

Glass, Bryan (2014), *The Scottish Nation at the Empire's End*, Basingstoke: Palgrave Macmillan.

Goffman, Erving (1990a [1959]), *The Presentation of Self in Everyday Life*, London: Penguin Books.

Goffman, Erving (1990b [1963]), *Stigma: Notes on the Management of Spoiled Identity*, London: Penguin Books.

Goldsmith, Belinda and Olivia Harris (2014), 'Violence, Threats, Prompt More Muslim Women in Britain to Wear a Veil', *Reuters*, 21 August, <http://uk.reuters.com/article/2014/08/21/uk-britain-muslim-veils-idUKKBN0GL0X720140821> (last accessed on 17 February 2016).

Goodall, Kay, Peter Hopkins, Simon McKerrell, John Markey, Stephen Millar, John Richardson and Michael Richardson (2015), *Community Experiences of Sectarianism*, Edinburgh: Scottish Government Social Research.

Goode, Erich and Nachman Ben-Yehuda (1994), 'Moral Panics: Culture, Politics, and Social Construction', *Annual Review of Sociology*, 20 (1): 149–71.

Goodhart, David (2013), *The British Dream: Successes and Failures of Post-War Immigration*, London: Atlantic Books.

Goodwin, Karin (2016), 'Human Rights Lawyer Aamer Anwar "Deeply Moved" by Support Following Death Threats', *The National*, 4 April, <http://www.thenational.scot/news/human-rights-lawyer-aamer-anwar-deeply-moved-by-support-following-death-threats.15896> (last accessed 12 April 2016).

Gray, Rebecca (2015), 'Muslim Cultural Centre Torched by Thugs in Bishopbriggs', *Evening Times*, 17 November, <http://www.eveningtimes.co.uk/news/14036512.Muslim_cultural_centre_torched_by_thugs_in_Bishopbriggs> (last accessed 19 January 2016).

Guardian, The (2012), 'Travel Awards 2012 Winners', *The Guardian*, 29 September, <http://www.guardian.co.uk/travel/2012/sep/29/travel-awards-2012-winners> (last accessed 21 February 2016).

Guardian, The (2015), 'British Muslims Gather in London to Protest Against Muhammad Cartoons', *The Guardian*, 8 February, <http://www.theguardian.com/world/2015/feb/08/british-muslims-london-protest-against-muhammad-cartoon-charlie-hebdo> (last accessed 24 February 2016).

Hafez, Farid (2014), 'Shifting Borders: Islamophobia as Common Ground for Building Pan-European Right-Wing Unity', *Patterns of Prejudice*, 48 (5): 479–99.

Hall, Stuart (2005), 'Whose Heritage? Un-settling "the Heritage", Re-imagining the Post-Nation', in Jo Littler and Roshi Naidoo (eds), *The Politics of Heritage: The Legacies of Race*, London: Routledge, pp. 23–35.

Hall, Robert (2014), 'World War One at Home. Perth, Scotland: Diaspora, Indian Troops and WW1', *BBC Radio Scotland*, 17 November, <http://www.bbc.co.uk/programmes/p02c4kpq> (last accessed 10 January 2016).

Hamid, Sadek (2011), 'British Muslim Young People: Facts, Features and Religious Trends', *Religion, State and Society*, 39 (2–3): 247–61.

Harari, Yuval Noah (2014), *Sapiens: A Brief History of Humankind*, London: Harvill Secker.

Hellyer, Hisham (2007a), 'British Muslims: Past, Present and Future', *Muslim World*, 97 (2): 225–58.

Hellyer, Hisham (2007b), *Engagement with the Muslim Community and Counter-Terrorism: British Lessons for the West*, Washington, DC: Brookings Institution, Analysis Paper 11.

Henne, Peter (2015), *Latest Trends in Religious Restrictions and Hostilities*, Washington, DC: Pew Research Centre.

Herald Scotland (2011), 'Muslims Quizzed 15 Times at Airport, Says MSP', *Herald Scotland*, 14 July, <http://www.heraldscotland.com/news/13033003.Muslims_quizzed_15_times_at_airport__says_MSP> (last accessed 16 January 2016).

Herald Scotland (2015a), 'How Scotland's Muslims are Fighting the Rise of Radical Islam at Home', *Herald Scotland*, 1 February, <http://m.heraldscotland.com/news/13199694.Revealed__how_Scotland_s_Muslims_are_fighting_the_rise_of_radical_Islam_at_home> (last accessed 15 February 2016).

Herald Scotland (2015b), 'Muslim Groups Unite against Terrorism', *Herald Scotland*, 2 July, <http://www.heraldscotland.com/news/13366460.Muslim_groups_unite_against_terrorism> (last accessed 16 February 2016).

Herald Scotland (2016a), 'Pakistani Rift Behind Turf War at Glasgow Mosque', *Herald Scotland*, 26 March, <http://www.heraldscotland.com/news/14385932.Pakistani_rift_behind_turf_war_at_Glasgow_mosque> (last accessed 29 March 2016).

Herald Scotland (2016b), 'Police Reassure Communities in Glasgow After Death of Asad Shah', *Herald Scotland*, 28 March, <http://www.heraldscotland.com/

news/14388063.Police_reassure_communities_in_Glasgow_after_death_of_ Asad_Shah> (last accessed 29 March 2016).

Herald Scotland (2016c), 'Muslim Council of Scotland "Deeply Concerned" by Murder Accused's Statement', *Herald Scotland*, 8 April, <http://m.herald scotland.com/news/14411961.Muslim_Council_of_Scotland__deeply_con cerned__by_murder_accused_s_statement> (last accessed 12 April 2016).

Herbert, David (2012), 'Shifting Securities in Northern Ireland: "Terror" and the "Troubles" in Global Media and Local Memory', *European Journal of Cultural Studies*, 10 (3): 343–59.

Herman, Arthur (2003), *The Scottish Enlightenment: The Scots' Invention of the Modern World*, London: Fourth Estate.

Herrington, Lewis (2015), *Incubating Extremist Terrorism: The UK Islamic Fundamentalist Movement 1989–2014*, unpublished PhD thesis, University of Warwick.

Higher Education Funding Council for England (2010), *Trends in Young Participation in Higher Education: Core Results for England*, <http://www.hefce. ac.uk/media/hefce/content/pubs/2010/201003/10_03.pdf> (last accessed 20 February 2016).

Hogg, Michael (2000), 'Subjective Uncertainty Reduction through Self-Categorization: A Motivational Theory of Social Identity Processes', *European Review of Social Psychology*, 11 (1): 223–55.

Home Office (2016), *Proscribed Terrorist Organisations*, <http://www.gov.uk/gov ernment/uploads/system/uploads/attachment_data/file/509003/20160318pros cription.pdf> (last accessed 31 March 2016).

Homes, Amy, Chris McLean and Lorraine Murray (2010), *Muslim Integration in Scotland*, Edinburgh: Ipsos MORI Scotland.

Hope Conference (2015), *Hope Conference: Conference of Knowledge and Inspiration*, <http://www.hopeconference.co.uk/speakers.php> (last accessed 20 February 2016).

Hopkins, Peter (2004a), 'Everyday Racism in Scotland: A Case Study of East Pollokshields', *Scottish Affairs*, 49 (Autumn): 88–103.

Hopkins, Peter (2004b), 'Young Muslim Men in Scotland: Inclusions and Exclusions', *Children's Geographies*, 2 (2): 257–72.

Hopkins, Peter (2007a), '"Blue Squares", "Proper" Muslims and Transnational Networks: Narratives of National and Religious Identities Amongst Young Muslim Men Living in Scotland', *Ethnicities*, 7 (1): 61–81.

Hopkins, Peter (2007b), 'Global Events, National Politics, Local Lives:

Young Muslim Men in Scotland', *Environment and Planning A*, 39 (5): 1119–33.

Hopkins, Peter (2009), 'Responding to the "Crisis of Masculinity": The Perspectives of Young Muslim Men from Glasgow and Edinburgh, Scotland', *Gender, Place and Culture*, 16 (3): 299–312.

Hopkins, Peter (2016), 'Deflections, Displacements and Disengagements', in Nasar Meer (ed.), *Scotland and Race Equality: Directions in Policy and Identity*, London: Runnymede Trust, pp. 30–1.

Hopkins, Nick and Leda Blackwood (2011), 'Everyday Citizenship: Identity and Recognition', *Journal of Community and Applied Social Psychology*, 21 (3): 215–27.

Hopkins, Nick and Ronni Greenwood (2013), 'Hijab, Visibility and the Performance of Identity', *European Journal of Social Psychology*, 43 (5): 438–47.

Hopkins, Peter and Susan Smith (2008), 'Scaling Segregation: Racialising Fear', in Rachel Pain and Susan Smith (eds), *Fear: Critical Geopolitics and Everyday Life*, Aldershot: Ashgate, pp. 103–16.

Hopkins, Nick, Ronni Greenwood and Maisha Birchall (2007), 'Minority Understandings of the Dynamics to Intergroup Contact Encounters: British Muslims' (Sometimes Ambivalent) Experience of Representing Their Group to Others', *South African Journal of Psychology*, 37 (4): 679–701.

Hopkins, Peter, Katherine Botterill, Gurchathen Sanghera and Rowena Arshad (2015), *Faith, Ethnicity, Place: Young People's Everyday Geopolitics in Scotland*, Research Report 2015, Swindon: Arts and Humanities Research Council.

House of Commons (2005), *Terrorism and Community Relations: Volume 1*, London: The Stationery Office.

Human Rights Watch (2010), *Without Suspicion: Stop and Search under the Terrorism Act 2000*, New York, NY: Human Rights Watch.

Huntington, Samuel (1993), 'The Clash of Civilizations?', *Foreign Affairs*, 72 (3): 22–49.

Huq, Rupa (2013), 'Situating Citizen Khan: Shifting Representations of Asians Onscreen and the Outrage Industry in the Social Media Age', *South Asian Popular Culture*, 11 (1): 77–83.

Hussain, Dilwar (2008), 'Islam', in Guy Lodge and Zaki Cooper (eds), *Faith in the Nation: Religion, Identity and the Public Realm in Britain*, London, Institute for Public Policy Research: pp. 39–46.

Hussain, Yasmin and Paul Bagguley (2012), 'Securitized Citizens: Islamophobia, Racism and the 7/7 London Bombings', *Sociological Review*, 60 (4): 716–34.

Hussain, Asifa and Mohammed Ishaq (2002), 'Scottish Pakistani Muslims' Perceptions of the Armed Forces', *Scottish Affairs*, 38 (Winter): 27–51.

Hussain, Asifa and Mohammed Ishaq (2008), 'Managing Race Equality in Scottish Local Councils in the Aftermath of the Race Relations (Amendment) Act 2000', *International Journal of Public Sector Management*, 21 (6): 586–610.

Hussain, Asifa and William Miller (2006), *Multicultural Nationalism: Islamophobia, Anglophobia, and Devolution*, Oxford: Oxford University Press.

Hutchison, Paul and Harriet Rosenthal (2011), 'Prejudice Against Muslims: Anxiety as a Mediator Between Intergroup Contact and Attitudes, Perceived Group Variability and Behavioural Intentions', *Ethnic and Racial Studies*, 34 (1): 40–61.

Hutnik, Nimmi (1991), *Ethnic Minority Identity*, Oxford: Oxford University Press.

Improvement Service (2013), *Scotland's Councillors 2013*, Broxburn: Improvement Service.

Islam Festival (2010), *Islam Festival Edinburgh Documentary: Part 1/8*, <http://www.youtube.com/watch?v=2U9zy37Mqq8> (last accessed 10 February 2016).

Jacobson, Jessica (1997), 'Perceptions of Britishness', *Nations and Nationalism*, 3 (2): 181–99.

Jaspal, Rusi (2011), 'Delineating Ethnic and Religious Identities in Research with British South Asians', *Psychology Studies*, 56 (2): 241–4.

Jeldtoft, Nadia (2010), 'Lived Islam: Religious Identity with "Non-Organized" Muslim Minorities', *Ethnic and Racial Studies*, 34 (7): 1134–51.

Jenkins, Richard (2008), *Social Identity*, 3rd edn, London: Routledge.

Jivraj, Stephen (2013), 'Muslims in England and Wales: Evidence from the 2011 Census', in Claire Alexander, Victoria Redclift and Ajmal Hussain (eds), *The New Muslims*, London: Runnymede Trust, pp. 16–19.

Johnston, Ron, Michael Poulsen and James Forrest (2016), 'Ethnic Residential Patterns in Urban England and Wales, 2001–2011: A System-wide Analysis', *Tijdschrift voor Economische en Sociale Geografie*, 107 (1): 1–15.

Joppke, Christian (2009), 'Limits of Integration Policy: Britain and Her Muslims', *Journal of Ethnic and Migration Studies*, 35 (3): 453–72.

Joppke, Christian (2014), 'Europe and Islam: Alarmists, Victimists, and Integration by Law', *West European Politics*, 37 (6): 1314–35.

Kabir, Nahid (2005), *Muslims in Australia: Immigration, Race Relations and Cultural History*, London: Kegan Paul.

Kabir, Nahid (2010), *Young British Muslims: Identity, Culture, Politics and the Media*, Edinburgh: Edinburgh University Press.

Kabir, Nahid (2012), *Young American Muslims: Dynamics of Identity*, Edinburgh: Edinburgh University Press.

Kalin, Ibrahim (2001), 'Islam and the West: Deconstructing Monolithic Perceptions – A Conversation with Professor John Esposito', *Journal of Muslim Minority Affairs*, 21 (1): 155–63.

Karlsen, Saffron and James Nazroo (2015), 'Ethnic and Religious Differences in the Attitudes of People Towards Being "British"', *Sociological Review*, 63 (4): 759–81.

Kelly, Brian and Stephen Ashe (2014a), 'Geographies of Deprivation and Diversity in Glasgow', *Local Dynamics of Diversity: Evidence from the 2011 Census*, Manchester: Centre on Dynamics of Diversity.

Kelly, Brian and Stephen Ashe (2014b), 'Ethnic Mixing in Glasgow', *Local Dynamics of Diversity: Evidence from the 2011 Census*, Manchester: Centre on Dynamics of Diversity.

Khan, Yasmin (2015), *The Raj at War: A People's History of India's Second World War*, London: Bodley Head.

Khattab, Nabil and Ron Johnston (2013), 'Ethnic and Religious Penalties in a Changing British Labour Market From 2002 to 2010: The Case of Unemployment', *Environment and Planning A*, 45 (6): 1358–71.

Khattab, Nabil and Tariq Modood (2015), 'Both Ethnic and Religious: Explaining Employment Penalties Across 14 Ethno-Religious Groups in the United Kingdom', *Journal for the Scientific Study of Religion*, 54 (3): 501–22.

Khattab, Nabil, Ibrahim Sirkeci, Ron Johnston and Tariq Modood (2011), 'Ethnicity, Religion, Residential Segregation and Life Chances', in Tariq Modood and John Salt (eds), *Global Migration, Ethnicity and Britishness*, Basingstoke: Palgrave Macmillan, pp. 153–76.

Khattab, Nabil, Ron Johnston and David Manley (2015), '"All in it Together?" Ethnoreligious Labour-Market Penalties and the Post-2008 Recession in the UK', *Environment and Planning A*, 47 (4): 977–95.

Kidd, Sara and Lynn Jamieson (2011), *Experiences of Muslims Living in Scotland*, Edinburgh: Scottish Executive.

Kiely, Richard, David McCrone, Frank Bechhofer and Robert Stewart (2000), 'Debatable Land: National and Local Identity in a Border Town', *Sociological Research Online*, 5 (2).

Kiely, Richard, Frank Bechhofer, Robert Stewart and David McCrone (2001), 'The Markers and Rules of Scottish National Identity', *Sociological Review*, 49 (1): 33–55.

Kiely, Richard, Frank Bechhofer and David McCrone (2005), 'Birth, Blood and

Belonging Claims in Post-Devolution Scotland', *Sociological Review*, 53 (1): 150–71.

Klausen, Jytte (2005), *The Islamic Challenge*, New York, NY: Oxford University Press.

Knott, Kim and Sajda Khokher (1993), 'Religious and Ethnic Identity among Young Muslim Women in Bradford', *New Community*, 19 (4): 593–610.

Kostakopoulou, Dora (2010), 'Matters of Control: Integration Tests, Naturalisation Reform and Probationary Citizenship in the United Kingdom', *Journal of Ethnic and Migration Studies*, 36 (5): 829–46.

Kundnani, Arun (2014), *The Muslims are Coming! Islamophobia, Extremism, and the Domestic War on Terror*, London: Verso Books.

Kymlicka, Will (2012), *Multiculturalism: Success, Failure and Future*, Washington, DC: Migration Policy Institute.

Kyriakides, Christopher, Satnam Virdee and Tariq Modood (2009), 'Racism, Muslims and the National Imagination', *Journal of Ethnic and Migration Studies*, 35 (2): 289–308.

Labott, Elise (2016), 'In Fighting ISIS, Canada not Trying to be "Little U.S."', *CNN*, 12 March, <http://edition.cnn.com/2016/03/11/world/canada-isis/index.html> (last accessed 27 January 2016).

Laliótou, Ioanna (2004), *Transatlantic Subjects: Acts of Migration and Cultures of Transnationalism between Greece and America*, Chicago: University of Chicago.

Lambert, Robert and Jonathan Githens-Mazer (2011), *Islamophobia and Anti Muslim Hate Crime: UK Case Studies 2010*, Exeter: University of Exeter, European Muslim Research Centre.

Lawson, Helen (2013), 'The Church that's Opened its Doors to Islam', *Mail Online*, 18 March, <http://www.dailymail.co.uk/news/article-2295149/Christians-roll-welcome-Muslims-having-pray-wind-rain-mosque-small.html> (last accessed 27 January 2016).

Leask, David (2016a), 'Charity Watchdog Slams Glasgow Central Mosque Elders Amid Concerns of Funding for Ultra-Orthodox Group', *Herald Scotland*, 19 January, <http://www.heraldscotland.com/news/14213225.Charity_watchdog_slams_Glasgow_Central_Mosque_elders_amid_concerns_of_funding_for_ultra_orthodox_group> (last accessed 2 February 2016).

Leask, David (2016b), 'Analysis: The New Generation of Liberal Scottish Muslims Taking Control of Scotland's Biggest Mosque', *Herald Scotland*, 19 January, <http://www.heraldscotland.com/news/14213213.Analysis__the_new_gen

eration_of_liberal_Scottish_Muslims_taking_control_of_Scotland_s_biggest_mosque> (last accessed 2 February 2016).

Leask, David (2016c), 'Scottish Muslims, Jews Braced for Racist Backlash After Brussels', *Herald Scotland*, 23 March, <http://www.heraldscotland.com/news/crime_courts/14376632.Scottish_Muslims__Jews_braced_for_racist_backlash_after_Brussels> (last accessed 29 March 2016).

Leask, David (2016d), 'Imam at Glasgow's Central Mosque Uses WhatsApp to Praise an Extremist Killer', *Herald Scotland*, 25 March, <http://www.heraldscotland.com/news/14383412.Imam_at_Scotland_s_biggest_mosque_praises_Islamist_assassin> (last accessed 29 March 2016).

Leask, David (2016e), 'Terror Police Intervene in Murderer Row at Mosque', *Herald Scotland*, 26 March, <http://www.heraldscotland.com/news/14385835.Terror_police_intervene_in_murderer_row_at_mosque> (last accessed 29 March 2016).

Leask, David (2016f), 'SNP's Yousaf: No Women on Glasgow Central Mosque Committee is a "Disgrace"', *Herald Scotland*, 20 January, <http://www.heraldscotland.com/news/14217328.SNP_s_Yousaf__no_women_on_Glasgow_Central_Mosque_committee_is_a__disgrace> (last accessed 29 March 2016).

Leask, David (2016g), 'Mosque Elders Warned They Could be Targeted by Corrupt Individuals', *Herald Scotland*, 1 February, <http://www.heraldscotland.com/news/14243675.Mosque_elders_warned_they_could_be_targeted_by_corrupt_individuals> (last accessed 29 March 2016).

Leask, David (2016h), 'Senior Muslim Calls for Charity Watchdog to Suspend Top Officials at Glasgow Mosque', *Herald Scotland*, 4 March, <http://www.heraldscotland.com/news/14321010.Senior_Muslim_calls_for_charity_watchdog_to_suspend_top_officials_at_Glasgow_Mosque> (last accessed 29 March 2016).

Leask, David (2016i), 'Glasgow Mosque Conservative: "You Have to Change for Islam. Islam Does not Change for You"', *Herald Scotland*, 4 February, <http://www.heraldscotland.com/news/14251236.Glasgow_Mosque_conservative___You_have_to_change_for_Islam__Islam_does_not_change_for_you> (last accessed 29 March 2016).

Leask, David (2016j), 'Mosque Conservatives Launch Attack Video on Scotland's Liberal Muslims', *Herald Scotland*, 26 February, <http://www.heraldscotland.com/news/14303667.Mosque_Conservatives_launch_attack_video_on_Scotland_s_liberal_Muslims> (last accessed 29 March 2016).

Leask, David (2016k), 'Reformer Leaders at Glasgow Mosque Resign Citing Threats of Violence', *Herald Scotland*, 3 February, <http://www.heraldscotland.com/news/homenews/14250945.Reformer_leaders_at_Glasgow_Mosque_resign_citing_threats_of_violence> (last accessed 29 March 2016).

Leask, David (2016l), 'Glasgow Mosque Cancels Weekly Lunches for Visitors and Worshippers', *Herald Scotland*, 15 March, <http://www.heraldscotland.com/news/14343500.Glasgow_Mosque_cancels_weekly_lunches_for_visitors_and_worshippers> (last accessed 29 March 2016).

Leask, David (2016m), 'Glasgow Mosque Selects its First Non-Pakistani Committee Member in Quiet Revolution', *Herald Scotland*, 2 May, <http://www.herald-scotland.com/news/homenews/14465852.Glasgow_Mosque_selects_its_first_Non_Pakistani_committee_member_in_quiet_revolution> (last accessed 2 May 2016).

Leiken, Robert (2005), 'Europe's Angry Muslims', *Foreign Affairs*, 84 (4): 120–35.

Leith, Murray (2012), 'The View from Above: Scottish National Identity as an Elite Concept', *National Identities*, 14 (1): 39–51.

Leith, Murray and Daniel Soule (2012), *Political Discourse and National Identity in Scotland*, Edinburgh: Edinburgh University Press.

Leith, Murray and Duncan Sim (2016), 'A Welcoming Scotland?', in Nasar Meer (ed.), *Scotland and Race Equality: Directions in Policy and Identity*, London: Runnymede Trust, pp. 27–9.

Lemert, Edwin (1951), *Social Pathology: A Systematic Approach to the Theory of Sociopathic Behavior*, New York, NY: McGraw-Hill.

Lemert, Edwin (1972), *Human Deviance, Social Problems and Social Control*, 2nd edn, Englewood Cliffs, NJ: Prentice-Hall.

Lemert, Edwin (1974), 'Beyond Mead: The Societal Reaction to Deviance', *Social Problems*, 21 (4): 457–68.

Lewis, Philip (2007), *Young, British and Muslim*, London: Continuum.

Lewis, Valerie and Ridhi Kashyap (2013), 'Are Muslims a Distinctive Minority? An Empirical Analysis of Religiosity, Social Attitudes, and Islam', *Journal for the Scientific Study of Religion*, 52 (3): 617–26.

Lindley, Joanne (2002), 'Race or Religion? The Impact of Religion on the Employment and Earnings of Britain's Ethnic Communities', *Journal of Ethnic and Migration Studies*, 28 (3): 427–42.

Lloyd, Katherine (2015), 'Negotiating Place, Heritage and Diversity: Young People's Narratives of Belonging and Exclusion in Scotland', in Christopher Whitehead, Katherine Lloyd, Susannah Eckersley and Rhiannon Mason (eds), *Museums,*

Migration and Identity in Europe: Peoples, Places and Identities, London: Routledge, pp. 149–82.

Loader, Ian and Aogán Mulcahy (2003), *Policing and the Condition of England: Memory, Politics and Culture*, Oxford: Oxford University Press.

Love, John, Steve Vertigans, Ann Love and Konrad Zdeb (2011), *A Scottish Health Council Report on Muslims, Hindus, Sikhs and Access to NHS Services in Scotland: Summary*, Glasgow: Scottish Health Council.

Maan, Bashir (1992), *The New Scots: The Story of Asians in Scotland*, Edinburgh: John Donald Publishers.

Maan, Bashir (2008), *The Thistle and the Crescent*, Glendaruel: Argyll Publishing.

Maan, Bashir (2014), *Muslims in Scotland*, Glendaruel: Argyll Publishing.

McBride, Maureen (2016), 'A Review of the Evidence on Hate Crime and Prejudice: Report for the Independent Advisory Group on Hate Crime, Prejudice and Community Cohesion', *SCCJR Report 07/2016*.

McCollum, David, Beata Nowok and Scott Tindal (2014), 'Public Attitudes Towards Migration in Scotland: Exceptionality and Possible Policy Implications', *Scottish Affairs*, 23 (1): 79–102.

McConaghy, Kieran (2015), *Scotland and Separatism: Reverberations of the Scottish Independence Referendum on Separatist Politics*, St Andrews: University of St Andrews, Handa Centre for the Study of Terrorism and Political Violence.

McCrone, David (2001), *Understanding Scotland: The Sociology of a Nation*, 2nd edn, London: Routledge.

McCrone, David (2002), 'Who Do You Say You Are? Making Sense of National Identities in Modern Britain', *Ethnicities*, 2 (3): 301–20.

McCrone, David and Frank Bechhofer (2008), 'National Identity and Social Inclusion', *Ethnic and Racial Studies*, 31 (7): 1245–66.

McCrone, David and Frank Bechhofer (2010), 'Claiming National Identity', *Ethnic and Racial Studies*, 33 (6): 921–48.

McCrone, David and Frank Bechhofer (2015), *Understanding National Identity*, Cambridge: Cambridge University Press.

McDonald, Zahra (2011), 'Securing Identities, Resisting Terror: Muslim Youth Work in the UK and its Implications for Security', *Religion, State and Society*, 39 (2–3): 177–89.

McGarvey, Neil and Gareth Mulvey (2016), 'Identities and Politics in the 2014 Scottish Independence Referendum: The Polish and Pakistani Experience', in Roberta Medda-Windischer and Patricia Popelier (eds), *Pro-independence Movements and Immigration: Discourse, Policy and Practice*, Leiden: Brill, pp. 134–62.

McGrath, Harry (2012), 'An Independent Scotland Could Look Like a Wee Canada', *New Statesman*, 26 March, <http://www.newstatesman.com/politics/2012/12/independent-scotland-could-look-wee-canada> (last accessed 27 April 2016).

McGuire, Jon (2016), 'Brexit Fallout: Nazi Stickers with Racist and Homophobic Messages Found in Glasgow Following EU Referendum', *Herald Scotland*, 28 June, <http://www.heraldscotland.com/news/14584292.Nazi_stickers_with_racist_and_homophobic_messages_found_in_Glasgow_following_EU_referendum> (last accessed 29 June 2016).

McIntosh, Ian, Douglas Robertson and Duncan Sim (2008), *English People in Scotland: An Invisible Minority*, Lampeter: Edwin Mellen Press.

Maclean, Colin and Kenneth Veitch (2006), *Scottish Life and Society. A Compendium of Scottish Ethnology, Vol. 12: Religion*, East Linton: Tuckwell Press.

McVie, Susan and Susan Wiltshire (2010), *Experience of Discrimination, Social Marginalisation and Violence: A Comparative Study of Muslim and non-Muslim Youth in Three EU Member States*, Vienna: European Commission Fundamental Rights Agency.

Macey, Marie (1999), 'Class, Gender and Religious Influences on Changing Patterns of Pakistani Muslim Male Violence in Bradford', *Ethnic and Racial Studies*, 22 (5): 845–66.

Maddox, David (2015), 'Scots Jihadist Killed by RAF Drone Strike in Syria', *The Scotsman*, 7 September, <http://www.scotsman.com/news/politics/scots-jihadist-killed-by-raf-drone-strike-in-syria-1-3879933> (last accessed 3 February 2016).

Madeley, John (2003), 'European Liberal Democracy and the Principle of State Religious Neutrality', *West European Politics*, 26 (1): 1–22.

Malik, Kenan (2005), 'The Islamophobia Myth', *Prospect*, 107 (February).

Malik, Shiv (2011), 'Muslim Rioters Say Police Discrimination Motivated Them', *The Guardian*, 8 December, <http://www.theguardian.com/uk/2011/dec/08/muslim-rioters-police-discrimination-motivated> (last accessed 3 February 2016).

Marranci, Gabriele (2008), *The Anthropology of Islam*. Oxford: Berg.

Marshall, Chris (2012), 'Pattern's Principles', *The Scotsman*, 8 July, <http://www.scotsman.com/news/scotland/top-stories/revealed-pattern-s-principles-1-2399186> (last accessed 16 February 2016).

Marshall, Chris (2016), 'Scots Counter-Terrorism Chief Fears Homegrown Attack', *The Scotsman*, 26 March, <http://www.scotsman.com/news/scots-counter-terrorism-chief-fears-homegrown-attack-1-4083407> (last accessed 29 March 2016).

Maxwell, Rahsaan (2010), 'Trust in Government among British Muslims: The Importance of Migration Status', *Political Behavior*, 32 (1): 89–109.

Maxwell, Rahsaan and Erik Bleich (2014), 'What Makes Muslims Feel French?', *Social Forces*, 93 (1): 155–79.

Meer, Nasar (2010), *Citizenship, Identity and the Politics of Multiculturalism: The Rise of Muslim Consciousness*, Basingstoke: Palgrave Macmillan.

Meer, Nasar (2011), 'What Would Independence Mean for Scotland's Racial Minorities?', *The Guardian*, 20 May, <http://www.theguardian.com/politics/2011/may/20/independence-scotland-racial-minorities> (last accessed 3 January 2016).

Meer, Nasar (2012), 'Misrecognizing Muslim Consciousness in Europe', *Ethnicities*, 12 (2): 178–96.

Meer, Nasar (2014a), *Race and Ethnicity*, London: Sage Publications.

Meer, Nasar (2014b), '"We're a' Jock Tamson's Bairns!" Race Equality, Migration and Citizenship in Scotland and the UK', *Discover Society*, 30 September, <http://www.discoversociety.org/2014/09/30/were-a-jock-tamsons-bairns-race-equality-migration-and-citizenship-in-scotland-and-the-uk> (last accessed 11 February 2016).

Meer, Nasar (2014c), 'Is it True that Muslims in Britain Are Not "Integrated" and How Can We Measure It?', *Research the Headlines*, 26 September, <http://researchtheheadlines.org/2014/09/26/is-it-true-that-muslims-in-britain-are-not-integrated-and-how-can-we-measure-this> (last accessed 10 February 2016).

Meer, Nasar (2014d), 'Islamophobia and Postcolonialism: Continuity, Orientalism and Muslim Consciousness', *Patterns of Prejudice*, 48 (5): 500–15.

Meer, Nasar (2015a), 'Looking Up in Scotland? Multinationalism, Multiculturalism and Political Elites', *Ethnic and Racial Studies*, 38 (9): 1477–96.

Meer, Nasar (2015b), 'Scottish BME Poll', *Survation*, <http://survation.com/wp-content/uploads/2015/09/Final-Strathclyde-Tables-5e0m21.pdf> (last accessed 20 January 2016).

Meer, Nasar (2016), 'Introduction: A "Scottish Approach" to Race Equality?', in Nasar Meer (ed.), *Scotland and Race Equality: Directions in Policy and Identity*, London: Runnymede Trust, pp. 3–4.

Meer, Nasar and Tariq Modood (2009), 'The Multicultural State We're In: Muslims, "Multiculture" and the "Civic Re-Balancing" of British Multiculturalism', *Political Studies*, 57: 473–97.

Meer, Nasar and Michael Rosie (2012), 'On an Equal Footing', *Holyrood*, 9 April,

<http://legacy.holyrood.com/2012/04/on-an-equal-footing> (last accessed 10 January 2016).

Meer, Nasar and Timothy Peace (2015), 'The 2015 Election: BME Groups in Scotland', in Omar Khan and Kjartan Sveinsson (eds), *Race and Elections*, London: Runnymede Trust, pp. 26–9.

Meer, Nasar, Varun Uberoi and Tariq Modood (2015), 'Nationhood and Muslims in Britain', in Nancy Foner and Patrick Simon (eds), *Fear and Anxiety Over National Identity*, New York, NY: Russell Sage, pp. 169–88.

MI5 (2016), *Terrorist Threat Levels*, <http://www.mi5.gov.uk/threat-levels> (last accessed 8 March 2016).

Migration Observatory (2016), *Immigration and Independence: Public Opinion on Immigration in Scotland in the Context of the Referendum Debate*, Oxford: University of Oxford, Migration Observatory.

Miles, Robert and Lesley Muirhead (1986), 'Racism in Scotland: A Matter for Further Investigation?', in David McCrone (ed.), *The Scottish Government Yearbook 1986*, Edinburgh: University of Edinburgh, Unit for the Study of Government in Scotland, pp. 108–36.

Miles, Robert and Anne Dunlop (1986), 'The Racialization of Politics in Britain: Why Scotland is Different', *Patterns of Prejudice*, 20 (1): 22–33.

Miles, Robert and Anne Dunlop (1987), 'Racism in Britain: The Scottish Dimension', in Peter Jackson (ed.), *Race and Racism: Essays in Social Geography*, London: Allen and Unwin, pp. 119–41.

Modood, Tariq (2003), "Muslims and the Politics of Difference", *The Political Quarterly*, 74 (s1): 100–15.

Modood, Tariq (2004), 'Capitals, Ethnic Identity and Educational Qualifications', *Cultural Trends*, 13 (12): 87–105.

Modood, Tariq (2005), *Multicultural Politics: Racism, Ethnicity and Muslims in Britain*, Minneapolis, MN: University of Minnesota Press.

Modood, Tariq (2010), 'Moderate Secularism, Religion as Identity and Respect for Religion', *Political Quarterly*, 81 (1): 4–14.

Modood, Tariq and John Salt (2011), 'Migration, Minorities and the Nation', in Tariq Modood and John Salt (eds), *Global Migration, Ethnicity and Britishness*, Basingstoke: Palgrave Macmillan, pp. 3–13.

Modood, Tariq, Richard Berthoud, Jane Lakey, James Nazroo, Patten Smith, Satnam Virdee and Sharon Beishon (1997), *The Fourth National Survey of Ethnic Minorities in Britain: Diversity and Disadvantage*, London: Policy Studies Institute.

Mogahed, Dalia (2007), *Beyond Multiculturalism vs. Assimilation*, Princeton, NJ: Gallup World Poll.

Moorey, Peter and Amina Yaqin (2010), 'Muslims in the Frame', *Interventions: International Journal of Postcolonial Studies*, 12 (2): 145–56.

Murray, Kath (2014), 'Stop and Search in Scotland: An Evaluation of Police Practice', *SCCJR Report 01/2014*.

Murray, Kath (2015), *Landscape Review on Stop and Search in Scotland*, Edinburgh: University of Edinburgh, Scottish Institute for Policing Research.

Murray, Kath and Diarmaid Harkin (2016), 'Policing in Cool and Hot Climates: Legitimacy, Power and the Rise and Fall of Mass Stop and Search in Scotland', *British Journal of Criminology*, DOI: 10.1093/bjc/azw007.

Mycock, Andrew (2012), 'SNP, Identity and Citizenship: Re-imagining State and Nation', *National Identities*, 14 (1): 53–69.

Mythen, Gabe (2012), 'Identities in the Third Space? Solidity, Elasticity and Resilience Amongst Young British Pakistani Muslims', *Journal of British Sociology*, 63 (3): 393–411.

Nachmani, Amikam (2016), 'The Past as a Yardstick: Europeans, Muslim Migrants and the Onus of European-Jewish Histories', *Israel Affairs*, 22 (2): 318–54.

Naqshbandi, Mehmood (2015a), *Muslims in Britain: UK Mosque/Masjid Directory*, <http://mosques.muslimsinbritain.org/index.php> (last accessed 16 June 2016).

Naqshbandi, Mehmood (2015b), *UK Mosque Statistics / Masjid Statistics*, <http://www.muslimsinbritain.org/resources/masjid_report.pdf> (last accessed 26 June 2016).

National Records of Scotland (2013), *2011 Census: Key Results on Population, Ethnicity, Identity, Language, Religion, Health, Housing and Accommodation in Scotland – Release 2A*, Edinburgh: National Records of Scotland.

Naysmith, Stephen (2015), 'Youth Radicalisation Debate Could be the Start of Something', *Herald Scotland*, 21 May, <http://www.heraldscotland.com/opin ion/13214765.Youth_radicalisation_debate_could_be_the_start_of_someth ing> (last accessed 16 February 2016).

Neuman, Keith (2016), *Survey of Muslims in Canada 2016*, Toronto: The Environics Institute for Survey Research.

Nicholson, Jonathan (2012), 'March in Solidarity with Palestinian Hunger Strikers – Edinburgh', *Demotix*, 28 April, <http://www.demotix.com/news/1173805/ march-solidarity-palestinian-hunger-strikers-edinburgh#media-1179544> (last accessed 2 November 2015).

Nielsen, Jørgen (2004), *Muslims in Western Europe*, 3rd edn, Edinburgh: Edinburgh University Press.

Noden, Philip, Michael Shiner and Tariq Modood (2014), 'University Offer Rates for Candidates from Different Ethnic Categories', *Oxford Review of Education*, 40 (3): 349–69.

Nyiri, Zsolt (2007), *European Muslims Show No Conflict Between Religious and National Identities*, Princeton, NJ: Gallup World Poll.

O'Leary, David (2014), 'Scottish Muslims Plan Rally against Islamic State', *The Scotsman*, 12 October, <http://www.scotsman.com/news/scottish-muslims-plan-rally-against-islamic-state-1-3570268> (last accessed 16 December 2015).

Ormston, Rachel, John Curtice, Susan McConville and Susan Reid (2011), *Scottish Social Attitudes Survey 2010: Attitudes to Discrimination and Positive Action*, Edinburgh: Scottish Government Social Research.

O'Toole, Therese, Daniel Nilsson DeHanas, Tariq Modood, Nasar Meer and Stephen Jones (2013), *Taking Part: Muslim Participation in Contemporary Governance*, Bristol: University of Bristol.

Palmer, Martin and Nigel Palmer (2000), *The Spiritual Traveler: England, Scotland, Wales. The Guide to Sacred Sites and Pilgrim Routes in Britain*, Mahwah, NJ: Hidden Spring.

Pantazis, Christina and Simon Pemberton (2009), 'From the "Old" to the "New" Suspect Community: Examining the Impacts of Recent UK Counter-Terrorist Legislation', *British Journal of Criminology*, 49 (5): 646–66.

Pantucci, Raffaello (2015), *'We Love Death as You Love Life'. Britain's Suburban Terrorists*, London: Hurst.

Parekh, Bhikhu (2000a), *Rethinking Multiculturalism: Cultural Diversity and Political Theory*, London: Macmillan.

Parekh, Bhikhu (2000b), *The Future of Multi-Ethnic Britain*, London: Profile Books.

Parmar, Alpa (2011), 'Stop and Search in London: Counter-Terrorist or Counter-Productive?', *Policing and Society: An International Journal of Research and Policy*, 21 (4): 369–82.

Peace, Timothy (2015a), *European Social Movements and Muslim Activism: Another World but with Whom?*, Basingstoke: Palgrave Macmillan.

Peace, Timothy (2015b), 'British Muslims and the Anti-War Movement', in Timothy Peace (ed.), *Muslims and Political Participation in Britain*, London: Routledge, pp. 124–37.

Peace, Timothy (ed.) (2015c), *Muslims and Political Participation in Britain*, London: Routledge.

Peach, Ceri (2005), 'Muslims in the UK', in Tahir Abbas (ed.), *Muslim Britain: Communities Under Pressure*, London: Zed Books, pp. 18–30.

Peach, Ceri (2006), 'Islam, Ethnicity and South Asian Religions in the London 2001 Census', *Transactions of the Institute of British Geographers*, 31 (3): 353–70.

Peach, Ceri and Richard Gale (2003), 'Muslims, Hindus and Sikhs in the New Religious Geography of England', *Geographical Review*, 93 (4): 469–90.

Peek, Lori (2005), 'Becoming Muslim: The Development of a Religious Identity', *Sociology of Religion*, 66 (3): 215–42.

Penrose, Jan (2013), 'Multiple Multiculturalisms: Insights from the Edinburgh Mela', *Social and Cultural Geography*, 14 (7): 829–51.

Pew Global Attitudes Project (2006), *The Great Divide: How Westerners and Muslims View Each Other*, Washington, DC: Pew Research Centre.

Pew Global Attitudes Project (2011), *Common Concerns About Islamic Extremism: Muslim–Western Tensions Persist*, Washington, DC: Pew Research Centre.

Pew Global Attitudes Project (2015), *Faith in European Project Reviving*, Washington, DC: Pew Research Centre.

Pew Global Attitudes Project (2016), *Europeans Fear Wave of Refugees Will Mean More Terrorism, Fewer Jobs*, Washington, DC: Pew Research Centre.

Phillips, Melanie (2006), *Londonistan: How Britain is Creating a Terror State Within*, London: Gibson Square Books.

Pinker, Steven (2002), *The Blank Slate: The Modern Denial of Human Nature*, New York, NY: Viking Press.

Police Scotland (2014), *Management Information Year End 2013/14*, Report to the Scottish Police Authority, <http://www.scotland.police.uk/assets/pdf/138327/232757/management-information-year-end-2013-14> (last accessed 16 February 2016).

Porter, Tom (2016), 'Glasgow Central Mosque Accused of Hiding Links to Anti-Ahmadi "Hate Speech" Group', *International Business Times*, 25 April, <http://www.ibtimes.co.uk/glasgow-central-mosque-accused-hiding-links-anti-ahmadi-hate-speech-group-1555662> (last accessed 25 April 2016).

Prokopiou, Evangelia, Tony Cline and Guida de Abreu (2012), '"Silent" Monologues, "Loud" Dialogues and the Emergence of Hibernated L-Positions in the Negotiation of Multivoiced Cultural Identities', *Culture and Psychology*, 18 (4): 494–509.

Putnam, Richard (2000), *Bowling Alone: The Collapse and Revival of Community in America*, New York, NY: Simon and Schuster.

Qureshi, Karen (2004), 'Respected and Respectable: The Centrality of "Performance" and "Audiences" in the (Re)production and Potential Revision of Gendered Ethnicities', *Particip@tions: Journal of Audience and Reception Studies*, 1 (2), <http://www.participations.org/volume%201/issue%202/1_02_qureshi_arti cle.htm> (last accessed 4 March 2016).

Qureshi, Karen (2006), 'Trans-Boundary Spaces: Scottish Pakistanis and Trans-Local/ National Identities', *International Journal of Cultural Studies*, 9 (2): 207–26.

Qureshi, Karen (2007), 'Shifting Proximities: News and "Belonging-Security"', *European Journal of Cultural Studies*, 10 (3): 294–310.

Qureshi, Karen and Shaun Moores (1999), 'Identity Remix: Tradition and Translation in the Lives of Young Pakistani Scots', *European Journal of Cultural Studies*, 2 (3): 311–30.

Rahim, Hajra (2015), 'Good Communty Relations Mean Young Muslims in Scotland Eschew Extremism', *The Guardian*, 14 July, <http://www.theguardian. com/society/2015/jul/14/good-community-relations-young-muslims-scotland- eschew-extremism> (last accessed 7 March 2016).

Renan, Ernst (1939), 'What is a Nation?' in Alfred Zimmern (ed.), *Modern Political Doctrines*, Oxford: Oxford University Press, pp. 186–205.

Revoir, Paul (2012), 'Heavily Made-Up Girl in a Hijab Provokes Storm of Complaints as BBC is Accused of Insulting Muslims with New Sitcom Citizen Khan', *Mail Online*, 28 August, <http://www.dailymail.co.uk/news/article-2194972/Citizen- Khan-provokes-200-complaints-BBC-accused-insulting-Muslims.html> (last accessed 14 January 2016).

Robinson, Lena (2009), 'South Asians in Britain: Acculturation, Cultural Identity and Perceived Discrimination', *International Journal of Diversity in Organisations, Communities and Nations*, 9 (4): 71–84.

Rosie, Michael and Ross Bond (2008), 'National Identities and Politics After Devolution', *Radical Statistics*, 97: 47–65.

Roy, Olivier (2004), *Globalised Islam: The Search for a New Ummah*, London: Hurst.

Roy, Olivier (2007), *Secularism Confronts Islam*, translated by George Holoch, New York, NY: Columbia University Press.

Ruthven, Malise (2012), *Islam: A Very Short Introduction*, 2nd edn, Oxford: Oxford University Press.

Saeed, Amir (2015), 'Racism and Islamophobia: A Personal Perspective', *Identity Papers: A Journal of British and Irish Studies*, 1 (1): 15–31.

Saeed, Amir, Neil Blain and Douglas Forbes (2001), 'New Ethnic and National Questions in Scotland: Post-British Identities Among Glasgow Pakistani Teenagers', *Ethnic and Racial Studies*, 22 (5): 821–44.

Saggar, Shamit and Will Sommerville (2012), *Building a British Model of Integration in an Era of Immigration: Policy Lessons for Government*, Washington, DC: Migration Policy Institute.

Saha, Anamik (2013), 'Citizen Smith More Than Citizen Kane? Genres-in-Progress and the Cultural Politics of Difference', *South Asian Popular Culture*, 11 (1): 97–102.

Sampson, Robert and John Laub (1990), 'Crime and Deviance Over the Life Course: The Salience of Adult Social Bonds', *American Sociological Review*, 55: 609–27.

Sampson, Robert and William Wilson (1995), 'Toward a Theory of Race, Crime and Urban Inequality', in John Hagan and Ruth Peterson (eds), *Crime and Inequality*, Stanford, CA: Stanford University Press, pp. 37–54.

Sander, Thomas and Robert Putnam (2010), 'Still Bowling Alone? The Post-9/11 Split', *Journal of Democracy*, 21 (1): 9–16.

Sartawi, Mohammed and Gordon Sammut (2012), 'Negotiating British Muslim Identity: Everyday Concerns of Practising Muslims in London', *Culture and Psychology*, 18 (4): 559–76.

Sartori, Giovanni (2000), *Pluralismo, Multiculturalismo e Estranei: Saggio sulla Società Multietnica* [Pluralism, Multiculturalism and Strangers: An Essay on the Multiethnic Society], Milan: Rizzoli.

Sarwar, Mohammad (2016), *My Remarkable Journey: The Autobiography of Britain's First Muslim MP*, Edinburgh: Birlinn.

Savage, Timothy (2004), 'Europe and Islam: Crescent Waxing, Cultures Clashing', *The Washington Quarterly*, 27 (3): 25–50.

Scharbrodt, Oliver, Tuula Sakaranaho, Adil Khan, Yafa Shanneik and Vivian Ibrahim (2015), *Muslims in Ireland: Past and Present*, Edinburgh: Edinburgh University Press.

ScotCen Social Research (2014), *Attitudes to Same-Sex Marriage in Scotland*, Edinburgh: ScotCen Social Research.

Scotsman, The (2003), 'Scots Butcher Creates Halal Haggis for Muslim Clientele', *The Scotsman*, 7 December, <http://www.scotsman.com/news/scotland/top-sto ries/scots-butcher-creates-halal-haggis-for-muslim-clientele-1-1296802> (last accessed 6 March 2016).

Scotsman, The (2015), 'Paris Attacks: Scotland Holds Minute's Silence', *The Scotsman*, 16 November, <http://www.scotsman.com/news/politics/paris-attacks-scot land-holds-minute-s-silence-1-3949502> (last accessed 9 March 2016).

Scotsman, The (2016), 'Edinburgh Voted the World's Fourth Most Beautiful City', *The Scotsman*, 19 February, <http://www.scotsman.com/edinburgh/edinburgh-

voted-the-world-s-fourth-most-beautiful-city-1-4034597> (last accessed 28 February 2016).

Scottish Executive (2002), *Police Stop and Search among White and Minority Ethnic Young People in Scotland*, Edinburgh: Scottish Executive.

Scottish Executive (2003), *Pride and Prejudice: A Review of Police Race Relations in Scotland*, Edinburgh: Scottish Executive.

Scottish Executive (2004), *Analysis of Ethnicity in the 2001 Census: Summary Report*, Edinburgh: Scottish Executive.

Scottish Executive (2005), *Analysis of Religion in the 2001 Census: Summary Report*, Edinburgh: Scottish Executive.

Scottish Executive (2006), *One Scotland Many Cultures 2005/06 – Waves 6 and 7 Campaign Evaluation*, Edinburgh: Scottish Executive.

Scottish Government (2012), *Scottish Index of Multiple Deprivation 2012: A National Statistics Publication for Scotland*, Edinburgh: Scottish Government.

Scottish Government (2013a), 'Racist Incidents Recorded by the Police in Scotland, 2012–13', *Statistical Bulletin: Crime and Justice Series*.

Scottish Government (2013b), *Scotland's Future: Your Guide to an Independent Scotland*, Edinburgh: Scottish Government.

Scottish Government (2015a), 'Recorded Crime in Scotland 2014–15', *Statistical Bulletin: Crime and Justice Series*.

Scottish Government (2015b), 'Religiously Aggravated Offending in Scotland 2014–15', *Crime and Justice Series*.

Scottish Government (2015c), 'Racist Incidents Recorded by the Police in Scotland, 2013–14', *Statistical Bulletin: Crime and Justice Series*.

Scottish Government (2016a), 'Religiously Aggravated Offending in Scotland 2015–16', *Crime and Justice Series*.

Scottish Government (2016b), *Race Equality Framework for Scotland 2016–2030*, Edinburgh: Scottish Government.

Scottish Government (2016c), 'Recorded Crime in Scotland 2015–16', *Statistical Bulletin: Crime and Justice Series*.

Scottish Government (2016d), *Scottish Social Attitudes 2015: Attitudes to Discrimination and Positive Action*, Edinburgh: ScotCen Social Research.

Scourfield, Jonathan, Chris Taylor, Graham Moore and Sophie Gilliat-Ray (2012), 'The Intergenerational Transmission of Islam in England and Wales: Evidence from the Citizenship Survey', *Sociology*, 46 (1): 91–108.

Scuzzarello, Sarah (2015), 'Political Participation and Dual Identification Among Migrants', *Journal of Ethnic and Migration Studies*, 41 (8): 1214–34.

Sendagorta, Fidel (2005), 'Jihad in Europe: The Wider Context', *Survival*, 47 (3): 63–72.

Shah, Bindi, Claire Dwyer and Tariq Modood (2010), 'Explaining Educational Achievement and Career Aspirations Among Young British Pakistanis: Mobilizing "Ethnic Capital"', *Sociology*, 44 (6): 1109–27.

Shaikh, Omar and Stefano Bonino (forthcoming), 'Feeling Scottish and Being Muslim: Findings from the Colourful Heritage Project', in Peter Hopkins (ed.), *Muslims in Scotland: Lived Experiences and Community Themes*, Edinburgh: Edinburgh University Press.

Sharp, Clare, Anna Marcinkiewicz and Lisa Rutherford (2014), *Attitudes Towards Alcohol in Scotland: Results From the 2013 Scottish Social Attitudes Survey*, Edinburgh: ScotCen Social Research.

Shaw, Alison (2001), 'Kinship, Cultural Preference and Immigration: Consanguineous Marriage Among British Pakistanis', *Journal of the Royal Anthropological Institute*, 7 (2): 315–34.

Sherwood, Marika (2003), 'Lascars in Glasgow and the West of Scotland During World War II', *Scottish Labour History Society Journal*, 38: 37–50.

Silke, Andrew (2008), 'Research on Terrorism: A Review of the Impact of 9/11 and the Global War on Terrorism', in Hsinchun Chen, Edna Reid, Joshua Sinai, Andrew Silke and Boaz Ganor (eds), *Terrorism Informatics: Knowledge Management and Data Mining for Homeland Security*, New York, NY: Springer, pp. 27–50.

Simpson, Ludi (2014), 'How Has Ethnic Diversity Changed in Scotland?', *The Dynamics of Diversity: Evidence from the 2011 Census*, Manchester: Centre on Dynamics of Diversity.

Siraj, Asifa (2011), 'Meanings of Modesty and the Hijab Amongst Muslim Women in Glasgow, Scotland', *Gender, Place and Culture: A Journal of Feminist Geography*, 18 (6): 716–31.

Siraj, Asifa (2012), '"Smoothing Down Ruffled Feathers": The Construction of Muslim Women's Feminine Identities', *Journal of Gender Studies*, 21 (2): 185–99.

Smith, David (2005), 'Ethnic Differences in Intergenerational Crime Patterns', *Crime and Justice*, 32: 59–129.

Spalek, Basia (2002), 'Hate Crimes against British Muslims in the Aftermath of September 11th', *Criminal Justice Matters*, 48 (1): 20–1.

Spalek, Basia (2005), 'British Muslims and the Criminal Justice System', in Tufyal Choudhury (ed.), *Muslims in the UK: Policies for Engaged Citizens*, Budapest: Open Society Institute, pp. 253–343.

Statham, Paul (2016), 'How Ordinary People View Muslim Group Rights in Britain, the Netherlands, France and Germany: Significant "Gaps" between Majorities and Muslims?', *Journal of Ethnic and Migration Studies*, 42 (2): 217–36.

Strabac, Zan and Ola Listhaug (2008), 'Anti-Muslim Prejudice in Europe: A Multilevel Analysis of Survey Data from 30 Countries', *Social Science Research*, 37 (1): 268–86.

Strathclyde Police (2011), *Chief Constable's Annual Report 2010/2011: Statistical Supplement*, Glasgow: Strathclyde Police.

Student Rights (2012), *Israeli Ambassador Shouted Down by Anti-Israel Activists*, <http://www.studentrights.org.uk/article/1985/breaking_israeli_ambassador_shouted_down_by_anti_israel_activists> (last accessed 6 March 2016).

Suleiman, Yasir (2009), *Contextualising Islam in Britain: Exploratory Perspectives*, Cambridge: University of Cambridge, Centre of Islamic Studies.

Suleiman, Yasir (2012), *Contextualising Islam in Britain II*, Cambridge: University of Cambridge, Centre of Islamic Studies.

Suleiman, Yasir (2013), *Narratives of Conversion to Islam in Britain: Female Perspectives*, Cambridge: University of Cambridge, Centre of Islamic Studies.

Suleiman, Yasir (2016), *Narratives of Conversion to Islam in Britain: Male Perspectives*, Cambridge: University of Cambridge, Centre of Islamic Studies.

Sumner, Ian (2001), *The Indian Army: 1914–1947*, Oxford: Osprey Publishing.

Sunak, Rishi and Saratha Rajeswaran (2014), *A Portrait of Modern Britain*, London: Policy Exchange.

Sutherland, Ruari (2012), '"The Scottish Hate Us More Than the Muslims . . .": The North/South Divide? A Comparative Analysis of the Agenda, Activities and Development of the English and Scottish Defence Leagues', *Reinvention: A Journal of Undergraduate Research*, British Conference of Undergraduate Research 2012 Special Issue, <http://www.warwick.ac.uk/go/reinventionjournal/issues/bcur2012specialissue/Sutherland> (last accessed 9 March 2016).

Swami, Viren, Jusnara Miah, Nazerine Noorani and Donna Taylor (2013), 'Is the Hijab Protective? An Investigation of Body Image and Related Constructs among British Muslim Women', *British Journal of Psychology*, 105 (3): 352–63.

Swindon, Peter (2016a), 'Asad Shah Family Fear for Safety After Killing Linked to Sectarian Tensions in Muslim Community', *Evening Times*, 27 March, <http://m.eveningtimes.co.uk/news/14386376.Asad_Shah_family_fear_for_safety_after_killing_linked_to_sectarian_tensions_in_Muslim_community> (last accessed 29 March 2016).

Swindon, Peter (2016b), 'Faith Groups Condemn Extremism as Police Probe

Links between Mosque Leaders and Pakistani Terrorists', *Evening Times*, 1 April, <http://m.eveningtimes.co.uk/news/14397384.Faith_groups_condemn_extremism_as_police_probe_links_between_Mosque_leaders_and_Pakistani_terrorists> (last accessed 12 April 2016).

Swindon, Peter (2016c), 'Scots Muslims Speak Out Over Racist Abuse After Terror Attacks', *Herald Scotland*, 31 July, <http://www.heraldscotland.com/news/14653092.Verbal_abuse__violence_and_suspicion__prominent_Scots_Muslims_speak_out_as_racism_ramps_up_amid_summer_of_terror> (last accessed 8 August 2016).

Syal, Rajeev (2009), 'Undercover Job Hunters Reveal Huge Race Bias in Britain', *The Observer*, 18 October, <http://www.theguardian.com/money/2009/oct/18/racism-discrimination-employment-undercover> (last accessed 20 February 2016).

Taspinar, Omer (2003), 'Europe's Muslim Streets', *Foreign Policy*, 135: 76–7.

Taylor, Charles (1994), 'The Politics of Recognition', in Amy Guttmann (ed.), *Multiculturalism: Examining the Politics of Recognition*, Princeton, NJ: Princeton University Press, pp. 25–73.

Tell MAMA (2016), 'Scottish Defence League Protest Falls Flat but Brings Together Hardened Neo-Nazis', *Tell MAMA*, 22 March, <http://tellmamauk.org/scottish-defence-league-protest-falls-flat-brings-together-hardened-neo-nazis> (last accessed 17 June 2016).

Tibi, Bassam (2007), 'A Migration Story: From Muslim Immigrants to European "Citizens of the Heart?"', *Fletcher Forum of World Affairs*, 31 (1): 147–68.

Tibi, Bassam (2010), 'Ethnicity of Fear? Islamic Migration and the Ethnicization of Islam in Europe', *Studies in Ethnicity and Nationalism*, 11 (1): 126–57.

Tönnies, Ferdinand (1974 [1887]), *Community and Society*, translated by Charles Loomis, New York, NY: Harper and Row.

Townsend, Mark (2016), 'Scotland Yard Warns Muslims Against Sectarian Feuds after Glasgow Murder', *The Observer*, 23 April, <http://www.theguardian.com/uk-news/2016/apr/23/asad-shah-stabbed-ahmadiyya-muslim-glasgow> (last accessed 26 April 2016).

Tyab, Imtiaz (2013), 'Fair Winds for Pakistan's Bagpipe Industry', *Al Jazeera*, 13 February, <http://www.aljazeera.com/video/asia/2013/02/201321371749190628.html> (last accessed 25 January 2016).

Uberoi, Varun, Nasar Meer, Tariq Modood and Claire Dwyer (2011), 'Feeling and Being Muslim and British', in Tariq Modood and John Salt (eds), *Global Migration, Ethnicity and Britishness*, Basingstoke: Palgrave Macmillan, pp. 205–24.

Understanding Glasgow (n.d.), *Glasgow Neighbourhood Data Profiles: Pollokshields*

East, <http://www.understandingglasgow.com/profiles/2_south_sector/46_pol-lokshields_east> (last accessed 26 February 2016).

Vaughan, Barry (2002), 'The Punitive Consequences of Consumer Culture', *Punishment and Society*, 4 (2): 195–211.

Vidgor, Jacob (2011), *Comparing Immigrant Assimilation in North America and Europe*, New York, NY: Manhattan Institute.

Virdee Satnam, Christopher Kyriakides and Tariq Modood (2006), 'Codes of Cultural Belonging: Racialised National Identities in a Multi-Ethnic Scottish Neighbourhood', *Sociological Research Online*, 11 (4).

Volpi, Frédéric (2007), 'Constructing the "Ummah" in European Security: Between Exit, Voice and Loyalty', *Government and Opposition*, 42 (3): 451–70.

Wacquant, Loïc (2009), *Punishing the Poor: The Neoliberal Government of Social Insecurity*, Durham, NC: Duke University Press.

Walsh, David, Neil Bendel, Richard Jones and Phil Hanlon (2010), 'It's not "Just Deprivation": Why do Equally Deprived UK Cities Experience Different Health Outcomes?', *Public Health*, 124 (9): 487–95.

Walsh, David, Martin Taulbut and Phil Hanlon (2010), 'The Aftershock of Deindustrialization: Trends in Mortality in Scotland and Other Parts of Post-Industrial Europe', *European Journal of Public Health*, 20 (1): 58–64.

Walsh, David, Gerry McCartney, Chik Collins, Martin Taulbut and David Batty (2016), *History, Politics and Vulnerability: Explaining Excess Mortality in Scotland and Glasgow*, Glasgow: Glasgow Centre for Population Health.

Wardak, Ali (2000), *Social Control and Deviance: A South Asian Community in Scotland*, Aldershot: Ashgate.

Wardak, Ali (2002), 'The Mosque and Social Control in Edinburgh's Muslim Community', *Culture and Religion: An Interdisciplinary Journal*, 3 (2): 201–19.

Weber, Victoria (n.d.), *Scottish, English, European Identities: A Literature Review*. Edinburgh: University of Edinburgh, Sociology Research Papers.

Webster, Alison (2003), 'The Contribution of the Scottish Enlightenment to the Abandonment of the Institution of Slavery', *The European Legacy: Towards New Paradigms*, 8 (4): 481–9.

Weedon, Elisabet, Sheila Riddell, Gillean McCluskey and Kristina Konstantoni (2013), *Muslim Families' Educational Experiences in England and Scotland*, Edinburgh: University of Edinburgh, Centre for Research in Education Inclusion and Diversity.

Weldon, Victoria (2014), 'Scottish Muslims Condemn "Barbaric" Murder', *Herald Scotland*, 15 September, <http://www.heraldscotland.com/news/13179985.

Scottish_Muslims_condemn__barbaric__murder> (last accessed 6 March 2016).

Werbner, Pnina (2012), 'Veiled Interventions in Pure Space: Honour, Shame and Embodied Struggles Among Muslims in Britain and France', in Max Farrar, Simon Robinson, Yasmin Valli and Paul Wetherly (eds), *Islam in the West: Key Issues in Multiculturalism*, Basingstoke: Palgrave Macmillan, pp. 103–20.

Whybrow, Paul, Julie Ramsay and Karen MacNee (2012), *The Scottish Health Survey: Equality Groups*, Edinburgh: Scottish Government.

Winkler, Beate (2006), *Racism, Xenophobia and the Media: Towards Respect and Understanding of All Religions and Cultures*, speech delivered at 'Euro-Mediterranean Seminar', Vienna, 22 May, <http://fra.europa.eu/sites/default/files/fra_uploads/153-euromed_en.pdf> (last accessed 14 February 2016).

Women and Equalities Committee (2016), *Employment Opportunities for Muslim Women in the UK*, London: House of Commons.

Yassine, Abdessalam (1998), *Islamiser la Modernité* [The Islamisation of Modernity], Casablanca: Al Ofok.

Zapata, Sarah (2010), 'Contesting Identities: Representing British South Asians in Damien O'Donnell's *East is East*', *Journal of English Studies*, 8: 175–86.

Zee, Machteld (2016), *Choosing Sharia? Multiculturalism, Islamic Fundamentalism and Sharia Councils*, The Hague: Eleven International Publishing.

INDEX